FROM THE INSIDE

A Half-Century of Michigan Athletics

Don B. Canham

with Larry Paladino

Olympia Sports Press
Ann Arbor, Michigan

Cover design by Betsy Lescosky
Photo technician, Robert J. Hird
Editorial services, Rita J. Stevens

Published by Olympia Sports Press
745 State Circle
Ann Arbor, Michigan 48108

Library of Congress Catalog Card Number:
96-92643

ISBN 0-9654263-0-0

Printed in the United States of America

To my grandchildren
Amelia C. Eaton and Don C. Eaton,
who brightened so many days for me —
I hope they also will remember those
who have gone before.

Contents

Contents

To the beautiful women in our home,
my wife Marilyn and daughters Sheri and Lisa, who work so hard
and deserve so much more.
To my mother Irene, for a lifetime of encouragement.
To my father Joe, for years of sound advice.
And to all the relatives and friends who have provided
motivation and inspiration for a half century.

— *Larry Paladino*

Introduction

Putting the legacy on paper

Young or old, if you've followed University of Michigan sports you know about Don Canham.

Even if your loyalties are Green and White, or Scarlet and Gray, or any other combination besides Maize 'n Blue, you at least have heard of him.

You've heard that he's the marketing genius who turned Michigan football Saturdays into full-blown, family-style events that have made crowds of 100,000-plus routine.

You've known he's the one who hired Bo Schembechler, the football coach who re-established the program to the glory days it had known under such legends as Fielding Yost and Fritz Crisler.

You've likely been aware of the NCAA Indoor Track and Field Championships that were such a success for two decades in Detroit, and that Canham was responsible.

And you've probably even had an inkling that he once was a track star at Michigan, then a track coach, before becoming athletic director in 1968.

But that's just the tip of the iceberg, as they say. There's a whole lot more you don't know about Canham — or about U-M sports over the half-century and more that he's been a Wolverine.

Oral histories have gone the way of the dodo and the passenger pigeon. To pass those stories on they must be put somewhere other than in the fleeting memories of some old coaches, friends, or relatives.

How many stories might Yost have been able to tell? Or Crisler? But they didn't tell them, not in a book, anyway. Canham doesn't want to make that same mistake and so has decided to write this book.

And what a book it is. There are anecdotes galore and he has covered so many aspects of Michigan sports that *Don Canham's From the*

Inside, A Half Century of Michigan Athletics will be a reference treasure for decades to come.

Readers will be introduced to some familiar tales of Yost, Crisler, Harry Kipke, Bob Ufer, and many others. But they'll also learn plenty of new things only Canham knows to tell.

They'll learn details of Michigan's marketing strategy, the hiring of Schembechler, the scheduling of Notre Dame, life among the presidents and coaches, and controversies involving Title IX, the College Football Association and the Amateur Athletic Union.

They'll be taken through more than a half-century of changes and get a glimpse of what lies ahead. And, of course, they'll learn of Canham himself: where he grew up, how he wound up at Michigan, how he became a coach and then athletic director, and who he learned to trust and admire.

Through it all, photos help give life to the stories. Many of the pictures had never been published and are from Canham's own collection or from that of his co-writer.

The new millennium that is upon us will bring untold changes in athletics. But will there be any more lasting than those Canham forged in his tenure at Michigan?

Although the book begins at the beginning — his days in Illinois and how he got to Ann Arbor — its heart is the chapter on marketing. Canham would be satisfied with a "marketing genius" legacy. His book proves that's just part of it.

— *Larry Paladino*

Preface

The idea for this book was sparked in the Michigan Press Box in the fall of 1993. Dave Strack and I were sitting in my booth watching a game along with 104,000 others. Dave, as Michigan fans know, had been a successful basketball coach at Michigan and then served as my assistant. Eventually he went to the University of Arizona as athletic director. He had retired and was visiting Ann Arbor during that fall. I probably was thinking out loud when I said, "Someone should write a book, Dave, on how Michigan became Michigan, with crowds like this every game day."

"You're correct," Dave said. "Why don't you do it? You're the only guy left who knew Yost, Kipke, Oosterbaan, and Crisler and all the coaches for the last half century." And we both knew that neither Fielding Yost or Fritz Crisler ever documented their times.

I really hadn't given much thought to my having been at Michigan for over a *half century*, but coming from Dave such a statement had impact. Actually, I had previously considered doing a picture history or something of that nature on the athletic department at Michigan. However, being unsure of how to get organized I had procrastinated.

Shortly after that football Saturday with Strack, a young sports reporter came to see me. He was writing about the early days of television. I had been there, so to speak, and tried to help him. During our talk I casually mentioned Cazzie Russell and was astounded when he looked puzzled and asked who Cazzie Russell was.

The young writer can't be blamed for his information gap — he wasn't even born when Russell, one of the greatest basketball players in Michigan history, played for Michigan and later for the New York Knicks. The realization struck me that much of the history of Michigan athletics had faded from the common memory. At that moment I decided to try and do something about it.

The nation now views Michigan as a leading intercollegiate athletic power, and one that is highly respected. Facilities for all sports are regarded as the nation's finest. Arriving at that point was not an accident. Few worthwhile things are the result of luck. Michigan athletics have reached a pinnacle of achievement through decades of effort. The credit goes to the hard work and dedication of countless individuals. In this book I hope to document the contributions of some of these people who have made Michigan the "Champions of the West." It goes without saying there is no possibility everyone who should share the credit will be recalled; they number in the thousands, not hundreds.

When I decided to proceed with this project, I had no idea how time-consuming it would become. Fifty years of my own scrap books came first; then I delved into 35 or 40 years of Board in Control of Intercollegiate Athletics minutes, plus reams of correspondence and magazine and newspaper articles spanning the years since the turn of the century. But most of the manuscript is from my own walk through Michigan history.

This is not a book of games played and scores made; nor is it a tribute to the great athletes who played on the fields and in the gymnasiums. In attempting to recall a particular time period I refer to some of the more significant athletes, but in general the teams and the scores are to be found in newspaper files and not in this book. Someone else will have to write about the contests played and races won; it is just too vast to be covered here. This work deals with the people and the places that figure notably in the story of how the Michigan athletic department became the premiere athletic department in the country. It will also deal with the mistakes we all have made, with the problems and mismanagement every institution uncovers if it looks hard enough.

If there is a key to Michigan's success it is attention to details. Yost once said it: "If you don't worry, you don't win." I had watched great coaches — Charlie Hoyt, Fritz Crisler, Ray Fisher, Cliff Keen, Matt Mann, Newt Loken and Strack — put aside everything that interfered with the details of coaching and winning. I believe attention to details had a large part to play in our success during my tenure. It was simply my nature to be involved in everything. Will Perry once told a reporter who asked him how it was to work for me: "If you ask Canham over for a drink, he's liable to ask you if you have enough ice. He simply watches everything." I wasn't quite that attentive, but anyone who worked with me can probably recall memos regarding the fine details of our program and association. Bo Schembechler, Bill Frieder, Red Berenson, Jon Urbanchek, and Gus Stager were detail guys. And winners, too.

Woody Hayes wrote a book titled, *You Win with People*. Of course he was correct; no one accomplishes anything alone. From the outset I was obsessed with that philosophy. During my time I made few mistakes in hiring. Although my record isn't perfect, the people I hired were the ones who moved Michigan forward with innovation. Michigan transformed intercollegiate athletics during the '70s and ''80s. Those who did it are identified here.

As early as 1837 student teams were competing against each other on the campus. In the early part of the book I've included a short history of the first century of Michigan athletics, before my own half-century.

My time at Michigan began in 1938 and I retired as athletic director in 1988. In those 50 years, I competed, coached, and became athletic director. All during my years as director I had great alumni, faculty and student support, probably second to none. I worked for four presidents and never had them attempt to interfere with the conduct of athletics under the Board in Control — not true in the 1990s during James Duderstadt's presidency.

Michigan is acknowledged as the institution that introduced modern marketing methods to intercollegiate athletics. We are also recognized as the pioneers in souvenir and premium development and sales. When we started it all in 1968 there was considerable criticism and consternation from faculty and some alumni. Advertising and marketing just weren't done in the conservative '60s. Universities were not a part of the marketing universe. Time, however, has silenced the critics as every educational institution in the nation followed Michigan's lead. Our program is now a vital part of everyone's public relations and revenue agenda. In that sense, we have "changed athletics forever."

Like everything else, we needed help. It came from the support of the presidents I served, from pragmatic Boards in Control of Athletics and finally from regents who understood the changing world.

I often heard criticism that I had too much power — absolute nonsense and an insult to the presidents I worked for. Those who made such statements simply confused support with power. On some occasions the Board in Control disagreed with me. We almost always had lengthy discussions on such issues, but since I never took unreasonable or stupid projects or plans to the board, our differences in 20 years were few. If that's power, so be it. Some of the brightest people I've ever associated with served on the board — alumni, faculty and students. That's why we got things done.

Some Acknowledgments

There were so many people who contributed to the great Michigan tradition during my half-century that it's impossible to mention them all. This includes those whose positions and jobs were absolutely essential, yet who did them without much recognition or supervision from my office. There are several people, however, who must be singled out who are not discussed otherwise in this book.

How could Michigan have a football game without Howard King announcing from the press box, a pro among pros; or Leon Tweedy getting the stadium ready for game day. Ken Hurst, Marv Tweedy, Archie Corzine and others were there, too.

Rod Grambeau and Mike Stevenson ran the Intramural Department and handled club sports. Bob Hurst and then Bob Flora, my right-hand man, for many years supervised and administered the maintenance and construction in the athletic complex. Hurst's father, by the way, had held the job before he did. Flora, in particular, solved problems for me before they ever surfaced on so many occasions, and we are friends to this day.

Dee Eddington and Steve Galletti were receptive when I suggested the formation of a School of Athletic Administration. They established it and it now ranks as one of the finest in the country. Following Marc Plant, faculty representatives Gwen Cruzat, Percy Bates and Paul Gikas gave so much time and effort, and were always supportive of what we were trying to do. I see them often.

The most important group, however, may be the office personnel, starting with Carol Coppersmith, who had been secretary to vice president Frank Rhodes before she came to the athletic department. She knew every university rule and it wasn't long before she knew NCAA and Big Ten rules and she kept me out of trouble for 20 years; Lilyan Duford, my secretary when I was track coach, who became business manager when I became athletic director; Maxine O'Neill, who ran the switchboard and knew every athlete by his first name during that 20-year period — of course before "voice mail." Pat Perry, Will Perry's wife, who had probably the best memory of anyone I ever knew. She ran our travel office and handled eligibility during my time as athletic director and did it without a problem; Fritz Seyfirth, who did so much for Michigan under four different athletic directors. And there was Jon Falk, the head equipment manager, who with his great sense of humor kept everyone in good spirit. He revolutionized the position with his efficiency; Bill Cusumano, with his barrage of ideas and photographic memory; Wilf Martin and Bob Hand, who would always get fields, arenas and parking ready for the big events without being reminded to do so and without much credit for jobs well done. These and others, too numerous to mention, made my coaching and administrative days so memorable and helped provide what some have referred to as "The Golden Era" for Michigan fans. I miss them all.

And since retirement and starting to work on this book, others must be acknowledged:

Tom and Trudy Driscoll who, without flaw, transcribed and organized my original material.

Bob Bauer for his great help with old pictures, the Bentley Historical Library for their help with pictures and history, and Jim Schneider for his suggestions and help on women's athletics.

Rita Stevens, who spent months on the manuscript organization, design and layout, was superb in all areas. Not a great Michigan fan when we started, she now knows who Harry Kipke was.

A special thanks to Larry Paladino, my long-time friend, who collaborated on the book from day one. His style, great memory and picture collection made the project fun to do — and he managed to Anglicize much of my English.

My wife, Margaret — who constantly "prodded and badgered" me to get this book done, on days when I wanted to do everything else but think about the book — must get credit for its completion. She wanted me to put more hockey in — she is Berenson's greatest fan. She also may be the best proofreader in my time.

Don Canham

Larry Paladino in the press box next to the Media Hall of Fame board with pictures of those who have been inducted. Larry, like the others, was inducted after long service covering Michigan athletic teams. We started the Hall in 1969 and some of the most famous press, radio and TV people in the nation have been honored.

Chapter 1

Early Years

◆————————————————————

Oak Park to Michigan

T he world was in turmoil in 1938, soon to be embroiled in its most massive war, one that would change its face forever. Americans, though, were still in their isolationist glory. They would soon find out how small the world really was. Meanwhile, the Great Depression was waning and life in the United States seemed headed for peace and prosperity. Gas was 20 cents or less a gallon and bread 10 cents a loaf. Income was pretty low, too.

It was a great time for a young athlete to leave home and head for one of the great universities of the nation. I was about to head for Ann Arbor, where it cost just $75 a semester for tuition — and, more importantly to me, the opportunity to compete in track at the University of Michigan.

With a pretty fair track and field record at Oak Park High School in Oak Park, Ill., outside Chicago, I was drawn to Michigan mainly because of its track coach, Charles B. Hoyt. His teams had won many Big Ten track championships, details of which were fully reported in my local papers, the *Chicago Tribune* and the *Chicago Daily News.* (The *News,* in fact, conducted a huge indoor track meet at the old stock yards on the south side, later moving it to Chicago Stadium.)

Interscholastic champions

MAY 1937

Don Canham, Oak Park, high jumped six feet four inches — the second highest leap in Interscholastic history.

Athletics consumed me. I was not a sensational student. The principal at Oak Park High, a Mr. McDonald, told my parents, "You're wasting your time if you think he's college material." Judging by my record, he was right. However, I was a good English student and during my years at Michigan my grades in English were among the best I received. I was awful in chemistry.

At Oak Park High School I played a lit-tle football and basketball as a freshman. In my sophomore year I developed into an above-average track athlete. I won the Illinois state outdoor high jump championship and was unofficial champion in the hurdles and high jump indoors, based on results of the Oak Park Relays, then the unofficial indoor championships. So I had a few college recruiting letters. Recruiting was low key and there were no athletic scholarships. I had visits from schools like Pittsburgh, Minnesota, Illinois and Wisconsin — but not Michigan.

In the summer I played sandlot baseball and for a time was torn between baseball and track. Had I not been so involved in track and field I might have been a pretty fair baseball player in high school and college. I could hit a little and was a pretty good first baseman.

My paternal grandfather, Samuel Canham, must have been a good athlete. He never went to college but in his youth he played a lot of sandlot baseball, the sport that attracted most amateur athletes in those days because opportunities in other

"Uncle Bill" —
"Don't call me
Grandpa."

Samuel Canham
The tree climber.

sports were few. He also had a short fuse. In his 20s he worked as a bookkeeper. One day when his boss crossed him in some way, he announced, "I quit," and walked out. He never worked at a regular job again. He spent his life raising canaries and selling them to Sears and Roebuck — and going to Chicago Cubs baseball games. In his time, he may have seen more Cubs games than anyone else, and he sold a lot of canaries so he could do it.

I remember grandfather Canham in his 60s and 70s climbing fruit trees in his backyard, swinging from branch to branch picking pears and apples. I suppose I inherited some of my athletic ability from the tree-climber. My father, Ernest, certainly did; he was very well-coordinated, even in later life, but never had much opportunity for athletic development. He went directly from grade school to an artist's studio.

My mother's father, William Burrell, had a major influence on my life. There's no question that my interest in business came from him. At his insistence all of us grandchildren called him "Uncle Bill" until his death. He never wanted to be known as a *grandfather*; he was just too young for that. He lived most of his life building businesses and losing them, one after another. Had he been an educated man, my guess is he would have become quite wealthy. As it was, he died in his 80s running a small machine shop in Kankakee, Ill., as happy as he could be.

When young, he had invented a gasoline engine called the Diamond B that he sold to Minnesota Mining Company. For many years he received royalties. The company had offered him Minnesota Mining stock instead but he refused. Had he accepted the stock and held it, he would have been one of the wealthier people in Illinois, what with the splits and re-splits and acquisitions.

My father, Ernest G. Canham, the teen-age artist.

Uncle Bill was one of the first to get into the miniature golf course business, accumulating a chain of them. When the activity lost popularity he tried indoor miniature golf, but it never caught on. His next endeavor was raising chickens under ultraviolet light and I remember visiting one of his buildings that housed 2,000 chickens. His biggest early venture was a machine shop in Bradley, Ill., that employed 200 machinists. When the building burned, the whole business went up in smoke. Uncle Bill had no insurance. But he frequently talked to the grandchildren about another new venture or new product or some business idea he was working on.

He was financially comfortable because, among other things, he received royalties from a road divider he'd developed. It was laid down the center of virtually all concrete highways in the early days to allow for expansion and contraction of the concrete. After he died, my grandmother lived off the royalties. I feel that whatever innovative ability and business imagination I have was inherited from my grandfather on my mother's side — W. C. Burrell, better known as Uncle Bill.

I was born in 1918 in Chicago. My father had a few years of tough times when I was a child and needed to get away from the city. So our family moved to a farm in Kankakee. Eventually we returned for good to Chicago where my father became a well-known magazine illustrator and an outstanding retouch artist. We had a comfortable existence. There was no log cabin in my youth.

My father did the artwork for the color furniture ads in Sears and

Roebuck catalogs prior to color photography. And he did virtually all the Maybelline eye shadow advertising and was the artist for Nash automobile and Shaeffer fountain pen ads. I still have some of the original drawings he did in the '20s and '30s — the color he added makes them look the way color photos do today.

My mother, Mary Frances Burrell, was an avid contract bridge player and also a pretty good horse handicapper. She placed more $2 bets than my father ever imagined. I probably inherited from her the instinct to take chances, although I never considered myself a riverboat gambler.

Mary Burrell Canham, my mother with me in 1919: before the $2 bets.

My brother Bob, three years younger than I, became a surgeon. For a time he was the team physician for Knox College in Galesburg, Ill. We had a sister, Grace Marie, who died at age 16. Her passing has had

Dr. Robert Canham, my brother, a dedicated surgeon.

Grace Marie Canham, my sister, whose death changed my life.

a tremendous impact on my life. As I look back, I think it was that tragedy in my early 20s that formed my philosophy: only a few of the things we fret about are truly important; losing a football game is not one of them. I still think of her often. One of the great tragedies in life is for a parent to bury a child. My folks never were the same after Grace passed away.

I often think how an incident or a circumstance shapes one's future. In my case, a grade school teacher, Mr. Goldthorpe, was the one person who pre-determined the course of my life. He had been a high jumper in a small teachers' college and, I think, a good one. He was fascinated with the event and had gym class contests. He had constructed a high jump pit on the playgrounds and during the winter his gym classes high jumped on old felt mats. I recall in seventh grade I was above average as a jumper, and in the eighth grade I could beat Mr. Goldthorpe with a jump of 5 feet, 8 inches — good in the 1930s for a 13-year-old. I became the state high school champion and high jumping led me to Michigan as an athlete, then as a coach. Had I not been on the Michigan scene, I would not have become athletic director. I probably would have ended up as a basketball or baseball coach at Whitewater State Teachers College.

Another teacher who was a great influence in my life was John Gaelman. He taught high school English and had been a personal friend of poets Vachel Lindsay and Carl Sandburg. He had even toured with Sandburg during the summer when the poet was giving readings throughout the state. Gaelman put life into the study of English. He could dramatize poetry better than any other teacher I ever had. We as students all looked forward to his hour each day. From his classes I developed a lasting interest in poetry and he got me into writing a little. Eventually I wrote five technical books and many magazine articles. None were especially noteworthy; some books, however, sold well. When Gaelman retired I wrote him a letter telling of his teaching abilities. I treasure his response.

It was not academics, though, but track that lured me to Michigan. In those days you could be a big high school star and still have to seek out your own college opportunities. You couldn't assume you'd get tuition and fees paid by a university eager for your services. Grant-inaids were a thing of the future. Although there were no scholarships as we know them today, there were jobs for room and board. And for tuition there was summer work — for athletes. Good summer jobs were not so easy to come by if you weren't a student athlete.

It wasn't until January 1938 that I enrolled at Michigan. I was sidetracked for a term trying to land a spot on the track team of the legendary Dean Cromwell at the University of Southern California. I corresponded with Cromwell and drove out there with some friends to meet him in person, but he was well-supplied with high jumpers. He

*Johnny Wilson with
the "western roll."*

*Don Canham using
the new "straddle style."*

already had both Johnny Wilson and Clark Mallory. (Ironically, I tied Wilson for the 1940 NCAA high jump championship four years later.)

After I started coaching, Cromwell became a friend, ten years after my trip to Los Angeles. Mallory became a well-known musician with the Firehouse Five Plus One group. I saw Wilson often in later years. He owned a restaurant in Los Angeles and always came to the Rose Bowl games when Michigan played. Cromwell wanted me to go to a southern California junior college and I didn't want to do that. Leaving California behind, I went to work in Hillsdale, Mich., on a construction job, building grain elevators for the Harold Stock Company. Stock turned out to be a Michigan fan. One day we piled into his car and he drove me to Ann Arbor to meet his friend, Charlie Hoyt, the Wolverines' track coach.

Hoyt encouraged me to come to Michigan. Stock, in Hoyt's presence, said, "Well, if he comes to Michigan I'll pay his tuition for four years." Today that would put you on probation in a hurry, but in those days it was completely legal for an alumnus to finance the education of an athlete. They often did it in football but it was a little unusual for a track man to be subsidized. Stock, true to his word, paid my tuition for four years. That amounted to $75 or $100 each semester until my senior year when, I recall, it rose to $150.

Athletic scandals were rare in those days. Perhaps it was due to lower stakes, few career opportunities in athletics, or just plain fear, but athletic departments were routinely scandal-free. I can't remember a time during my student days when athletes caused problems at Michigan or at any other school. In general, we felt it a privilege to compete. I suppose we were also afraid we'd be thrown off the team and out of school, as most of the coaches were disciplinarians. Athletes were expected to conform to behavioral standards with dignity and grace. Earrings, trash talk, baggy uniforms and police blotters were in the future.

It was too late in 1937 to enroll for the fall semester when Stock made his tuition offer. I went back to Oak Park and returned to Michigan in January. During that six month period I attended Oak Park Junior College and received good grades. Michigan accepted me on that basis. I could not have made it on my high school record.

My first home in Ann Arbor was a rooming house on Forest Avenue. After six months I joined Theta Delta Chi fraternity on South State Street — because it was the closest to the athletic department. I worked at the Chi Psi fraternity and the Beta Theta Pi house, making some of my best undergraduate friends there. Among them was Lynn

BOARD IN CONTROL OF PHYSICAL EDUCATION
UNIVERSITY OF MICHIGAN
DEPARTMENT OF INTERCOLLEGIATE ATHLETICS
FERRY FIELD — ANN ARBOR

February 3, 1938

Mr. Donald Canham
1134 S. Scoville Avenue
Oak Park, Illinois

Dear Don:

    I have just been informed by the Dean's Office that you are going to be admitted to the University to start the second semester. No doubt the Dean will notify you right away of his action.

    When you arrive in Ann Arbor, come directly to the Athletic Office and see me before going to the University.

    Looking forward to seeing you, I am

Cordially yours

Charles B. Hoyt
Track Coach

CBH/NB

Townsend, who would go on to become president of Chrysler Corporation. Lynn and I washed dishes together in the Beta house for a time. We met frequently in later years.

Obviously not an honor student, I didn't have much difficulty getting through school despite spending most of my time with the track team and in the movie houses. I think I saw every movie produced during the years I was in college. The old Worth Theater, Michigan Theater and State Theater in Ann Arbor — they provided an escape, I suppose, in a time when there was so much tension in the world. With World War II looming, we all knew that come graduation it was war service for us. Some athletes even left school early to serve. Many never came back.

Since then I've seen few movies. I don't watch much

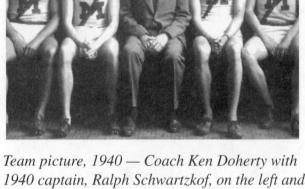

Team picture, 1940 — Coach Ken Doherty with 1940 captain, Ralph Schwartzkof, on the left and me, the incoming 1941 captain, on the right.

television either, but I read three or four hours an evening, mostly non-fiction, and subscribe to three newspapers and more than 10 magazines, all because a high school English teacher got me interested in reading and poetry.

Alexander Ruthven was U-M's president when I arrived at Michigan, and the university was celebrating its centennial. Composer George Gershwin had just died; *Snow White and the Seven Dwarfs* was first-run movie fare at the Worth Theater; book stores displayed John Steinbeck's latest novel, *Of Mice and Men*; and the Dodgers still played baseball in Brooklyn. I found myself in the same class with Tom Harmon, a football player from Gary, Ind., who became a good friend. Harmon, "Ol' 98," would become the triple-threat Heisman

Trophy-winning halfback who went on to become a World War II hero. He survived being shot down over China, married a movie star, Elyse Knox, and became a prominent sportscaster in California. Tom died in 1990. Other athletes at Michigan during that era who became friends included Jim Tobin, Ed Frutig, Bob Flora and Bill Watson.

It was a time when Michigan dominated the news in sports pages around the state and the nation. Michigan Agricultural College hadn't yet become Michigan State. Eastern Michigan University was Michigan Normal, a teacher's college. The University of Detroit, though, was prominent in football and basketball.

Among the lures to U-M for athletes was the lustrous array of coaches. Individually and collectively they were generally considered the best in college athletics: Ray Fisher in baseball, Hoyt in track, Matt Mann in swimming, Cliff Keen in wrestling and Fritz Crisler in football. Michigan was not a major factor in basketball, however, until Dave Strack began to coach years later.

The first coach I encountered was football assistant Wally Weber. I took some freshman classes from him. He called everybody by his home town so I was "Oak Park" to him until I became track coach at Michigan 10 years later. Wally was a fixture in the department from Fielding Yost's era to mine. He retired a few years after I became athletic director.

Harrry Kipke's Michigan teams had won national football championships in 1932 and 1933, but the 1938-39 season would be his last. Michigan hired Princeton coach Crisler as his replacement because of four seasons when Kipke's teams won only 10 of 32 games. Kipke was the last Wolverine football coach to be fired for his record — unless you feel that Gary Moeller's record was a factor in his 1995 dismissal.

I knew all the coaches as an athlete and later became a close friend of several. From them I learned first hand how important tradition is, and how fragile. These associations would serve me well three decades later. Bennie Oosterbaan, Kipke, Fisher, and Keen were of tremendous help to me in my first few years as coach and then as athletic director.

During my college days I started several businesses. One of them was a clothing business with Johnny Barr, a golfer, and Jeff Hall, a hurdler, roommates of mine at Theta Delta Chi fraternity. We would go into the mills, some of them in Detroit, and buy surplus clothing or seconds which we'd bring back to the campus: sweat socks, knit ties, jackets and belts.

Because we were athletes and familiar with all the fraternities, we could lay out displays of our goods in fraternity houses during dinner hours. We set it up so that students could put purchases on their house bills. That was long before credit cards were commonplace and you might say we were credit card pioneers. For many fraternity members it was their first opportunity for credit. We sold knit ties for 50 cents each, ties for which we paid 17 cents. Those and five pairs of sweat socks for $1 were our hot sellers. We paid 45 cents for the five socks. We often made from $50 to $100 profit a night, a small fortune in 1939, '40 and '41. Although our fraternity friends hadn't yet paid for their merchandise, the house managers would pay us in cash. We'd go down the

Business partners and room-mates, Jeff Hall and John Barr.

street to the Parrot Restaurant and divide up the profits over a late dinner each weeknight.

I would guess that to earn from $20 to $30 each night as we were doing was highly unusual on the Michigan campus or any campus at that time. Frankly, I made more money in the clothing sales business my senior year at Michigan than the contract amount for my first year of teaching in Kankakee — $1,600 a year, and mine was one of the better teaching contracts signed from my graduation class. Those were the days when one could buy a Ford for $750.

I also began to invest in the stock market during those years, but after graduation I abandoned the clothing business. Barr, Hall and I considered franchising our idea at other Big Ten schools and might

Father-in-law Walter Norris and my father, 1952.

have done so if World War II hadn't been on the horizon. All three of us were headed for the service. Barr saw considerable action on an aircraft carrier.

During my junior year at Michigan I met Marilyn Norris of Grand Rapids and we married in August of 1941, after my graduation. We were married for nearly 50 years before Marilyn, whom everyone called "Bunny," passed away in December 1990. We have two children, both U-M graduates: Clare Ann Eaton and Donald Norris Canham. Clare, a Michigan cheerleader, married Don Eaton, a player on Bo Schembechler's first team. Their two children, Don and Amelia, have made many times bright for me. Don, my son, is president of the family business.

After graduation in 1941 I went to Kankakee to visit my grandparents and there I saw an item in the newspaper about the high school looking for a track and cross-country coach and an assistant football coach. I applied. Some relatives, the Small family, whose patriarch, Len Small, had been governor of Illinois, were influential in Kankakee. I'm afraid my first job was due more to their recommendation than my abilities. I coached cross-country and was the assistant to head football coach Gene Dykstra, the former Illinois football player. But then came Pearl Harbor. A month later, in January 1942, I found myself in the Air Corps. I served until the spring of 1946, primarily in the training command. I wound up as a captain with no desire for a military career and no service decorations, either.

My father-in-law, Walter Norris from Grand Rapids, had plans to buy a theater in Coloma, Mich., and after my discharge I was going to run it. We hesitated when Walter saw the threat of the new medium, television, to the small town theater. How right he was. Before TV came on the scene, however, a small town theater was a road to riches.

At about this time, Chester Stack-house, the assistant track coach at U-M, was leaving to go to Lincoln University as head coach. That opened up a spot on the Wolverines' staff. I had had little coaching experience but I knew I would like to coach at Michigan. Ken Doherty, who had become head track coach when Hoyt went to Yale before my junior year in 1940, offered the assistant's job to me. On the advice of everyone I talked with, and with my own affection for the University of Michigan, I decided to accept. It wasn't hard to forego the theater business for that offer and it was the most fortunate decision I ever made. Most great decisions, I've learned, come about through lucky opportunities.

My involvement with investments helped me develop friendships with Ralph Aigler, the faculty representative for athletics, and baseball coach Fisher. We often discussed the market and traded information. Aigler once told me, "Only buy good securities and never sell." If he'd never sold a single share of stock in his lifetime, he said, he'd have been one of the wealthiest men in Michigan. Even so, Aigler held IBM, General Motors, General Electric, and other blue chips for which he paid $2 or $3 a share, adjusted for splits. I pretty much have followed Aigler's advice and have passed that advice on to anyone who would listen.

With daughter Clare at 3, in 1956...

...and son Don, the official at the NCAA indoor track meet in 1969.

Fisher related a story to me about an expensive baseball trip. When the stock market crashed in 1929, Fisher was in Japan with the U-M baseball team. Like many other speculators and investors at that time, Fisher had bought a great deal of stock on margin when the market was climbing through the roof in 1928. By the time he got back from Japan he had lost a sizable fortune. His Japan trip, Fisher told me, was the most expensive ever taken by any Michigan team. But Ray was a shrewd investor. He immediately went to the university and borrowed $10,000, using his house as collateral, and went back into the market at the very bottom. Those investments made him a wealthy man before he died.

I served as an assistant to Doherty in 1946 and 1947. In 1948 he was offered the head job at the University of Pennsylvania and asked if I would become his assistant there. I had no interest in going east. In fact, some months earlier I had been offered the assistant's job at Harvard and turned it down. I had also refused an interview for the head track coach job at Drake University in Iowa. I just didn't want to leave the University of Michigan. But not knowing who was going to come in, I had some anxious moments trying to make up my mind. The theater business loomed again.

As the assistant track coach I shared an office with Weber, the freshman football coach; Ozzie Cowles, the head basketball coach; and two other assistant coaches — five in one office with just two telephones. Today, the norm is two telephones for each coach. The building we were housed in is now the Michigan ticket department and later was named after the former women's athletic director, Marie Hartwig.

In the spring of 1948, Crisler, the athletic director, appointed me head track coach and I moved from the office with five coaches and two telephones to one with three coaches and one telephone. I shared that office with Keen and Fisher. The present office building on the corner of State and Hoover was constructed by Crisler in 1951 and after that we all had more space and our own phones.

Doherty and Crisler always had my loyalty and affection. Had Doherty not appointed me assistant in 1945 and Crisler to the head job in 1948, I certainly would not have had the opportunity to be the Michigan athletic director from 1968 to 1988. Just think — Shippensburg State and Slippery Rock would never have played in Michigan Stadium.

◆◆◆

Chapter 2

Fielding H. Yost

◆────────────────────────────

And How It All Began

F ielding H. Yost's legend is such that some people assume he started competitive athletics at Michigan. That certainly isn't the case, but he did have tremendous influence on the course it took. The fact is, we can trace competition back to 1837 when student clubs were formed to play each other. The structure came from England and the European continent where even today a great deal of athletic competition takes place between clubs from various towns. By the 1860s Michigan clubs had begun competing against similar student organizations at other schools — more than 30 years before Yost's arrival.

The origins of Michigan athletics were thoroughly detailed in a 1937 "M" Club publication written by Phil Pack, a 1918 graduate and the athletic department sports publicity director from 1925

through 1938. Pack's research and detailed documentation provide the best information we have of the early athletic history of the University of Michigan. His *100 Years of Michigan Athletics* has been out of print for decades.

Michigan played its first football game in 1879, more than a half century before I came to Michigan from Illinois. In 1890 the Athletic Association of the University of Michigan was formed. It brought all the clubs and their associations under one authority, run by the students. Any student who opted to pay $3 made himself "a participant in the management of athletics." Five officers and nine directors were elected by those who had paid their $3 — actually, a sizable sum then.

In 1893 a problem arose when several athletes were found to have competed without being enrolled in school. So, in December of 1893, the regents created a Board in Control of Athletics. This board was given full control in matters of eligibility, scheduling, and the handling of any accusations of misconduct. It would also approve the hiring of coaches. Included in its mission was the charge, "to foster the spirit of honor and gentlemanliness in athletics" and "to suppress evil tendencies." No definition of *evil tendencies* was provided. With this board,

First University of Michigan football team, 1879

control of university athletics rested in the hands of the faculty for the first time.

Five years later, in 1898, the faculty board created the position of "Graduate Manager of Athletics," in actuality, Michigan's first athletic director. He was Charles A. Baird, who had graduated just three years before. The youngest athletic director in Michigan history, Baird served until 1909 when Philip G. Bartelme was appointed. In 1921 football coach Yost took over from Bartelme and the first two directorships soon became overshadowed.

The first faculty board also participated in creating the Intercollegiate (Western) Conference, when representatives of seven institutions met in Chicago on Feb. 8, 1896: Purdue, Michigan, Wisconsin, Minnesota, Illinois, Chicago, and Northwestern. From that time on, athletics at Michigan expanded

Charles A. Baird

dramatically, as it did at the other six schools. The Western Conference became the Big Ten when three additional schools, Iowa, Indiana and, in 1912, Ohio, joined the group.

Just after the turn of the century, the popularity of track and baseball assured those sports of their own facilities but others had poor facilities. Football was the exception. Football games were first played at Regents Field, at the far south end of present Ferry Field. The first stands at Regents Field in 1893 accommodated 400 spectators. Year by year more stands were added and for the last game in 1905 a record crowd of 17,000 filled the wooden stands. As attendance continued to increase each year, demand for a new stadium was building. Yost led the move.

In 1906 the new football field was constructed at Ferry Field, the present location of the track and field facility. Again the stands were built of wood, but in 1914 new concrete stands were started. University officials contemplated constructing a "U" shaped stadium, but only the stands on the south side of the field ever were built. In 1969 I had those stands condemned. An interesting footnote is that both of these early fields ran east and west, with players facing the sun morning and afternoon, for practice and for games. Today all football fields run north and south.

Spectator interest steadily grew and at the end, in 1927, Ferry Field was at capacity with 46,000 spectators. In 1924 Yost began to talk of a large, efficient stadium. The public, the press, and the regents liked his ideas. Not so enthusiastic were the faculty and administrative officers, partly because Yost often revealed his plans to the press before clearing with anyone. Outside pressure from alumni and the legislature eventually forced university approval. Yost had engineered the pressure, as usual.

The land was purchased in 1925 for $240,000 and two years later Michigan Stadium was completed at Main Street and Stadium Boulevard. The "hole in the ground" that was to be the foundation for the future magnificent Michigan athletic plant was a reality. The stadium wasn't quite as we know it today. "Just" 87,000 people could watch football games from its seats, not more than 102,501 as is now the case.

One of the most frequently asked questions I got when I was athletic director concerned announced football attendance. How could we announce that 3,000 or 4,000 *more* people were watching the game than we had seats? Not a tough question. We often had close to 1,000 in the press box, on the photo deck and in the TV and radio booths. The bands of both schools totaled about 700. Security people, ticket takers, plumbers, electricians, and concessionaires made up the rest. We even counted cheerleaders, officials, and, on occasion, a streaker or two.

In the 1920s most spectators came on foot or by train, so parking spaces for 25,000 cars weren't necessary. Excursion trains chugged in from Detroit, Chicago, and Ohio and parked along the east side of the stadium on four or five siding tracks. Greyhound and Trailways buses also delivered thousands. On the east side of the stadium — where several thousand cars now park — was a practice golf green and fairway. Golf was a favorite Yost sport.

The Michigan Stadium complex is on 15 acres and was built for less than $2 million. In the 1970s we spent nearly that much adding women's restrooms, an item not much in demand when the stadium was built. Women seldom attended football games; football crowds were decidedly male. Old photos show thousands of men in derby hats and fedoras, holding cigars. College football became extremely popular in the 1920s and '30s, and the Western Conference, as the Big Ten does today, led the nation in attendance. Michigan, with the largest

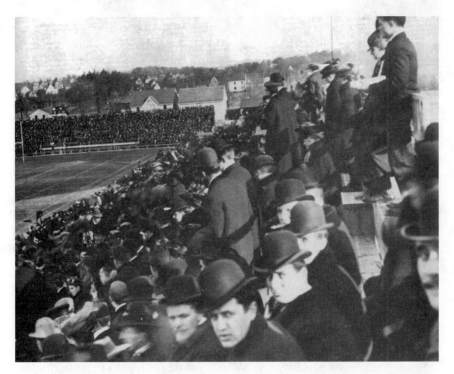

Derby hats and cigars — and very few brought dates.

stadium, nonetheless didn't always have the biggest crowds. Ohio State usually claimed that distinction.

The Western Conference became the Big Nine when Chicago dropped out in the 1940s, and it reverted to the Big Ten when Michigan State was admitted May 20, 1949. In 1988 Penn State joined, so the Big Ten now has 11 members — but hasn't changed the name. Someone can't count. (Actually, the conference redesigned its logo so that the name reveals a numeral 11 within the letters.)

Alexander Ruthven, university president from 1929 to 1951 and Ralph Aigler, the faculty representative to the Big Ten from 1917 to

Ralph Aigler   *Alexander Ruthven*

1955, had the greatest initial influence on national and Michigan athletics. Aigler served as chairman of the Board in Control of Athletics and was a renowned law professor on the faculty. Those two made the future greatness of Michigan possible, yet never have been adequately credited.

Ruthven was a master delegator. He was, for example, perfectly at ease with deans running their own departments. He had great confidence in Aigler and his knowledge of athletics. Aigler had ushered in the "age of Yost," a 20-year period that saw Michigan's and the nation's greatest building program for athletics. It also saw the beginning of an administrative structure, designed by Aigler, in which the athletic department was a separate corporation and a separate operating unit like the hospital and law school. That plan was soon copied by most of the country's major institutions.

Aigler was also instrumental in getting Yost appointed athletic director in 1921. The university and the Athletic Association were never to be the same. Yost engineered programs and buildings beyond those seen until then by any university. In a few short years he built a magnificent athletic plant that was, until the 1950s, second to none. The details of how he did it are mind-boggling.

Yost the Builder

The first fieldhouse ever built went up in 1923. Now Yost Ice Arena, it was originally called Yost Field House. The floor was dirt, with an eight-lap cinder track and a 75-yard straightaway down the middle. Outside dimensions of the building were 342 feet by 165 feet. The concept was entirely Yost's and some felt he built it primarily for indoor football practice. That was a factor, but track and field, basketball, wrestling, and baseball also were housed there.

The seating capacity of the building was to be 12,500. Eliminating a second balcony reduced it to 8,500, but the footings and beaming for the second balcony are still in place. A portable basketball floor was installed in the center of the structure. Varsity games were played there until 1967, when Crisler Arena was built. In the 1965-66 season, Cazzie Russell and

Yost Field House, photo circa 1935

his teammates were the last to play in Yost. Dave Strack was the last basketball coach to climb the steps to the second floor locker rooms.

The erection of Yost Field House required moving the baseball stands and diamond about 150 feet west of their old site. The diamond remains there to this day. It was completely rebuilt by Crisler and then I remodeled the baseball stadium in the early '70s.

Yost Field House replaced the previous Club House that had provided locker and shower facilities for athletes in intercollegiate competition at Ferry Field since 1912. It had been built that year to provide facilities previously available only at Waterman Gymnasium. Following the construction of the fieldhouse, the Club House was altered in

1925 to become the Athletic Administration Building. It is now the athletic ticket office, named after Marie Hartwig, my first women's athletic director.

The Michigan Coliseum, purchased in 1926, was another move in the expansion of the athletic plant. Rebuilding took it from its previous life as a roller skating rink into that of an indoor ice rink with artificial ice and a seating capacity of 1,200. In the 1970s I converted it to an intramural facility when we transformed Yost Field House into an ice rink seating over 7,000, then the largest college-owned ice rink in the nation. The seats are filled for every game.

In 1928 the athletic campus became larger by 112 acres. Purchased for $344,000, this land lay to the south of the 40-acre plat (acquired in 1925) south of the present Stadium Boulevard. Another 15 acres were added in 1936. The Michigan Golf Course, designed by famed golf course architect Alexander MacKenzie, was constructed on this land.

The Intramural Sports Building, part of the "athletics-for-all" program that Yost talked about, was built in 1929 at Ferry Field, paralleling the gridiron on the north side. Its erection involved tearing down the old wooden stands on the north side. Put up at a cost of $743,000, this building was, again, the first of its kind. Heavily used to this day, it contains four basketball or tennis courts, 13 squash courts, 14 walled handball courts, a golf driving net, and an auxiliary gym equipped with gymnastic apparatus. At one time, varsity teams in fencing, wrestling, boxing, and swimming used the facility. It is a magnificent structure that shows little depreciation.

Forty clay and concrete tennis courts for intercollegiate and intramural play were constructed by Yost at Ferry Field along the west and northwest fences. The Canham Natatorium and Revelli Hall, the band building, replaced them in the '70s and '80s.

The athletic plant covered 235 acres in the late '30s and was valued at more than $3.5 million. More than $3 million worth of expansion had taken place since 1921 when Yost became athletic director. It was a phenomenal figure, probably equal to $300 million or more in the 1990s. The construction was made possible by revenues of the department itself. The only other monies included in the total are the original grants for Barbour Gymnasium, Palmer Field (both for women), Waterman Gymnasium, Regents Field, and the land for Ferry

The first Intramural Sports Building, photo circa 1935

Field. Ruthven had determined that no general funds would be used for athletics. To the present time that philosophy and practice have not changed. Since Yost, no general fund money has been used for athletic construction or operations.

The area has changed little since then, but the value of the plant has increased beyond comprehension. It would now cost more than $20 million to duplicate Yost Field House; the $2 million stadium could not be duplicated for $200 million. Yost was not only an innovator, he was a shrewd investor. The "hole in the ground" made Michigan's remarkable athletics tradition and sports leadership possible.

The stadium construction is a story in itself and a tribute to Yost's vision. When he built Michigan Stadium some felt the university might never dig its way out from under the costs. Yost was the target of severe criticism. The stadium was built without the blessings of the faculty and many of the townspeople, to say nothing of the university administration.

The organized faculty opposition to constructing the stadium arose from an opinion that it represented extreme overemphasis on athletics. Other critics maintained there would never be any need for a football stadium that could hold 87,000 people. Some questioned the proposed location —out in the wilderness, so far from the campus.

Most concerns proved to be short-sighted, but those who worried about financing the stadium showed some vision. Yost had to borrow $1.5 million. Three thousand $500 bonds were issued, at 3 percent. Michigan's football team had been playing to standing room only in the Ferry Field stadium and it seemed that paying off the bonds would pose no problem. For the most part that was true, but it took much longer than planned.

The new stadium had to turn down ticket requests for Ohio State, Minnesota, and Navy. But just about the time everyone thought the attendance boom would go on forever, the Great Depression struck and the athletic department fell behind in paying the debt service on the stadium bonds. More than half the bonds had not been repaid when Yost retired in 1941, no surprise to some critics. A combination of Fritz Crisler's winning teams and wartime spirit filled seats. The last bonds, totaling $867,000, were eventually retired by Crisler, Yost's successor.

Yost's great contribution was his almost religious belief that you cannot win without facilities. His remarkable attention to details served Michigan well. Yost's legacy is thus solidly constructed in brick and mortar. He conceived and engineered facilities at Ferry Field that are second to none in the world. All of his construction was paid for by revenue from "the hole in the ground on the hill."

His initial difficulty getting university support for his stadium idea is easy to understand. He never enjoyed a solid working relationship with the administration or the faculties. Academics, in his opinion, was an area that had to be tolerated, even ignored where possible, although publicly he spoke otherwise. There is some question, for instance, of whether Willie Heston, one of our greatest football players, attended many classes. Some claim Heston was not alone in that practice.

The alumni, however, were Yost supporters. He was popular with the press because he was excellent copy. And he also spent countless days cultivating the state legislature. When it came time to put on the pressure to build the Michigan Stadium and other structures, Yost generated so much positive publicity using those three groups that even prominent faculty people finally gave in. In fairness, there were some faculty who felt Yost could do no wrong. Many of those served with distinction on the Board in Control.

Now, of course, the Michigan community and alumni throughout the world marvel at Yost's wisdom and tenacity in pushing ahead with the stadium project. For seven decades the games played there have provided the major funding for intercollegiate athletics for both men and women at Michigan.

Michigan's early success in ice hockey was due to Yost's

*Michigan Stadium construction, 1926-27:
excavating, grading, laying the footings.*

construction of the Coliseum on Hill Street, one of the first indoor ice rinks in the nation. Michigan has had great success in swimming. A major factor was the varsity swimming pool Yost put into the Intramu-

ral Building. Few schools could claim one equal to it at the time. Prior to the pool's construction it was said to be for students, but general use never really developed. Matt Mann coached his national championship teams in that intramural swimming pool without much student interruption. Faculty water polo at noon was about the only recreational use.

On Michigan Stadium's dedica-tion day in 1927 Detroit alumni presented Yost with a new car.

Yost constantly said, "athletics for all," but some thought he really meant "intercollegiate athletics for all."

Yost was an engineer and every facility he had constructed was made of the finest materials and always overbuilt. It has been said that Yost's construction of the Intramural Building, the first in the nation, was not out of love for students or to provide for their recreation, but to pacify the faculty and the university community who opposed his stadium plans. Regardless, the students were the beneficiaries.

The intramural pool in which Mann won so many championships was covered and made into a gymnastics center when Crisler built the varsity pool on the corner of Hoover and State Street. That pool in turn was converted into a gymnasium in 1990 and named after the great wrestling coach Cliff Keen when we built the Canham Natatorium.

It cannot be forgotten that without Fielding Yost, Michigan wouldn't be the power in athletics that it is today. Illinois, Yale, and Ohio State were building stadiums at the same time. None have the capacity or the beauty and efficiency of the nation's largest college-owned stadium at Michigan. And no other institution built the variety of facilities that Michigan did in Yost's time.

His remarkable vision becomes apparent when one reads some of his old memoranda and looks at some of his blueprints. Michigan Stadium is the best example. At the time of construction, Yost said he wished he could double the size because one day Michigan would need 300,000 seats for football. His statement, made in 1928, attracted ridicule. But had not television and professional football and a host of other pro sports come along to claim fan interest, Yost would likely have been correct. Yost gave the new stadium double footings because he was sure that someday it would have to be enlarged. Due to his foresight that possibility still exists. One day seats around the top of the stadium, a larger press box, and heavier scoreboards might be needed. That same construction shows in every facility touched by Yost.

Baird hired "point-a-minute" Yost away from Stanford University in 1901. Yost had graduated from West Virginia Law School in 1897. In his first season as Michigan's football coach the team won 10 games, didn't lose any, and scored more than 500 points. From that time on his teams were publicized as scoring "a point-a-minute," and his name remained synonymous with the phrase throughout his life.

The spectacular 1901 season ended in the first Tournament of Roses game against Stanford University. Yost took 15 players on a four-day train trip to California and had only one practice before the game. Michigan faculty were not happy. They didn't like the "emphasis" and the expense. They probably weren't ecstatic, either, over the publicity an athletic team was receiving or the rumors floating around concerning irregularities in the football program. The game was to be played in two 35-minute halves on a very dusty field. In the middle of the second half Michigan had a 49-0 lead and Stanford left the field and didn't come back.

Following that trip the Big Ten voted to end all post-season games, as other faculties across the conference also were opposed to the emphasis placed on football. The Big Ten ban on bowl games lasted for more than 40 years. Michigan's *next* bowl trip was to the Rose Bowl in 1948, with Crisler as coach. Wrote Braven Dyer of the *Los Angeles Times*, "Showing no improvement, Michigan won by the same score that they did in 1901, 49-0, against Southern California."

The athletic area as we know it today can be credited primarily to Dexter M. Ferry, owner of the Ferry Seed Company and a close friend of Yost's. Yost convinced Ferry that Michigan needed space for athletic expansion, particularly for a football field. Thus Ferry bought 17 acres on South State Street, forever to be known as Ferry Field.

Rose Bowl Game No. 1, the Wolverines in California: How many were enrolled in school? Yost, standing far right, back row; Athletic Director Baird, in the derby hat, third from left, middle row.

Problems Surrounding Football

1905 brought Yost his first major crisis. During that season, 18 players died in football games nationwide, although none from Michigan. The reason was that players wore little protection. President Theodore Roosevelt called for abolishing football. President A. A. Angell of Michigan, not a great fan of Yost's, organized the Western Conference, primarily in an attempt to control football. At the meeting, Wisconsin proposed that football be dropped for two years to assess the situation, asking for an examination of cases in the conference where ineligible athletes were being used. Michigan was a suspect. Other questionable practices were firing up faculty concerns on virtually all campuses.

Michigan's faculty representative was sympathetic to dropping football. Yost was furious. Although football did escape being dropped completely, some sensible rules were legislated. The schedule limited teams to five games a season, training tables were eliminated, minimum player progress toward a degree was mandated, and coaches were to be full-time appointments of the university with pay no higher than that of a faculty member of the same rank. Of particular impact were rules dictating that players must be full-time students and that freshmen were not eligible.

One of the most controversial decisions to come out of the Angell Conference was that players could not compete for more than three years. Seniors who had played as freshmen became immediately ineligible, a strange retroactive ruling. Yost was infuriated and started a campaign to get out of the league. Students and alumni were angry because football was extremely popular and, in the students' case, some of their friends were made ineligible. Their anger grew when they found out that all this was primarily due to Angell's recommendations.

To no one's surprise, the faculty senate endorsed the conference action and also recommended dropping paid coaches at all conference universities. Yost had a four-year contract — which meant that after four years he would not be employed by Michigan. The faculty senate suggestion was never implemented, but it illustrates the animosity most faculty held for Fielding Yost.

Michigan's Board in Control of Athletics, however, appealed the conference decisions, asking for seven games, not five, and requesting that fourth-year seniors be allowed to play — reasonable requests, most Michigan people thought. The conference thought otherwise and turned down these modifications, triggering anger among players, sympathetic students, and alumni. They were publicly encouraged by Yost and began to demand that Michigan withdraw from the Western Conference. They saw its rules as aimed at Michigan, not considering that Angell had recommended virtually all the restrictions.

Those who recommended withdrawal assumed that other Big Ten schools would continue to play Michigan in football and in other sports, an assumption that today is hard

President A. A. Angell
He tried to control
Yost and football.

Fielding H. Yost

1901: He arrives.   *1915: the successful coach*   *1921: Finally the A.D.*

to comprehend. Conferences are designed to provide competition. Few independents besides Notre Dame can survive out of conferences. Amazingly, the regents recommended to the Board in Control that they vote to withdraw. The board, with a faculty majority, disagreed. It deferred the matter to the full faculty senate, which resented the regents suggesting any action concerning athletics. The senate declined to act on the recommendation and stated opposition to withdrawing. But Yost continued putting pressure on the newspapers, legislature, and alumni.

Finally, in October 1907, the regents abolished the sitting faculty Board of Intercollegiate Athletics and created a new one, rigged to vote for withdrawal. That violated conference rules requiring faculty control. In January 1908 Michigan was expelled from the conference because it had abandoned that control. Furthermore, the conference mandated that members *not* compete against Michigan in any sport. Ohio State, not a member then, continued to play Michigan. Competition for U-M in all sports, particularly football, became a serious problem. Michigan history always has contended that we withdrew from the Big Ten, but league minutes clearly show we were ejected.

Yost teams had won five of six Big Ten football championships to that point and finished second in 1905. In most years, Michigan played 11 games. In 1908, when conference schools were prohibited from playing Michigan, Yost looked east and scheduled Syracuse and Pennsylvania. He turned to the south and scheduled Vanderbilt and Kentucky, two teams simply not in Michigan's class. Michigan Agricultural College also appeared on the schedule. Today, of course, it is known as Michigan State University. Most of the time Yost's Wolverines defeated the Spartans easily, but in 1915 the Spartans beat Michigan 24-0. They didn't win another game against Michigan until the Aggies, as they were called, defeated Harry Kipke's team in 1934, and then continued to beat Michigan for the next three years. It was a factor in the firing of Kipke and the hiring of Fritz Crisler.

The schedules from 1907 on show that Michigan missed the Western Conference more than the conference missed Michigan. The southern and eastern schools that Yost's teams were forced to play weren't in a class with the Wolverines. Attendance declined dramatically, alumni began to complain, and incoming students couldn't understand the stupidity of Michigan's administration in "forcing the conference to kick Michigan out."

The hand-picked faculty board was of no help. Its agenda came from the regents and everyone knew it. Except to complain, most did little about the situation. Yost stubbornly insisted that all was well. A look at schedules and attendance proves it wasn't. Even the press called for re-entry. Yost had lost a reliable ally.

In 1913 the students began in earnest to urge a return to the conference. The faculty still was upset about its lack of control of intercollegiate athletics. The regents still were trying to justify their mistakes and their recommendation to withdraw. By 1915 the regents bowed to faculty and alumni pressure and again let the faculty senate select the majority of the board members and to make all decisions regarding intercollegiate athletics, as required by the Western Conference.

Aigler became chairman of the Board in Control in 1915 and served until Crisler succeeded him in 1938. Aigler, a master of mediation, immediately began exploratory talks with members of the Western Conference. By 1917 he had single-handedly convinced the conference and the board at Michigan that U-M should return. He assured the conference the board would report directly to the university's faculty senate. (Not until 1990, under President James Duderstadt, was this procedure altered, once again putting faculty control in jeopardy.)

The conference quickly invited Michigan back. And in November 1917 Michigan rejoined. In 1913 Ohio State had become a new member and so now the conference was known as the Big Ten.

The 1919 season saw the Big Ten expand the number of games played, and Illinois, Minnesota, Northwestern, and Chicago once again appeared on the Michigan schedule. But from 1908 until 1919, such teams as Carroll, Case, Mount Union, Kalamazoo, Detroit, South Dakota and Marietta had provided Michigan's competition. Michigan lost few games during that period.

Yost As A.D.

Philip Bartelme, athletic director from 1909 until 1921, had supported the disastrous situation that forced Michigan out of the conference and he never lived it down. For years there were rumblings that he should be removed. In 1921 he resigned and Yost became the athletic director.

On many occasions Yost had not been loyal to Bartelme, often forcing his agenda upon him. Correspondence and hearsay suggest that Yost engineered the pressure to remove Bartelme. In fact, when Michigan returned to the Big Ten, Yost took most of the credit — even though his actions had led to Michigan being forced out in the first place. The person entirely responsible for cleaning up the program and influencing the Big Ten to invite Michigan to rejoin was Aigler.

While Michigan's athletic fortunes were sinking during the non-conference period, most of the other conference schools had expanded programs and facilities. In 1919 U-M won only three football games and lost four. By 1921 it was no longer considered dominant in Midwest intercollegiate athletics. Those years were Yost's worst as a coach and led to widespread dissatisfaction among students and the administration. Always a poor loser, Yost blamed others for his lack of success.

There was some truth to Yost's charges because Bartelme was not a very astute financial manager. In addition to some financial difficulties, there were eligibility problems during the last few years of his administration. Once again it was Aigler who stepped in, engineering the appointment of Yost to take Bartelme's place. Aigler felt quite simply that Yost's popularity with the press, legislature and students could not be ignored. Whether he could handle Yost was another matter; two of Yost's athletic directors couldn't.

Even with Aigler's support, Yost's appointment wasn't a sure thing. There were several other applicants, mostly former Michigan athletes. In faculty circles, Yost had little support. Objections to him grew from their conviction that he had too little concern for the athletes' academic progress. As he did many times, Yost bypassed the university community and went directly to the press and to state legislators. Through them the regents were pressured to vote for Yost. But it was probably the alumni, who lionized Yost and remembered his victories, who insured his appointment. Fanatic alumni at institutions nationwide are consistently oblivious to the faults of winning coaches.

Yost governed the athletic department not only with ideas and innovations but with boundless energy and enthusiasm. During his directorship he added six varsity sports and laid plans to make Michigan the premiere athletic institution in the na-

Philip G. Bartelme, A.D. 1909-1921
Yost had his way — always.

tion. His keen rivalry on the football field with Bob Zuppke at Illinois and L.W. St. Johns at Ohio State spilled over into other areas as he made every attempt to out-build them with an athletic plant second to none. He succeeded. Those who knew him well said he was consistently upbeat. It lasted until the end. During the short time I knew him, I was constantly amazed. In 1940, returning from a track meet in Illinois, I sat with him on a train for most of the night, I still recall his enthusiasm and love for Michigan.

Yost was obviously an egomaniac and often talked too much to the press about things better left unsaid. He was called an "unabashed ham" by some of the press and an "exhibitionist" by others. One reporter stated, "He was a person who could boast and who could still be liked for doing so." Yost seldom had bad press because he was good copy. The writer Ring Lardner was asked, "Do you ever talk to Fielding Yost?" "No," replied Lardner, "my father taught me never to interrupt." That summarized Fielding H. Yost's relationship with the press.

It was fortunate for him that, following World War I, post-war prosperity settled upon the nation. He was able to finance the Intramural Building, the fieldhouse and, in large part, Michigan Stadium, all on gate receipts because of the spiraling attendance growing out of prosperity. During Yost's entire career as football coach and as athletic director his obsessions were to keep Michigan athletics at the forefront of development and conspicuously in the press. He succeeded beautifully with both.

And it was also Yost who first realized the value of the marching band. The Michigan Band broadened the interest people already had in the football program. To this day there's hardly a football game played anywhere on any level in the United States without a band in attendance. Yost was the pioneer who brought that about.

One of his most bitter defeats, however, came from the Board in Control after Michigan fired Kipke and was looking for a replacement. Yost had been a personal friend of Tom Hamilton, the coach at Navy, who had been highly successful all through his career and in recent years had had great success at the Naval Academy. Yost began his letter campaign and wrote to legislators, alumni, and friends, urging them to write letters to him in support of Hamilton. Aigler, on the other hand, had made up his mind long before that the next football coach at Michigan was going to be Crisler, formerly an assistant to Amos Alonzo Stagg at Chicago, head coach at Minnesota and then at Princeton.

President Ruthven had supported Aigler on many occasions and had great respect for him. Correspondence indicates that Ruthven had been less than pleased with the pressure tactics Yost exerted from time to time. On the other hand, he was grateful to Yost for what he had done with the athletic department without asking his office to solve problems or begging for funds to balance the budget.

As early as 1937 Aigler had gone to New York to talk with Crisler about leaving Princeton. Subsequently, Crisler came to Ann Arbor by train and met privately with Ruthven and Aigler in nearby Ypsilanti.

Yost knew nothing about the plans or the meeting and continued to push for Hamilton.

I knew Hamilton well when he became commissioner of the Pacific Coast Conference. I saw him often and was on several committees with him during my early years as coach and later as athletic director. He would certainly not have been a disaster had Yost prevailed and Michigan hired him. As a football coach, however, he was never as highly regarded as Crisler.

A strange thing happened upon Crisler's appointment. The board was split in its opinions, some siding with Yost, and they actually agreed to hire Hamilton on a close vote, Aigler voting against. Before there was any publicity or Hamilton could be notified, Ruthven reconvened the board in a special meeting at Aigler's suggestion and asked that they reconsider.

Elmer Mitchell, the long-time director of intramurals at Michigan and a giant in his field, was a member of the board. He recounted the situation to several of us years later. Mitchell received a phone call three or four days after the special meeting. The call, surprisingly enough, came from Yost himself, asking Elmer if he would change his vote and cast it for Crisler and not Hamilton. Mitchell had voted with Yost for Hamilton at the original meeting. With Mitchell changing his vote and the three alumni board members who had sided with Yost changing theirs, Crisler received a majority.

It appears that all four changed their votes not because of favoring Crisler, but only as a favor for Yost — who no doubt had heard from Ruthven. It's pretty clear that is what occurred because the three alumni members resigned from the board a short time after that. Yost, surprisingly enough, explained to Mitchell that

Yost signed this picture at his retirement dinner in 1941.

In 1969 with Mrs. Yost at her birthday party, held at Bennie Oosterbaan's house. I never asked if she changed the vote.

it was Yost's wife who told him to change the votes, not the president. The reasoning she gave was that he'd soon be retiring and it was unfair to impose his wishes upon those who remained responsible for the athletic department and physical education. True or not, that was Yost's story. He retired in 1941 and Crisler assumed the chair.

Yost's legacy cannot really be measured; his vision and ability made it possible for those of us who followed to build on what he, through his genius, began.

Yost retires in 1941: Mrs. Yost, and Illinois coach Bob Zuppke congratulating him at a huge party in Waterman Gymnasium called "A Toast to Yost from Coast to Coast." I was an usher, as were all team captains.

Chapter 3

Herbert O. "Fritz" Crisler

◆────────────────────────────

"Chairman of the Board"

Fielding Yost's successor as athletic director was Herbert Orin "Fritz" Crisler. He took over in 1941, coming to the job without a search committee and with no other proposed candidates. Faculty representative Ralph Aigler of the Michigan law school was chairman of the Board in Control of Intercollegiate Athletics and he alone engineered the succession.

Aigler had made an agreement with Crisler when Fritz left Princeton to coach Michigan football in 1938 that when Yost retired, Fritz would get the A.D. job. It was part of the inducement to get Crisler to come to the University of Michigan. President Alexander Ruthven and the Board in Control had agreed to it in private meetings. Freedom of Information Acts and fair employment laws were far in the future.

Crisler led the Michigan athletic department for the next three decades. In the 1930s and '40s, with smaller programs of men only and far less emphasis on athletics and winning than there is today, many football coaches also were athletic directors. It was not until the '60s that separating the jobs of athletic director and football coach became the norm. By the '80s and '90s it was rare to find a major college football coach who had enough time, energy and background to also handle the duties of athletic director.

Crisler held the dual position only until 1948 when he gave up football and appointed Bennie Oosterbaan as the new coach. He went on serving as athletic director until he was 70. I succeeded him July 1, 1968 (after having been appointed March 15).

Crisler, born Jan. 12, 1898, was from Earlville, Ill. He attended the University of Chicago after having an outstanding athletic career at Earlville High School. I never could get him to talk much about his youth. I had the feeling that it was not a happy one. I have no proof of that, but he seldom mentioned anything in his life prior to playing for Amos Alonzo Stagg at the University of Chicago.

There he was a nine-letterman, starting in football, baseball, and basketball, and he was listed on the Walter Camp football All-America third team. In 1921 he captained the Chicago baseball team as a pitcher. It isn't surprising to find out he was an outstanding student. The story went that he was a Phi Beta Kappa. I was unable to verify it and Fritz never mentioned it to me. He did receive the Western Conference medal for scholarship and proficiency in athletics.

He was a pre-medical student at Chicago until Stagg hired him as a graduate assistant in football in 1922, intending to work with Stagg for a year or two to accumulate enough money to go to medical school.

As a player under Stagg at Chicago

A year or two stretched into eight and medical school was forgotten. Then, in 1930, he accepted the position as athletic director and football coach at the University of Minnesota. He had been there for only two years and had a record of 10-7-1 when Princeton offered him its football job and he left for what later would become the Ivy League. He was not, however, athletic director at Princeton.

He never mentioned why he left Minnesota for Princeton, other than to say one time that he found " too much politics in Minneapolis for me." There were rumors at Minnesota about other reasons for Fritz leaving, but none has been substantiated, to my satisfaction, anyway. His record at Princeton was outstanding, a 35-9-5 record in six years.

Aigler had been greatly impressed with Crisler at NCAA and Big Ten meetings during Fritz's short stay at Minnesota. Several years later, as a committee of one, he engineered Crisler's transfer to Michigan. But Fritz was not an easy man to move. He was happy at Princeton and had been successful. It took an institution with the stature of the University of Michigan to make him relocate.

Crisler did not move quickly, however. He made use of the leverage he knew he had with Aigler and eventually with Ruthven. One of the most unnoticed and unrecognized features of the move was Fritz's insistence he become chairman of the Board in Control of Intercollegiate Athletics, a position Aigler held at that time. Fritz often told me it was the greatest buffer an athletic director could have. It was made up of faculty, alumni, and students; yet unless the athletic director was chairman, half the time the meetings were spent deciding about moving benches on the golf course or settling disputes over intramural facilities, while more pressing matters were put aside.

During my time I saw exactly those situations at various institutions where athletic directors could not direct the agenda of their athletic boards. In the '90s some university presidents have completely negated the faculty-controlled boards as Duderstadt attempted to do at Michigan in 1995-1996. Where administrators have taken over athletic departments, critical decisions often are made in some vice president's office. In schools where faculty and alumni and students have been by-passed, problems have multiplied.

In any case, Crisler became chairman of the board with Aigler's blessing. Ruthven, a master delegator, approved it. He had known Crisler through the Big Ten relationship at Chicago and Minnesota and had great respect for him. As chairman, Crisler ran the athletic department for 30 years with faculty control, and I ran it the same way for 20 more. In 1991 faculty control gave way at Michigan to presidential control; but that's another story for later.

In 1968 on two occasions I sat on Ruthven's porch beside the Huron

*"The Chairman of the Board" in suit coat and tie — and always with
shoes shined. His assistants were similarly dressed. Unlike Nike today,
Brooks Brothers didn't pay him a dime.*

River with him and Bennie Oosterbaan, one of Ruthven's favorites,
and discussed the role of athletic director. I recall Ruthven's words: "I
attempt to hire people I think are capable and I delegate authority to
them." He remarked that one of the best administrators he ever had
was Dr. Albert Kerlikowski, head of the hospital. Kerlikowski never
came to him with problems, never embarrassed him, and settled everything to his satisfaction. Few presidents today have enough confidence to place such trust in their administrators, although the presidents I served under — Robben Fleming, Allan Smith, and Harold
Shapiro — in my view certainly did.

Crisler was not an easy person to get close to. He told me he had
three friends and thousands of acquaintances. In fact, he used that phrase
many times to emphasize his isolation. He seemed to make an effort
not to become close to anyone. I often wondered what caused him to
keep his distance from people. I always thought that among his "three
friends" was Henry DeKoening, the contractor who built most of the
athletic facilities during Fritz's time. Another was Bill Snyder, a local
businessman. The third was probably Myron Steinberg, a printer who

did the Michigan football programs and tickets during most of Crisler's administration.

I knew all three of them and I can understand the friendship. They were very confidential people and I think Fritz not only trusted them in business but personally. In any case, those three were who I saw him with the most. Of the coaching staff, I think there's not much doubt that I was as close to him as anyone. During the later years, Bob Ufer, the broadcaster, and I spent more time with him than even the un-named friends.

Ufer had purchased Crisler's house in Ann Arbor Hills and lived a block away from the house Fritz had built in the 1960s. Ufer idolized Crisler and spent hours with him talking football. When I was track coach my close association with Fritz began after he found I had a 36-foot Egg Harbor cruiser on the Detroit River. Crisler was a great boater and he often would come by on a summer afternoon and say, "Let's take a cruise." It's very difficult for a track coach to turn down the athletic director, so off we'd go to the river, sometimes with faculty representative Marcus Plant and sometimes with a coach or two, for a cruise out onto Lake Erie and dinner. It was only on those trips that some of us got close to Fritz. Yet the next morning it was back to reality and the chairman of the board was back in character. We'd wonder if yesterday had really happened. He kept everyone, even his former players, at arm's length. I'd guess Tom Harmon knew him best.

Crisler was a compelling public speaker and, like all great coaches I have known, he was a great actor. I could just see him doing Shakespeare somewhere. He had distinct likes and dis-likes and one of the persons he disliked most was Frank Leahy, the football coach at Notre Dame. Because of this it wasn't until I became athletic director that we began to schedule Notre

Bob Ufer with Fritz Crisler at a Friday night press party in 1979.

"Let's take a boat ride!" How could a track coach say no?

Dame. Fritz thought Leahy was a phony and he would tell the story to anyone who listened that, if someone offered Leahy a drink he would take it and hold it and never touch it; if he was offered a cigarette he would take it but never smoke it. I can still hear Fritz in his deep voice saying, "Why the hell didn't he just say he doesn't drink or smoke?" Fritz did a little of both, but I think we all did in those days.

Crisler always claimed that, "the newspaper people can't help you if you're losing and you don't need them if you're winning." He therefore cared little what people said or wrote about him. I watched criticism roll off his back on many occasions. That's not to say he wasn't vain and didn't like to read the papers when they were writing about him, as they did a great deal. But almost without exception Crisler had a favorable press. The grumbling you heard about Crisler was not that he wasn't newsworthy, but that he talked very little about his accomplishments and his plans. He had no friends that I know of in newspapers or in the radio or TV world. The nearest thing to a close acquaintance was Mill Marsh, the *Ann Arbor News* sportswriter, who on occasion played cards with Fritz on trips. Mill never wrote a bad line about Michigan or Crisler.

Crisler made no attempt to make friends or keep in touch with them. An illustration of this happened shortly after I became athletic director

As a coach with captain Fred Janke in 1938

Crisler with Michigan's most famous backfield in 1940: Forest Evashevski, Bob Westphal, Tom Harmon, Fred Trosko

in 1968. Lynn "Pappy" Waldorf had coached at Northwestern and at the University of California at Berkeley, and had known Fritz for many years. He came by the office while he was scouting for the San Francisco 49ers. We talked about mutual friends, primarily Bill Reed, Stu Holcomb, Red Mackey, and Biggie Munn. He asked about Fritz. "He hasn't been feeling well," I told him, "and he's usually alone. Why don't you drive out and see him?" I drew a little map to show where Fritz lived out in the Hills, not too far from where I lived. Pappy looked at me, winked and said, "I may do that." He never did. A year later when he came back I asked him why he didn't go see Fritz. He just shrugged his shoulders. It was pretty obvious he had never felt he was even a close acquaintance of Crisler's.

It bothered me to see people ignore Crisler during his retirement, and they certainly did. He had always been wonderful to me and even though we were never close friends, he was always generous to me. The first occurrence of his kindness came in 1949, my first year as track coach. I was certainly not a very good one in those days, finishing eighth in the Big Ten. At Michigan you almost have to *try* to do that. Fritz never said a word to me and gave me a substantial raise three weeks later. We finished second the next year and won our share after that.

Another instance was when I was invited by the U. S. State Department to go to Africa in 1956 to coach the first Kenya and Uganda Olympic teams for the Melbourne Games. I was to be paid $750 a month, as I recall, more than I was earning at Michigan; I think my salary in those days was $8,200 a year. There were no Michigan track meets scheduled, but I would be gone for six weeks or two months during the fall. When I told Fritz about the invitation, that was the fall of '55, I suggested he take me off the payroll until I returned. That was common in those days when people took leaves of absence. He looked up from his desk, didn't smile, just looked at me and said, "I don't think we'll do that. You have a new house; you could use the money." And that was the end of the conversation. It was a particular surprise because Fritz was cost-conscious and the coaching staff was constantly concerned over what Fritz might think about their expenditures on one thing or another. I realized then he was more human and kind than he wanted anyone to believe.

Fritz's contributions to intercollegiate athletics at Michigan are leg-

The department "limo" was passed on to Oosterbaan when he became coach; Crisler with George Ceithaml, Ben Oosterbaan, and Al Wistert.

endary. Everyone knows he was the founder of two-platoon football, born out of necessity when he was playing Earl Blake's great Army team in Yankee Stadium during World War II with a bunch of unheralded Michigan students. He was a long-time member of the NCAA rules committee, actually "for life," and was instrumental in the two-point conversion and many other college football rules being adopted.

Few remember that Crisler was a dominant figure in aligning the Big Ten with the Pacific 10 on the Rose Bowl agreement. Lay Leishman, Bill Nicholas, and Stanley Hahn, three members of the Rose Bowl football committee and giants in the bowl picture, referred many times to Fritz's contributions to the Rose Bowl. Prior to the Big Ten alliance the Rose Bowl did not sell out. Afterward, it was standing room only for decades. In 1996 there was a change in the Rose Bowl agreement that opened it up to a coalition game that might pit No. 1 against No. 2 in the Rose Bowl. Many feel it was a serious mistake that both conferences will one day regret. The original Rose Bowl pact was unique and the most prestigious, lucrative, and traditional Bowl of all time. To gamble that package seems foolish. The presidents were responsible and the Big Ten

Two giants of the Rose Bowl, Stan Hahn and Lay Leishman. They always gave Crisler credit as the one who put the Big Ten–Pac-10 Bowl agreement together in the 1940s.

has little leadership in the office of commissioner Jim Delany.

Crisler, like all athletic directors during their time, served through great change. He was confronted with television for the first time. He fought and lost the battle against moving from strict amateurism to paid athletic scholarships, something he never believed in and warned would be a ruination of intercollegiate athletics. He, along with Aigler, practically wrote the Big Ten and NCAA rules on recruiting and the rules on the conduct of an athlete. In the history of the NCAA, both are mentioned frequently as the Michigan contribution to intercollegiate sports in that area. Some of the recruiting rules they introduced are still in the NCAA handbook.

Crisler also witnessed the tremendous inflation that occurred in intercollegiate athletics, starting after World War II. He fostered the inclusion of the black athlete at Michigan and that led other institutions to follow. When Michigan played California in Berkeley in 1940 he was the first football coach to use air travel to fly the team. In addition to all that, he built and financed a men's varsity swimming pool, now called the Cliff Keen Gymnasium, and the Margaret Bell pool for women. He twice enlarged Michigan Stadium, erected a modern scoreboard in the stadium, and built Crisler Arena, the Ray Fisher Baseball Stadium, a golf course club house, and the athletic offices at the corner of Hoover and State Street.

When Crisler retired at 70, he did it reluctantly. It was almost humorous to me, except that I understood his love for the position. When I was named, March 15, 1968, I was to take over July 1. In that span, the only overture Fritz made to me was to take me to two Big Ten meetings and one Board in Control meeting. We never discussed the job and I wasn't privy to any of the problems that faced the department during those four months. I just kept on coaching track.

It was not until July 1 that he called me down to the office and we talked for two or three hours, with him sitting behind the desk as he always did. He gave advice, showed files and financial statements I'd never seen before, and then got up and walked out, saying, "I won't be back unless you call me." He had spent most of the time warning me there would probably be a move to take over the athletic department administration and finances and to take the authority away from the Board in Control. He was correct, but I wasn't really concerned about it because I had assurances from Fleming that things were not going to change. The issue did not come up again until the 1990s after I had retired.

Crisler's contributions to the University of Michigan and to intercollegiate athletics were monumental. Michigan and those who follow its teams will be forever in his debt. He was simply the most respected and admired man in intercollegiate athletics during his time.

Crisler's last backfield: Chalmers (Bump) Elliott, Howard Yerges, Jack Weisenburger, and Bob Chappuis. They won the Rose Bowl game against Southern California 49-0 in 1948.

◆◆◆

Chapter **4**

Legends

◆ ────────────────────────────

Harry Kipke and Others

A handful of people in Michigan athletics stand out larger than life. Some names may not be household words, even for U-M followers, and not all have had buildings named after them. But their contributions to the university were exceptional in some way. Five of these unique individuals are gathered here, all appropriately under the heading, "Legends."

Harry Kipke — Dedicated

Harry Kipke gets his name in the Michigan history books in three categories: athlete, coach, and regent of the university. Time has eroded memory of his achievements. Few remember he was a football All-American who won nine sports letters at Michigan, three each in football, basketball and baseball. That was in the early '20s when athletes were allowed to compete for only three years. (In 1902, Neil Snow won 10 letters, but under slightly different eligibility standards.) One of Kipke's athletic highlights came in 1922 when 72,500 spectators crammed into Ohio State's new stadium for the dedication game against Michigan. The Buckeyes had beaten the Wolverines three consecutive years and expected the string to hit four, but Kipke took a pitchout and scored the winning touchdown. "This place is really dedicated now," he remarked, holding the ball aloft as he crossed the goal line. Kipke's claim to football fame, though, is in his kicking — he was one of the greatest kickers in Michigan history.

In 1924, while a senior at Michigan, he accepted the job as head baseball coach at the University of Missouri. Primarily, though, the Tigers wanted him as an assistant football and basketball coach. From there Kipke moved on to a coaching job at Michigan State before winding up back at Michigan in 1929 as football coach, replacing E.E. "Tad" Wieman.

In his nine-year tenure as coach of the Wolverines, Kipke's record was 46-26-5. In the four-year span from 1930 to 1933, Michigan went 31-1-3, with four consecutive Big Ten titles, plus national championships in 1932 and 1933. No other Michigan coach has equaled that record.

Unfortunately, after Kipke's initial four-year success, Michigan football fell on hard times. The next four years were disastrous: the 1934 team won only one game and lost seven, 1935 brought a four and four split and 1936 saw a 1-7 repeat. Following another 4-4 record in 1937, Athletic Director Fielding Yost simply had to fire the man he still thought of as one of his old players.

It wasn't easy, however. Kipke had solid support from many Michigan people who liked him personally. In fact, Kipke was one of the University of Michigan's most popular football coaches ever. He had been a great athlete, he was modest and possessed a genuine sense of humor; and he had led Michigan to two national championships in eight years, all factors that endeared Kipke to many people.

Stories began to spring up regarding the reasons behind his firing and it's not clear who started them. They were reinforced by a statement from Yost. "Michigan never fires people for losing games," he said.

"Then why?" wondered the press.

Yost wouldn't comment, but he seemed to be alluding to other

Athletic Director Yost, left, with football coach Harry Kipke, far right, in 1931. The Little Brown Jug, traditional trophy for the winner of the annual Michigan-Minnesota game, was stolen and found. The duplicate is often on display. Kip's staff: Wally Weber, Ben Oosterbaan, Jack Blott, Frank Cappon. The situation here appears to be a serious discussion about what to do with two jugs.

problems. It was revealed there had been an early season practice in Canada at which Ivy Williamson (who later became athletic director at the University of Wisconsin) had been injured. The incident received widespread publicity. In addition, Kipke and his line coach, Frank Cappon, had had a public squabble that ended up in the newspapers. The disagreement was pointed to as evidence of widespread dissension. Actually it wasn't, but when Michigan lost, Kipke's friends tended to pick out the line play as the reason.

But there were general staff problems. When any team is losing, that's usually the first effect. Kipke began to overreach as he tried to shore up the team, requiring most of his players, even those who were also baseball, basketball, and track athletes, to report to spring football practice. Only some of the varsity football players and outstanding athletes in the spring sports were excused.

Kipke's friends and defenders cited statements Yost had made from time to time that undermined Kipke's leadership. During his tenure as athletic director Yost had developed a habit of commenting frankly about the football program to the press. Ralph Aigler, the faculty representative for athletics, finally stepped in and sent Yost a letter suggesting he discontinue talking about the faults of Kipke and his staff.

Kipke's relationship with Harry Bennett, who ran the Ford Motor Company for Henry Ford II, was criticized by many. It was revealed that most of the football team had jobs at a Ford factory during the summer and were permitted to practice rather than work. The most serious charge against Kipke involved a slush fund set up by some people from Chicago, alumni who operated in Ann Arbor to assist football candidates. It was true: two athletes who had received illegal aid had quit the football team and dropped out of the university some time before the situation was discovered.

The violations would be a quick invitation these days for NCAA probation. In Kipke's time they may have been improper, but they were not NCAA violations. Later on, Aigler promoted some restrictive legislation in the NCAA because of matters discovered in the Michigan program just prior to Fritz Crisler taking over.

"I should have been fired. I just had lost interest in coaching," Kipke told me in 1969 on Lake St. Claire. He and Dr. Albert Kerlikowski had included me on one of their weekly bass fishing trips. I've fished the same area 100 times since.

Kipke never exhibited any bitterness over being fired. After his ousting as coach in favor of Crisler, he ran for a spot on the Board of Regents at U-M and was elected, serving for eight years during the '40s. He also was a member of the Board in Control of Intercollegiate Athletics for six years. Minutes of meetings reveal his great contributions on both boards and President Alexander Ruthven said he was an exceptional regent.

In 1944 Kipke became president of the Coca-Cola Co.'s Chicago office, holding that title until 1958 when he was elected chairman of the board. In 1962 he was appointed assistant to the company's national president. Kipke was elected in 1958 to the National Football Foundation Hall of Fame and 10 years later was inducted into the Michigan Sports Hall of Fame. He was 73 when he died in 1972.

William D. Revelli — Strike Up the Band

March king John Phillip Sousa proclaimed Michigan's fight song, "The Victors," by Louis Elbel, to be the greatest fight song ever written. And William D. Revelli certainly ranks among the greatest band directors of all time. He was the man who replaced military drill with marching in step to the arrangement, an innovation that changed marching bands everywhere.

By the time I arrived at Michigan as a student, Revelli already had been there for three of his 36 years with the university. He replaced Nicholas Falcone as the director of bands and chairman of the wind instrument department in 1935, beginning an era in which the university had perhaps the finest collegiate marching band in the country.

William D. Revelli, the guy in the center in the dark hat, burned a hole in the stadium Tartan Turf.

I knew Revelli well, from when I was track coach in 1948. Football coach Crisler had evicted the marching band from practice on the baseball outfield because it interfered with his adjacent practice too much. When Bill asked me if he could bring the band over to the inside of the running track at Ferry Field, I agreed. For many years we held our fall track and field practice early so Revelli could have his band work out at Ferry Field. It was no picnic for us, inconvenient, in fact, and I regretted I'd made the agreement. But I liked him so well I just couldn't change the situation.

In 1949 Michigan's band played in Yankee Stadium, then traveled to Pasadena to play at the Rose Bowl, both firsts that helped tag the band with the title, "Transcontinental All-American Band," in an era when airplane travel was less common than today.

Television was fascinated with Revelli and his marching bands in the early days, and without question TV had a lot to do with the popularity of the spectacle of Michigan football. We always tried to make room and provide time for Revelli's halftime, pregame, and postgame shows. I remember asking him if he'd give a postgame concert because I wanted people to stay in the stands and have a more orderly exit from the parking lots. He did it enthusiastically. It is now a ritual followed by most schools.

The master Bill Revelli with his capable successor, George Cavender. Cavender carried on the great tradition started by Revelli. They made football Saturdays special.

The year after we laid artificial turf in Michigan Stadium, one of Revelli's halftime shows backfired on him. Even years later Bill didn't much appreciate the comedy of the situation. The plan was for him to shoot a rocket 10 or 20 feet into the air, a fireworks display that was supposed to turn into a flower pot or some such thing. Maybe it was placed on the stand upside down or maybe it was defective. In any case, it made a hole in the artificial turf, and not a small one. With a second half to play we had a burned carpet.

The fans were horrified and Revelli was upset. Actually, although it had blackened a few square feet of the carpet, it looked much worse than it was. Officials inspected it and said there was no problem. The game went on and Michigan won. The next day, Sunday, I was in my office about 11 a.m. when I heard a rap on the window and there was Bill. I let him in and I could see he was still extremely upset. I said to forget about it, it was something easily repaired and we had plenty of spare carpet. All that had to be done was cut out the damaged square yard and cement a patch in place. He was not convinced. To relieve his mind I invited him down to the stadium on Monday afternoon to prove there were no permanent effects. We couldn't even see where the damage had occurred. Revelli never forgot that. On more than one occasion when he was speaking and I happened to be in the audience he would refer to our great friendship and how it didn't change, "even when he set fire to the Michigan Stadium."

Under Revelli's direction the University of Michigan Symphonic Band owned a truly international reputation. In 1961 the band defied the Cold War and traveled to the Soviet Union, Poland, and Romania, as well as Greece, Turkey, Jordan, Cyprus, and Lebanon — 30,000 miles and dozens of hours of concerts, all in 16 weeks.

Revelli's halftime innovations were copied nationwide as week after week, throughout his years at Michigan, his bands performed intricate formations on the field. Revelli led the band through 1971 and his influence continues. George Cavender, his assistant for 19 years, was the director through 1978. Eric Becher held the position through 1989, then came Gary Lewis for five years and, in 1995, former assistant Jeff Grogan took over — all with Michigan's tradition for excellent marching bands intact. During much of that time the band's announcer, whose voice became very familiar to football fans, was Carl Grapentine. In 1996 he was still going strong, and still driving from Chicago for each home game.

Under Revelli the band department expanded from one band and one department — made up only of himself — to a program of seven bands, more than 500 members and a nationally-recognized faculty of 15. The Michigan Marching Band was acclaimed worldwide.

On two occasions during my tenure Revelli had the band spell out my name in the middle of the field during the halftime show. When I was about to retire he offered to see that it was done again. Twice is enough, I said.

The band building on Hoover Street is named Revelli Hall. It was my affection for Revelli that gave me an idea when the university was seeking a location: I knew we were going to build indoor tennis courts, so I offered the outdoor tennis court site. Revelli was touched and the

The band even spelled my name right.
Twice was enough.

band people immediately accepted. So where Revelli Hall now stands, our former tennis courts once were. And that's why I'm the only ex-track coach who is a lifetime member of the Marching Band Alumni Association.

Henry Hatch — Behind the Scenes

Probably the first man in the nation to receive the title "Manager of Athletic Equipment," Henry Hatch started at Michigan during the directorship of Yost and remained for 44 years. Seven head football coaches and two long-term athletic directors had the good fortune to be served by Henry. Hatch died unexpectedly on April 7, 1964, four years before I became the athletic director. I worked with Henry for 16 years as a track coach and for two years before that as an assistant. And, of course, he was the equipment manager for the four years I was an athlete. I still think of him when I go into Yost Arena.

Hatch was more than an equipment manager. He was a great psychologist and probably knew the athletes better than the coaches. The lowest substitute received the same treatment from Hatch as the All-Americans and national champions who came by his cage for equipment every evening. If anything, he attempted to encourage the also-rans more than he did the stars. Few All-Americans got big heads around Henry. He would remind one and all that, "No one is ever so good that we can't find someone better." That usually was directed at some athlete who had started to believe his press clippings.

Never acknowledging the possibility Michigan might lose any contest, Hatch felt it his duty to keep individuals and teams from getting depressed. That attitude coming from the cage on the second floor of Yost Field House had a tremendous influence on how some players played the game.

Hatch had a way of defusing situations with humor. I recall a Saturday afternoon when Tom Harmon fumbled on a critical play. The next Monday Henry had a small ceremony in the equipment cage where, with Harmon's teammates looking on, he presented the great halfback with a football. Hatch had glued a handle on one side. Harmon, for a time at least, kept the ball with Henry's handle in place.

Hatch's friendship with Elroy "Crazy Legs" Hirsch, who had played for Michigan during the war and later became athletic director at the University of Wisconsin, led to Henry being portrayed in Hirsch's movie biography. From Bennie Oosterbaan, to Tom Harmon, to Terry Barr and Ron Kramer, he was the confidant of the athlete.

His devotion to the job was obvious. The lights would go on in Yost Field House early in the morning and stay lit into the evening. Henry was not only a dispenser of equipment, he was a master shoe cobbler, an excellent seamstress, and an innovator of protective equipment. His work shop was always busy. Equipment he designed and made became standard.

Under Yost and Crisler, equipment wasn't as sophisticated as it is

Henry Hatch with football jerseys showing the three numbers retired during his time: Bennie Oosterbaan, No. 47, Tom Harmon, No. 98, and the Wistert brothers — all three became All-Americans in the 1930s and '40s — No. 11. Only one other number was retired in the long history of Michigan football — No. 87, belonging to Ron Kramer.

today, or as plentiful. In my early days as track coach, Henry sewed new soles and put new spikes in the track shoes rather than issue a new pair to each athlete three or four times a year as we presently do. If an athlete lost a jock strap, it wouldn't be replaced unless the athlete had a note from the coach. Not many jock straps were lost. Today, athletes, men and women, walk through the campus with athletic department T-shirts and shorts and sweat socks that were issued for competition. That never happened in Henry's time. He guarded the equipment like it was his own.

The athletic equipment room for all sports was in a small area on the second floor of Yost Field House. It wasn't until I had the first football building constructed in the early 1970s that the equipment manager had adequate space for all sports. When we moved the equipment into other sports areas we found shelves of shoes, shirts and shorts in corners that had been there since the 1920s. Every inch of space was used — and nothing was thrown away.

Wanda, Henry's wife, was a delightful lady who worked in the Michigan ticket office for many years. Their daughter, Pat, subsequently did the same, when she wasn't teaching school.

When Henry died, a young man, Ron Pulliam, took his place, but Ron died during my time as athletic director and I hired Jon Falk, from Miami of Ohio. Falk would be a story in himself, but suffice it to say he is an equipment manager from the old school. He handles the job with remarkable skill, a job that is now far more complex with women's teams, larger squads, more men's teams, more athletes and more equipment for all sports than even a decade ago.

Jon Falk

In 1964 several of us in the graduate M Club, including Oosterbaan, were planning a special Henry Hatch Day for May 23. Hatch's old friends from all over the country had been sending in letters and gifts and contributions for the event. When Henry died in April, Oosterbaan had already received a stack of over 200 messages, letters and telegrams. We had planned to present them in a portfolio to Hatch on M Day but never had the chance.

Henry was a shrewd analyst of people. I would have loved to hear his assessment of the coaches he came to know and the hundreds of athletes he served and talked with for those 44 years. Of all the people who operated behind the scenes in the Michigan athletic department from the '20s to the '90s, no one was more anonymous to the public and yet did more to promote athletic success for the university than Henry Hatch.

Bennie Oosterbaan — In the Record Books

Benjamin Gaylord Oosterbaan was born in Muskegon, Mich., in 1906. He won nine letters at Michigan, in football, basketball, and baseball. In football he led the Big Ten in touchdowns in 1925, and in 1928 he led the Big Ten in scoring in basketball and was selected as a

Two of America's greatest football legends met in the late '20s: Bennie Oosterbaan, on the left, with Red Grange,"The Galloping Ghost" of Illinois.

first team All-American in that sport. He was a football captain in 1927 and the Most Valuable Player. And as a first baseman he led the Big Ten in hitting in 1928 and won the Western Conference medal for proficiency and scholarship as a senior.

Although he played in the '20s, Oosterbaan is still listed on many all-time football teams. One of college football's most gifted athletes, Oosterbaan was three times an All-American under Yost, the only three-time end until Anthony Carter came along in the early '80s. In 1927 the Helms Athletic Foundation of California named Bennie the Amateur Athlete of the Year, an award that was the forerunner of the

Heisman Trophy.

As a coach, Oosterbaan led his teams to Big Ten, Rose Bowl, and national titles. He succeeded Crisler as coach in 1948 and was followed in 1958 by Chalmers "Bump" Elliott who had played for Fritz and coached with Bennie. A national coach of the year, Oosterbaan retired with a .656 winning percentage, having won 63 games, lost 33

Bennie Oosterbaan
Always dignified and poised.

and tied 4. Although I never saw Oosterbaan play, I knew him well as a coach and as one of my administrative assistants when I became athletic director.

Although Oosterbaan is more famous for his remarkable pass receiving, he was a master of all other departments in football. He was probably one of the most accomplished defensive ends in Michigan history. Yost said that Oosterbaan's position at end, "was never turned by an opponent in his three years of play." But his main fame arose from his relationship with Benny Friedman, another of

Michigan's All-Americans and one of the most proficient passers of his day. Oosterbaan and Friedman formed one of the most celebrated passing combinations in football. "From Friedman to Oosterbaan" has gone down in football history. As proof of Bennie's all-around athletic ability, he turned into a passer in his senior year against Ohio State, threw two passes for touchdowns, and lateraled for another as Michigan beat Ohio.

In baseball, Oosterbaan pitched and played first base, led the Big Ten in hitting, and was called by his coach, Ray Fisher, "one of the two greatest players I ever coached." Ray never did say who the other was, possibly George Sisler. Steve Farrell, Michigan's track coach at the time, regretted Bennie's decision to play baseball. Ben had been a state discus champion in high school. Farrell, one of the great track coaches, maintained that Oosterbaan could easily have been an

Olympic discus champion. There are stories of how Oosterbaan would stroll by the track, pick up the discus, and throw it farther than the Big Ten champion who was on the Michigan team at the time. Yet he never did compete in track. Baseball was his spring sport.

"Just remember, Canham," he'd say, "I could have been a track star." He was joking, of course; he was one of the most modest men I ever knew.

Under Yost, Oosterbaan was the freshman coach. When Crisler arrived, Bennie became an end coach and doubled as the basketball coach for a time. In 1946 he became Crisler's number one assistant and his backfield coach. And when Fritz retired in 1948, Bennie was his successor.

When I became athletic director, Bennie had been retired for some years as coach and wasn't very active in athletic affairs. We immediately gave him a nice office and used him constantly for alumni affairs where he was outstanding. His help during my early years was instrumental in my being accepted by many Michigan people who weren't quite sure about "that track coach who took Fritz Crisler's place."

Marie Hartwig — First Women's A.D.

The first women's athletic director at Michigan, Marie Dorothy Hartwig, appointed in 1973, couldn't have been a better selection. I had only one regret about the choice I made — I lost her to retirement less than halfway through my directorship. Marie had been on the staff since 1932, more than five years before I came to Michigan as a student. A real trailblazer for women's sports, she worked for Yost and for Crisler before me, but in the physical education department.

The new post was an outgrowth of Title IX, part of the Educational Amendment Act passed by Congress in 1972 mandating "equal opportunity for men's and women's athletic programs." University President Robben Fleming and the regents created a separate women's athletic department in 1973. Because it was placed under the director of intercollegiate athletics, the responsibility was mine to choose an associate director for women. Hartwig was a remarkable person with the right credentials. Long before Title IX began to flex its muscles, Marie and I had met numerous times to discuss women's athletics and she understood the financial and organizational problems. She ran Michigan's club sports and recreation programs for women and taught classes on organization and administration in the school of physical education.

We wanted to officially field women's teams. Hartwig insisted on moving cautiously into women's intercollegiate competition, to take enough time to plan carefully. She constantly warned against making the same mistakes the men's program suffered from, specifically in recruiting and scholarships which, disregarding need, were based on performance. Probably she had discussed these matters with Crisler and, before that, with Yost. She felt the men had let athletics move in the wrong direction with financial aid and recruiting practices.

Marie Hartwig
She had everyone's respect.

In 1970 a single department of physical education under the intercollegiate athletic department had been established, a change from separate units for men and women. Paul Hunsicker, my associate director, headed it up. Hartwig was a professor of physical education and Paul's assistant in charge of the women's program. This 1970 move put the women's intramural program and club sports programs together with the men's. That led to a strong women's recreation program, but the club arrangement for women had only meager financial support from the university, unlike men's intercollegiate competition under the athletic department. Dissatisfaction about funding was inevitable, and the athletic department provided some early help. Unfortunately, our problem was trying to fund intercollegiate athletics. Recreation was another matter for both men and women.

Already two club sports for women had become well-established under resourceful coaches "Red" Simmons in track and Joyce Lindeman in synchronized swimming, although there were few varsity teams to compete against. That kind of arrangement was the forerunner of intercollegiate competition. In the early '70s when Hartwig and I attempted to start women's intercollegiate athletics at Michigan, there was little history to build on.

Marie was not satisfied with the scope of competition or the available financing. In May 1973 the regents appointed Eunice Burns as chairman of a committee to study the matter. Title IX, passed the year before, obviously forced the action. In November the Burns committee recommended to the regents that, "intercollegiate athletics [for women] at Michigan be started immediately." The regents funded the program with $175,000, as I recall. Since that day, however, women's athletics has been totally funded by the intercollegiate athletic program. With the funds mostly coming from the men's revenue sports, the budget now is in the millions.

We officially started the women's intercollegiate program in 1974 with six sports for which Marie felt there was the most interest and talent available. Track and field was not one of them because of the scarcity of schools to compete against. It was not until more interest in track developed, following the 1976 Olympics, that women's track and field became a varsity sport at Michigan.

Despite the clamor for more teams, Marie was right. The initial six provided enough problems for her and her staff: swimming, diving, basketball, volleyball, tennis, and golf. We didn't have to recruit to get started. The teams filled up quickly.

At the time Michigan belonged to an organization called the Association for Intercollegiate Athletics for Women (AIAW). Sadly, that organization disbanded when the NCAA took over women's athletics in the '80s. By then we had added five more sports for women — track, field hockey, cross country, swimming, and gymnastics. We dropped one, synchronized swimming, for lack of competition and no collegiate governing body.

Hartwig knew how to get things done. Her charm and wit brought support for her program from those who might otherwise have been reluctant. And she was a realist. A group connected with the women's basketball team complained I didn't promote and market it, under the first coach, Gloria Soluk, like I did football. Marie merely said, "Win some games and I'll talk with Don." Michigan had won three games that season.

The Marie Hartwig Building

After Hartwig's retirement she was my leading advisor on women's athletics for the next 10 years of my directorship and is still a good friend. She left the university before she could get proper credit. Her knowledge, patience and cooperation were the launching pad for Michigan's women's athletic program. Deservedly, she has two lasting memorials to her service — The Marie Hartwig Award, presented to the Michigan Women's Athlete of the Year, and the Marie Hartwig Building. Two buildings, connected back to back, make up the Hartwig building. The older, now the Ferry Field ticket office, once housed the football locker rooms and Yost's office during his entire tenure. The other I had constructed as a women's office building.

Phyllis Ocker

Phyllis Ocker succeeded Marie upon her retirement and served the remaining years until my retirement in 1988. The program continues to grow on the foundation Marie Hartwig built.

◆◆◆

Chapter 5

Coaching Track

◆ ───────────────────────────────────

Championships and Foreign Athletes

I n the spring of 1948, Fritz Crisler told me I would be the track coach at Michigan, succeeding Ken Doherty who had taken the same position at the University of Pennsylvania. Actually it was not quite that simple. For weeks Crisler had delayed naming someone while he interviewed many of the country's outstanding track coaches. I had no assurances he would appoint me. I watched him interview established coaches from across the country, Chick Werner of Penn State, Bill Easton of Kansas, and a few I didn't recognize.

As assistant track coach I was sharing an office with Ozzie Cowles, then the basketball coach; Wally Weber, assistant football

Tony Seth, of Guiana, the most talented runner I ever coached. No one ever knew it. He fell in love and left school in his sophomore year. What might have been has bothered me since.

coach; and two others. Ozzie knew I didn't want to go to Pennsylvania with Doherty and one day said, "Go across the hall and ask the old man for the job." With nothing to lose I did just that one noon when Norma Bentley, Crisler's secretary, was at lunch. She would have scheduled an appointment a week in the future. I said to Fritz, "Why don't you give me the track job?" His answer was, "Can you handle it?" My reply was, "Sure." Crisler said, "OK, you have it." That was the interview, evaluation and offer. It took two minutes. I was stunned. Of course, Fritz had intended to hire me in the first place. He didn't do things on the spur of the moment. I think he wanted me to ask first, though.

I returned to the office across the hall and said to Ozzie, "I got the job, now what do I do? I don't know where to start." In his wisdom he replied, "Just be enthusiastic, it covers up a lot of shortcomings." I was the most enthusiastic coach in history.

Michigan's football team, coached by Crisler, had just won the 1948 Rose Bowl and then he announced his retirement from coaching to become a full-time athletic director. Bennie Oosterbaan was to be the new football coach. Track and field was not a high priority at that time.

One of my relay teams that set American and world records: Jack Carroll, George Jacoby, Don McEwen and John Ross. Carroll, McEwen and Ross were also Big Ten champions and all were from Canada.

The 20 years I was to be track coach at Michigan was not one of our golden times in football. In fact, during that period Michigan State, with Biggie Munn and Duffy Daugherty, captivated the state of Michigan and the nation with their successes and for the most part dominated Michigan in football. The publicity and reputation of Michigan was carried by sports other than football. It wasn't until Bo Schembechler arrived in 1969 to coach football that things would change.

Ken Doherty
He left for Pennsylvania.

Before Doherty left for Pennsylvania, he asked me to go with him to be his assistant coach. He told me that, at age 27, I probably hadn't had enough experience to be the head coach at Michigan. He was right, but at the time I didn't see it that way. I had been Ken's assistant for only two years and before that had briefly coached in high school prior to World War II. I went on hoping for the job, oblivious to my lack of qualifications, and I got it. Ignorance was bliss, I guess.

Ken was an enigma to many, including Crisler. They seldom spoke to each other. I knew Fritz and Ken did not get along and I was afraid Crisler would not appoint an assistant of Doherty's as his replacement.

Ken, I recall, had a picture of Charlie Hoyt, his predecessor, hanging over his desk. Fritz walked into Ken's office one afternoon, saw the picture and said, "I thought Hoyt went to Yale. I don't think I'd have that picture hanging there." Fritz had always resented Hoyt for leaving Michigan because he was extremely popular and a successful coach. He could never understand why anyone would leave a coaching position at Michigan to go to Yale. Neither could I.

Doherty gave the impression he could never relax and have a good time. He constantly analyzed life, athletes, and how people reacted to situations. But he probably knew more about track and field techniques than any man who ever coached. In fact, his book, *Modern Track and Field*, made him famous throughout the world. It was a masterpiece and to this day, some 25 years later, is still widely used.

Ken did not believe much in recruiting, but in those days it was very low-key compared with today. His idea of recruiting was to send a letter or two to an outstanding high school prospect. He also never understood public relations. He had been a national decathlon track champion and third in the Olympic decathlon, so no one doubted his knowledge and qualifications. However, communicating was difficult for him. Yet I suppose I learned as much about coaching, good and bad, in two years under him as one could learn anywhere.

Doherty left for Penn in the spring and I hired Elmer Swanson as my assistant, a lucky appointment for me. Elmer was a giant in every respect. He had played baseball for Ray Fisher and hurdled for Doherty. Elmer and I made a few mistakes our first year.

When I looked around the league I saw Leo Johnson at Illinois, who had won national championships; Larry Snyder of Ohio State, coach of Jesse Owens and Mal Witfield; and Karl Schlaedeman, veteran coach at Michigan State, who had won national cross country championships and was regarded as one of the leading distance coaches in the country. I should have been scared to death.

I made plans to go to Europe the second summer I was coaching to work with Armas Valste of Finland — regarded as the leading coach in the world. I also attended just about every track and field clinic in the United States and kept copious notes of every time I talked with anyone who had any knowledge of track. It was a cram course on how to become a track coach. However, it was Phil Diamond, former German instructor at Michigan and also former owner of Liberty Music Shop in Ann Arbor, who was my closest confidant. He was the man

In 1952 Armas Valste, center, visited me from Finland. Lloyd Olds from Eastern Michigan University joined us. They were two of the giants in track and field.

who helped me most during my early years. He had actually been an unofficial coach for Hoyt and Doherty, and probably was their closest friend. His knowledge of track and field was considerable.

I had seen a book on baseball illustrated by a man named Tyler Micoleau, whom I later learned was the Leroy Neiman of his day. His remarkably fluid baseball illustrations made it obvious that Micoleau had a feeling for athletics. I wrote to the publisher's president, Lowell Pratt of A.S. Barnes Books, and asked if he would be interested in a series of books on track, to be illustrated by Micoleau, and if so, would he please contact him. Immediately I got an answer saying he had talked with Micoleau, who would like to do the books. Obviously it was not my name that influenced Pratt but the fact I was the track coach at Michigan. I was about to put to good use the hundreds of pages of notes I'd accumulated in my travels.

Micoleau came to Ann Arbor and spent three weeks at my home. Tyler illustrated every conceivable technique in track and field to be used in the books. Phil and I did the text. The books can be described as a series of drawings by Micoleau filled in with my commentary, followed by a section on training and techniques I had learned from the great coaches.

The books were called *Track Techniques Illustrated, Field Techniques Illustrated,* and *Cross Country Techniques Illustrated.* To my great surprise these books, published in 1950, became the best-selling track and field books in the world for the next 15 years. This was mostly due to Micoleau and his talent for simplifying, with beautiful drawings, a complicated event like the pole vault. The books were translated into Spanish, French, Russian, and Japanese. Micoleau and I collected royalties for many years, but the Russians, and I think some others, simply pirated the books. We received no royalties from Moscow.

I received better benefits than royalties, however; I became known throughout Europe and in subsequent years received many invitations to coach in foreign countries. Michigan was becoming regarded throughout the world as a great track and field institution — not quite true maybe, but who would argue the point?

A footnote to this is that, when the books were published in England, Harold Abrahams, who won a gold medal in the 100-meter sprint at the 1924 Olympic Games and the hero portrayed in the movie *Chariots of Fire*, was the English editor. After his Olympic victory he became a sports reporter and an author in London.

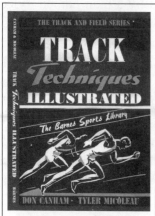

U.S., Japanese and English editions

In 1954 at the European Championships in Bern, Switzerland, I was coaching the Finnish field event squad. We stayed near Bern in a small town called Thun. One day on the street someone mentioned that the English team was staying at a hotel not far from ours. I walked over, stepped up on the porch and approached a man sitting in a swing.

"Do you know Harold Abrahams?" I asked.

"Yes, my friend, you're talking to him," came the reply.

I knew Abrahams traveled with the British team on occasion; it was just on a hunch I met the man who had written a very flattering foreword in the English editions of my books. We sat and talked for two hours or more. It was a memorable afternoon.

An athletic director at Eastern Michigan University probably had as much effect on my career as anyone. His name was Lloyd Olds. He had been track coach there and later athletic director. Incidentally, Lloyd was the person who first dressed basketball and football officials in striped shirts. Whenever I see officials so garbed I think of Olds. Almost immediately after I became track coach, Lloyd came to see me and asked if I would be interested in becoming involved in the Amateur Athletic Union. Both Hoyt and Doherty had refused to hold AAU-organized track meets on the Michigan campus. I had no idea why they felt this way, so I told Lloyd we were certainly interested. For several years, until 1953, I conducted indoor and outdoor AAU championships at Michigan.

In 1953 Lloyd engineered a summer trip to Europe where I was to be the head coach with five or six 1952 Olympic champions on a 16-man team. That trip changed my life. We competed for three or four weeks throughout Scandinavia. When we got to Finland I saw what later became known as the "loopfilm." All coaches used 16-mm film in those days to teach and coach. The Finns had taken 10 or 12 feet of film and made a loop. Put it into a movie projector and you could watch, for example, Jesse Owens running continuously on the screen. A coach could point out the good and bad as Jesse performed over and over — no more reversing the projector. I was impressed with the simplicity of it and planned to use it with my own track team at Michigan. The innovation was to become the foundation for our family corporation, now known as School-Tech Inc., with more than 80 employees.

When we went to Germany I heard that someone was selling the negatives of the 1936 Olympic Games for $280. I immediately bought them. Back in the United States I cut them into 22 loops with all the Olympic champions demonstrating techniques. Then I packaged them to track coaches in the U.S. and in three months had made more than $10,000. For those days that was a windfall.

With the profits from *Champions on Film*, we began to import stop watches from Switzerland and German starting guns. I say "we" because Diamond handled the storage and shipping of the films and other items. And we started at once to make a series of "loops" on 22 different sports: a football series with Forest Evashevski, a coach at Iowa and former U-M football star; a diving film with Bruce Harlan, a former Olympic champion who was coaching at Michigan; a cheerleading film with Newt Loken, the Michigan gymnastics coach; plus others featuring well-known coaches. Now the business is a manufacturing company in athletic equipment, health care, games, and scientific equipment. Video production is a small part. The business grew rapidly and it was put in trust when I became athletic director. Until 1968, though, I continued to coach track and run the business.

Conversations on planes are usually quickly forgotten. One, however,

I recall quite well. In December of 1964 Biggie Munn, then the athletic director at Michigan State, and Doc Greene, the noted columnist for *The Detroit News*, and I were flying back from a meeting in Washington, D.C.

Munn, a former shot putter from Minnesota, was a friend dating back to his days on Crisler's staff. During the flight, he turned to me and said, "Why don't we have an indoor track meet in Detroit? They have indoor track meets all over this country but nothing in Detroit."

I responded, "Well, if somebody will buy a track, I'll run the meet."

Greene threw in his opinion that *The News* would buy a track. He had no idea it would cost $55,000. But about a week later I got a call from Peter Clark, publisher of *The News*, asking to see me in Detroit.

Biggie Munn, who helped me start the NCAA Indoor Track Championships in Detroit.

Realizing then that the track meet idea might become more than a casual idea, I called Walter Byers, executive director of the NCAA, and said, "Walter, how about starting an indoor track meet, the National Championships, in Detroit? I'll do all the work and I think we can make it self-financing."

Byers, always willing to try something that would help intercollegiate athletics, responded, "Go ahead. Give me some ideas. Give me some plans. And give me a financial breakdown."

Then I talked with Clark and several on his staff at *The News*, including promotion director Bob Reese and his assistant Jim Stower. *The News* agreed to buy a track that would fit into Cobo Arena and would give it to the city.

For the next 14 years the meet was held at Cobo, with sellouts both for the Friday night and Saturday night competition. Record crowds followed when it moved next door to Joe Louis Arena, and again when it moved to the Silverdome in Pontiac. There we drew 25,000 spectators two consecutive years.

U-M was the tournament's host, but eventually the NCAA wanted to change the format to include women. We tried running the meet for a year or two on a combined basis but it just didn't work. We had doubled the size of the meet and instead of a two-hour program we had a five-hour program and fans don't sit still that long. In addition, the NCAA felt it had to go out on bid for hosts — a stupid thing to do. *The Detroit News*, the games committee, and the school were infuriated. In Detroit we had the most successful indoor track meet in the country and yet the NCAA was looking around. Later the NCAA said it was just a formality. We had a meeting and agreed the NCAA could find a new location. We'd had enough.

Subsequently it moved, going to Syracuse, Oklahoma City and Indianapolis with dismal turnouts in each place since. There

In 1985, the last year of the NCAA meet, we drew 25,000 spectators to the Silverdome — but with the women's events it ran five hours. The NCAA had ruined a great spectacle.

were two requests to return to Detroit, but we were no longer interested.

The sponsorship of *The Detroit News* was unique. Neither the NCAA nor the schools fully recognized the impact the newspaper had on the success of the meet. Radio and television helped, of course, as well as other newspapers. Friends in all branches of the media were responsible for its success. To start and conduct a track meet with the success we had during the same week of the NCAA basketball tournament was quite a feat. The NCAA found that out as they went to other locations.

It's difficult now to realize that, just 30 years ago, track and field was a major sport in the United States. On the front pages of their sports sections, the Detroit papers would headline the results of the

Big Ten championship and would carry full summaries of track meets throughout the country. Looking through old scrap books, I note that it wasn't unusual for almost a whole page of *The Detroit News* and the *Free Press* to be devoted to Michigan and Michigan State performances at the Penn and Drake Relays each year.

In the '50s and the '60s there were two major indoor track meets in Boston, six in Madison Square Garden in New York, one in Chicago, one in Cleveland, two in Los Angeles, one in San Francisco, one in Portland, Ore., and many others at indoor arenas around the nation. The college track coaches followed a regular circuit with their outstanding relay teams and individuals. Dual meet contests between major colleges were well-attended. The Michigan-Illinois dual meets during my time were always held before capacity crowds. When we ran at the Armory at Illinois the doors would have to be closed and locked an hour before the meet started because of the crush of people. At Ann Arbor, for almost all of the indoor track meets, we would fill the spectator half of Yost Field House. The Michigan State Relays drew teams from all over the country and always had capacity crowds.

Responsibility for the decline of track in the United States has to fall on the shoulders of the coaches as well as on the great surge of professional indoor sports, particularly basketball, both college and professional.

Madison Square Garden can present a basketball game now with Villanova and Georgetown at far less expense than it can put on a major track meet. It has college basketball teams standing in line to play in "The Garden." The increase in the popularity of hockey, Arena Football, touring ice shows, circuses and events of that nature, have taken venues away from what once made up the great collegiate track and field circuit.

The finger must be pointed at the coaches of the United States because they totally miscalculated public reaction to the switch to the metric system. The magic of the four-minute mile, when arenas were packed to see it attacked by a Glenn Cunningham or a Gene Venske or a Jim Ryan, is gone. There is no "magic" mile race in track now. It disappeared when the event was changed to the 1,500-meter race — and how many track and field fans even know how far 1,500 meters is? Worse was losing the magic of the 18-foot and then the 20-foot pole vault when measurements went to meters. What is a 7-foot high jump in meters? Few seem to know, or care. The drama that was built at a track meet by an approach to a 7-foot high jump or an 18-foot pole vault just isn't there. The excitement surrounding Jesse Owens and the 100-yard dash is a thing of the past — it's now 100 meters. Football fields are still 100 yards long, not 100 meters.

In addition, track coaches realized that running the big dual meets put pressure on the coaches; it was much easier to take a relay team to a major track meet where no score was kept. Track and field today in the United States is mostly conducted in relay meets. The great Southern California-UCLA dual track meet that used to draw 25,000 or 30,000 people is a distant memory.

Michigan recently put in a multi-million dollar track. It is hoped that the university, with its great track tradition, will be in the forefront of revival. In Jack Harvey and Ron Warhurst, it certainly has the coaches to get it done.

In 1956 I had coached the Kenya and Uganda Olympic teams, the first in East Africa, and saw some of the most remarkable athletes I'd ever encountered. I worked with some youngsters over there who later must have become world champions.

It was my coaching trips to Europe and the Caribbean that started foreign athletes coming to Michigan. Eeles Landstrom, the European pole vault champion, Fritz Neilsen, the Swedish discus champion, and Tom Robinson, the Bahamian four-time Olympian, were the first to arrive.

Each year saw Michigan with foreign athletes, particularly from the Caribbean countries. Canada, due to proximity, has always had athletes on our teams. The first of note was Don McEwen in 1948. Since McEwen, more than 50 Canadians have competed in track for Michigan. Mostly,

In 1956 in east Africa I helped pick and coach the first Uganda and Kenya Olympic teams.

though, U-M teams were and are made up of U.S. athletes. Not so nationally. The NCAA Championships now usually have more foreigners scoring than Americans.

Ron Kramer, one of Michigan's greatest athletes — and a nice guy, too.

Among my fondest memories in track is Ron Kramer. He and Bennie Oosterbaan are acknowledged by most as the greatest all-around athletes Michigan ever produced and I'd vote for that. I think Tom Harmon was probably the best football player, but fans of Kramer and Bennie might contest that. Kramer was certainly not the best basketball player nor the best track man, but he was dominating in football.

A particular track performance was remarkable. It was 1956, Ron's senior year, and I was the track coach. Kramer had competed on the team as a high jumper, an outstanding one for someone weighing more than 235 pounds. He came to my office and said, "Don, I am simply tired of athletics. I've had three years of football, three years of basketball, two years of track, and would you mind if I didn't come out for track this spring?"

As it happened, Diamond, a great prognosticator for track and field competition, and I had recently gone over the chances of Michigan winning the Big Ten track championship. We had concluded that with everybody healthy and breaks going our way we might be able to beat the University of Iowa for the Big Ten championships that were going to be held at Minnesota. I explained to Kramer how close the meet was going to be and that his points probably would mean the difference between winning and losing. I almost said to him, "Ron, I understand. Forget track." But I didn't. He got up and said, "OK, we can't let Iowa beat Michigan," and walked out of the office and I never heard another word about it.

In late May at Minnesota, Kramer high jumped 6 feet, 4 inches, a remarkable jump for someone his size and a pretty fair high jump for anyone in those days. Michigan won the meet by the points Kramer scored. My recollection is that he scored three or four points with his great jump. To this day, Kramer's devotion to Michigan is the same. He constantly does anything he can to help the program — an all-around athlete in many ways. I still remind him he would only be an eight-letter man if it weren't for his senior year in track.

Leaving my last NCAA Indoor Track and Field Championships as a coach was bittersweet, even though I knew I'd go on running the annual meet and would continue to get together with the other people involved. Some of the great track coaches in America were helping me conduct the meet in Detroit. The group included such men as Elliot Noyes from Dartmouth; Arthur O'Connor from Fordham; Bill McClure from Abilene Christian and later South Carolina; Weems Baskin, the great coach from South Carolina prior to McClure taking the job; Stanley Hiserman from the University of Washington, and Ralph Higgins from Oklahoma State.

We had become pretty close friends. They weren't so sure I'd keep my heart in track and field so they all contributed, probably more than they should have, to commission a nationally-prominent artist to paint a picture of me high jumping as a student. It hangs on my office wall to this day. Only McClure and Hiserman of the group were still living when I wrote this book, but when I look at that painting I think of all of them.

I was at that NCAA meet when I was notified Michigan had appointed me as athletic director. It wasn't announced from the floor and I didn't tell many people, but I did tell Dave Diles — who immediately took me over to the TV cameras. The story went over the air in Detroit and nationally because Diles was on the *Wide World of Sports* and on local TV as well. The coaches, though, were busy and few, if any, of them saw the broadcast.

After the broadcast I returned to my room at the old Book-Cadillac Hotel. I went up on the elevator with Karl Schlaedeman and his wife. He was the coach at Michigan State when I coached at Michigan. We had bitter rivalries and we both won a few. He was probably 25 years older than I and at the end of his career. We talked briefly about the meet, then they got off on one floor and I got off on another.

About 20 minutes later my phone rang and it was Karl. He said, "Don, I just saw on television where you were named director of athletics. I'm so sorry I didn't say something when we were on the eleva-

tor, but I didn't know. But I do want to congratulate you and say one thing: I wish I was 35 years younger so I could be your track coach." That, without question, was the nicest compliment I've ever received.

Long before I went to Michigan, the NCAA and the Amateur Athletic Union were into what would be a seven-decade dispute. It finally ended by an Act of Congress in 1978, after President Gerald Ford forced legislation. The NCAA for years fought the AAU over its autocratic restrictions on amateur athletes.

Karl Schlaedeman

At the turn of the century most amateur competition was in athletic clubs, not schools. In 1906 the AAU organized the clubs and became recognized by foreign associations as being "in control" of amateur athletics in the U.S. In addition, the U.S. Olympic Committee for decades was made up of AAU guys just wearing different hats. It was so outrageous in my time that no athlete could compete in any Olympic sport without an AAU card at a cost of $2 or $3. It had to be carried by grade school athletes as well as college graduates if they wanted to compete in open competition. If a playground had a track meet, an AAU permit was required and all athletes had to be card carriers.

American coaches started the modern-day rebellion in the '60s. I became involved when track coaches Ollie Jackson at Abilene Christian, Bill Bowerman at Oregon, and I, with the assistance of the NCAA, formed the U.S. Track and Field Federation. Several other coaching associations in other sports had formed their own federation to go head-to-head with the AAU. The purpose was to establish truly representative governing bodies in order to apply for the international recognition. Of course, it started a bitter fight lasting for years.

The first step in the solution began in 1967 when the Sports Arbitration Board was appointed by vice president Hubert Humphrey. I served on that board as an NCAA representative. The AAU never agreed that the board had authority, an attitude that focused its disdain for the athlete for all to see. It just wanted to hold control. It was a critical mistake and Congress took note.

The board met at various times with Douglas MacArthur, Bobby Kennedy and Humphrey. They all tried to find a solution. After two years everyone quit trying. The AAU wouldn't mediate on anything.

In the end when we disbanded, chairman Theodore Kheel said there was no possibility of settlement, "as neither side needs the other." The AAU had the international paper membership. Everyone else involved had the athletes (i.e. high schools, junior colleges, NCAA, etc.)

Some congressmen began to consider legislation. Movement finally began when Ford, a former Michigan football player, appointed the Commission of Olympic Sports in 1975. The chairman was the widely respected Gerald B. Zornow, chairman of the board of Eastman Kodak. More importantly, a man with a background in international competition, Mike Harrigan, was appointed director of the commission and was really the architect of its final report, which

The Sports Arbitration Board: standing l-r, Phil Brown, NCAA lawyer; Chuck Neinas, asst. director, NCAA; Walter Byers, director, NCAA; Eppy Barnes, Colgate, NCAA president; Don Canham. Seated l-r, General Shoup, Marine commandant; Ralph Metcalfe, congressman from Illinois; Hubert Humphrey, vice president of the U.S.; Theodore Kheel, lawyer from New York, committee chairman; Tom Vail, publisher from Ohio; and Archibald Cox, law professor, Harvard University.

became the law.

The unsung hero of the settlement that took more than 70 years to achieve was Walter Byers, executive director of the NCAA. It was Walter whose behind-the-scenes organizing of the various federations provided the leverage for change. He then persuaded the NCAA council to finance the federations. It was also Byers who had influenced Ford to form the commission.

President Ford and Mike Harrigan: key individuals who influenced legislation ending A.A.U. monopoly practices.

The commission took 18 months and released two volumes, more than 600 pages, recommending a national organization that was to 1) decide who would receive international recognition in each sport, 2) provide a means to decide how all groups could be equitably represented on any national governing body, and 3) set up a fund-raising policy board for amateur sports and particularly for the Olympic Association. The key recommendation was that jurisdictional disputes had to be settled by the American Arbitration Association. The NCAA had always been in favor of that.

The commission report became the Amateur Sports Act and ended the AAU as the group controlling amateur athletics in the U.S. It completely revamped the U.S. Olympic Committee, increasing its scope and power. However, the makeup of the governing bodies and specific language of the bill, stating that the U.S. Olympic Committee had no direct power over other organizations, pacified almost everybody. By this time I was no longer track coach and the elimination of the AAU made my 30-year involvement worth the work and effort.

◆◆◆

Chapter **6**

Athletic Director

◆————————————————

Deficits and Profits

My appointment as athletic director March 15, 1968, got ink in newspapers across the country — but not in the minutes of the athletic board meeting a few days later. You'll find no clues about the identity of the new A.D. to replace Fritz Crisler in the minutes of the Board in Control of Intercollegiate Athletics for March of 1968. There is absolutely no reference to a successor to Fritz, yet it was national news.

As I read over those old minutes it's almost humorous, because I knew at the time I was not a popular choice with Norma Bentley, Crisler's secretary (and Fielding Yost's before that.) It was Norma who took the minutes and typed them up. It's possible the board discussed Crisler's successor and my appointment and Norma simply re-fused to record it. It's

The Canhams, 1968: Don, Bunny and Clare

also possible — because we all knew that during his last year Crisler was hoping the regents would change their minds and extend his contract — that he never did discuss my appointment with the board.

As the chairman, Crisler explicitly controlled the agenda for the monthly board meetings. The only reference to me in the board minutes following my appointment is for May 3, 1968. Board member Hugh Rader, an alumnus from Detroit, made the motion that Donald B. Canham be authorized to sign checks for bank withdrawals, replacing the name of H.O. Crisler.

I understood Norma's loyalty to Fritz and in fairness to her I should say that it was a matter of days, not even weeks, after I took over that she became fiercely loyal to me as well. She had such vast knowledge and deep affection for the department that I never, ever resented her early reservations about me.

What I inherited on July 1 is reflected in the minutes of my first year or two: football tickets were $6 per seat and a student coupon book for six games was selling for $14. The faculty and staff had to pay $3 to see a game at Michigan Stadium. Crisler Arena had been dedicated in February 1968. That same month the *Michigan Daily* reported widespread illegal aid to athletes, namely in the guise of discounted clothing and free theater tickets. In those days, the NCAA had a very limited investigative department. The conference, not the NCAA, was the enforcement agency. Big Ten commissioner Bill Reed and I worked out a solution with a minimum of publicity and no inquiry whatsoever from the NCAA. Today, in my opinion, the problem would result in major sanctions.

Various athletic staff changes occurred. Don James left the football staff for the head football coaching job at Kent State. From there he went on to an illustrious career at the University of Washington. Longtime sports information director Les Etter also resigned. Golf coach Bert Katzenmeier was offered the athletic director's job at the University of Wichita. (A few years later Bert and his wife were killed in a plane crash. One of two planes carrying the Wichita football team went down in the mountains on its way to a game in the west.)

The best things I inherited were some individuals on the Board in Control who led me safely through the mine fields during my first six or eight months: Marcus Plant, the faculty representative and a close friend for 20 years; Doug Hayes, a professor in the business school; Ralph Gibson from the medical school, who had been a teammate at Michigan and was a life-long friend; plus Dr. Dorn Heinemann, who always felt I could do no wrong. These faculty people, along with Rader and Ward Quall, president of WGN in Chicago and a former classmate, were those I conferred with as I got my feet on the ground to make the changes I felt were necessary. Without them, my settling in would have been much more difficult, maybe impossible.

Marcus Plant, NCAA president, 1968, and outstanding faculty representative.

The first board meeting in my tenure was July 23, 1968. I asked that Plant keep the minutes because I felt Fritz and Norma had never included enough detail. The minutes from 1968 until I retired in 1988 give a clearer picture of what actually transpired in the athletic department. Those first minutes record our first effort to market our program: A motion was made that the board approve my turning to the J.L. Hudson Co. to help market our football tickets by enclosing applications in their 300,000 billing envelopes. They did it, as I recall, for $1,500.

My first meeting also brought a motion to put new scoreboards in Michigan Stadium at a cost of $75,000. I'd been told by the U-M plant department the old ones were virtually nonfunctional and unrepairable. This venture almost ended in a fiasco. The night before the first game the scoreboards still didn't work. Not until the Saturday of the game were the new ones up and running. I imagined the headlines if we didn't have scoreboards; the former track coach's first attempt at administration would have been newsworthy.

The board voted to change Don Weir's title from ticket manager to ticket and promotion manager. Weir was probably as good a ticket manager as you'd find, but he had no inclination whatsoever to delve into promotion and I should have known that. Three years before, when ticket sales were low, I had mentioned to Crisler we should test a direct-mail marketing campaign in some small town nearby. This would show us if my theory of marketing football tickets by direct mail might work. He gave the go-ahead and allotted me $3,000. Weir, I'm sure, resented it because in the negotiations with Crisler I had stupidly forgotten to include Weir. It would have been better if I'd made it appear as though it were his idea. In any case, we picked Plymouth, Mich., a northwestern Detroit suburb, and saturated the town with direct-mail ticket applications. We sold $14,000 worth of football tickets in Plymouth that we'd never sold before. But instead of our picking up on the idea and expanding it, nothing ever happened. It was that experiment that led me to believe we hadn't lived up to our potential in the marketing of tickets. Weir never became comfortable with promotion. From my first year, all of our promotions were run through Will Perry's sports information office. He was a pro.

A serious problem I faced in my first three weeks was the resignation of Jim Hunt as our head trainer. A great trainer who had succeeded Ray Roberts, Jim wanted to retire and I couldn't change his mind. I hired J. Lindsy McLean Jr., who had just accepted a job with the San Francisco 49ers. I flew out and persuaded him to come to Michigan for the same $11,500 a year the 49ers were to pay him, but eventually he returned to San Francisco and the 49ers. Also in my first month on the job I moved Johnny Orr up to replace Dave Strack as basketball coach and hired the first full-time black coach in Michigan history, Fred Snowden, to assist him. Snowden was outstanding and eventually left Michigan to become one of the nation's first black head coaches under Strack at the University of Arizona.

At the October meeting of 1968, the Board in Control approved my recommendation that we sell advertising in the basketball program. We had done so in the football program on a limited basis, but never in basketball. Frankly, there were no people on the staff under Crisler who had the time or inclination to sell advertising. Fritz's administrative staff consisted of Katzenmeier and his assistant, and Bentley, his do-everything secretary. The only other office people in the whole building were Lilyan Duford, Katzenmeier's secretary; Dorothy Johnson, secretary for the football staff; and Betty Bacon, secretary for all coaches' correspondence. It was a far cry from the large staffing of today.

It must be remembered that universities then, particularly Michigan, tended to be low-key in marketing and promotion. When I proposed, for instance, charging for parking around Crisler Arena and letting Sears, Roebuck and J.L. Hudson sell football tickets in their invoices, there was some resistance from faculty representatives on the Board in Control. But Hayes and Gibson convinced the rest of the board we should adopt a different attitude toward marketing, for survival.

In my first six months the first project we did was to remove the last remnants of the Ferry Field football stands. When football moved to Michigan Stadium a running track had been constructed at Ferry Field using the south stands for spectators. It was those stands that held a full house, 10,000 people, in 1935 when Jesse Owens set his world records there. Since then the stands had become a hazard. Crisler had talked for several years about removing them but hadn't done so. The university put wooden barriers across the top 15 or 20 rows so people wouldn't go up to the worst crumbling seats at the very top. I knew I had to do something about those deteriorated stands for liability reasons. They were torn down in the fall of 1968.

The last Ferry Field football stands. I had them taken down my first year as A.D. They were falling down; I could have saved the money had I waited.

Another interesting challenge in the early months involved clearing out the press box. Quall asked what we were going to do about it. Perry also mentioned we had too many people in the press box. He had no idea who some of them were and couldn't figure out how they were getting in. An investigation got us some answers. It seems the long-time guardians of the press box door were passing in their friends and more than a few got in with passes signed by Fielding H. Yost, who'd been gone for more than 25 years. We had sons and daughters using

Yost passes.

Perry immediately canceled all press box passes and removed the old-timers. We hired Burns Security to man the door, creating more than a few enemies in the process. But during Perry's tenure Michigan had a reputation for having the cleanest and most efficient press box in all of college football. The enemies we made in the process have faded from memory, but at the time they were furious that the "new group" was changing things.

I have been accused of adding female cheerleaders to basketball and football games because my daughter Clare was a high school cheerleader and had just become a freshman at Michigan. Not quite so. In November 1968 Hayes brought the matter up to the board, presenting a motion to plan for girl cheerleaders at basketball games. The motion was later expanded to football. It all met with my approval which, of course, quickly took me off the hook at home and Clare did become one of the first female cheerleaders. In 1969 female cheerleaders appeared at U-M football and basketball games. Some resistance came from the male cheerleading club and for a time we didn't mingle them, even placing women and men at different ends of the stadium. Gradually they integrated and today collegiate

The criticism when we started to use girl cheerleaders in 1969 didn't bother my daughter Clare — she finished third in a national contest in Cypress Gardens, Florida in 1970.

cheerleading squads across the country are made up of both sexes.

In December 1968, six months after I became director, Glen Edward "Bo" Schembechler was approved as head football coach. He had been a successful coach at Miami University in Oxford, Ohio, and had been an assistant at Northwestern under Ara Parseghian and an assistant at Ohio State under Woody Hayes. His qualifications were impeccable. Plant, Gibson, and several other members of the board had met Schembechler and were impressed with him so I had no worry he wouldn't be approved. However, the board spent well over an hour discussing Schembechler's qualifications. I suppose it was in self-defense: should there be criticism over hiring a non-Michigan man they could at least refer to a lengthy discussion. From 1949 to 1968 a Michigan graduate and athlete had been coach of the Michigan team. But I saw no Michigan men out there coaching with whom I felt comfortable for the job. And Plant, Gibson, Strack — assistant athletic director for business — and I all had the feeling Schembechler would be successful.

When the board approved Bo I told them we had to give him a five-year assurance, although there were no contracts of any kind for coaches and no one ever gave me one during my 20 years. Bo and I had a five year *agreement*, backed up by the board. He would have that time to turn the Michigan football program around. His annual salary was $21,000 and his predecessor, Bump Elliott, became an associate athletic director at a salary of $20,000 a year. I made $27,500.

In 1969, six months into my directorship, the Board in Control took an action destined to affect intercollegiate athletics forever. It was the motion proposed by Heinemann and Gibson to allow freshmen to compete in varsity athletics, with the exception of basketball and football. The NCAA at the January 1969 convention had just approved it. Michigan and the Big Ten had to follow, of course, or we would have been at a tremendous disadvantage in recruiting throughout the nation. Very few Big Ten athletic directors or faculty were in favor — it was a case of a vote carried by economics and the smaller NCAA schools. The point was made at the convention that we had millions of dollars invested in freshmen on scholarships without being able to use them. The argument went that we could reduce the overall number of scholarships if we used freshmen immediately for varsity teams.

Those of us who resisted freshman eligibility in the first place (as Michigan did on the floor of the convention in January of 1969) did so because we saw trouble ahead. Most of us realized when freshmen were made eligible for sports other than football and basketball it was only a matter of days before someone filed a court case based upon discrimination against football and basketball players.

That's exactly what happened. And when freshmen became eligible it led to the submission of phony transcripts from high schools and junior colleges to get instant-help athletes in school. High school transcripts were tampered with for that one year of instant help.

Another unfortunate result was student-athletes jumping from one institution to another when they didn't immediately compete as freshmen. It also led to dropouts because some freshmen simply couldn't handle the big-time athletic program plus a big-time academic load. And in schools on the quarter system, high school athletes were coming to the campus and playing in football games two and three weeks before classes even started. They were running for touchdowns on the college gridirons before they knew where the school library was. That's a common occurrence today and it hardly seems sensible to those of us who have regard for academic integrity. The presidents will not face up to these facts; and that letting freshmen compete is the cause of most campus problems with athletics.

In retrospect, virtually all of our major problems occurred as we predicted they would when freshmen were declared eligible by the NCAA. The major institutions initially and almost unanimously voted against freshman use. However, before the divisions in the NCAA, smaller institutions controlled the vote. There were just more of them. It was the smaller schools and not the larger ones that put freshmen in competition in 1969 — and forevermore, it appears.

My early days as A.D. also brought some positive changes as we struggled to wipe out a $250,000 inherited deficit. Changing our image was high on the priority list. Marketing became a high priority. Selling of Michigan and tickets had just not been done before. No institutions in the nation were doing what we knew had to be done. When we started marketing with ticket ads in *The Detroit News* and *Detroit Free Press* it caused a stir. Back at the campus, heads shook over that; it had never been done before in college sports. But I had a Board in

Control, and President Robben Fleming, who understood the pragmatic side of trying to run an athletic department with a projected deficit without using university funds. It was just the beginning.

I had a quick introduction to the real world in 1969. Tony Mason, who had been on Elliott's staff and whom Schembechler declined to keep, came to me and said that as of April 1 he would be employed by Purdue University. He wanted to know if he could stay on our payroll until that time. I said yes — and a week or so later heard from an alumnus in Chicago that Mason had been recruiting in February for Purdue in the Chicago area. A call to Purdue's athletic director Red Mackey gave me the date of Mason's employment at Purdue: he'd gone on the payroll in January. Red was furious when I told him about Mason's claim that he wasn't going to report there until April. I often wondered how Mackey and Mason got along after that because Red was one of the most honorable and tough athletic directors I ever served with. In any case, I stopped Mason's pay immediately and never heard a word. Following his stop at Purdue, Mason became head coach at Arizona and had reasonably good success there until he got into difficulty with the NCAA on rules violations. Later he earned a reputation as a motivational speaker.

It was early in 1969 that I began discussions to start a home-and-home series with the University of Notre Dame. We just had to improve our schedule. We also explored the possibility of putting up an air bubble for practicing football in inclement weather. Upon studying the problems inherent with an air bubble, we rejected that idea. Some years later we built probably the first free-standing building that housed a full 100-yard football field. During a Wisconsin football game on a rainy afternoon in Michigan Stadium in 1968, as Ron Johnson scored five times for the Wolverines, we decided to be the second school in the nation (Tennessee being the first) to install artificial turf. While Johnson scored at will, the muddy field made it impossible to see who had the ball. The board approved the plan with enthusiasm and we were on our way toward some of the goals set on July 1, 1968.

In 1969 when Schembechler's team won the Big Ten championship and an invitation to the 1970 Rose Bowl, we began to get the first proposals to put our football games on the new media called cable and closed circuit television. The games could not be done live, but we began to negotiate contracts to put our games tape-delayed on cable systems. The NCAA limited schools to one or two live TV appearances per year. Although cable money was not exceptional, it certainly helped and we relished the exposure. Cable was completely new and we were looking down the road at pay TV that everyone thought would make all schools rich. In college sports, though, it never developed as a huge money maker.

Following the Rose Bowl game we gave the assistant coaches each a $1,000 raise and Schembechler's salary was increased by $5,000. After 18 months we had balanced the budget, made a profit, and played in our first Rose Bowl game since 1965.

We all could relax a little.

◆◆◆

Chapter 7

Schembechler Hired

Paterno Passes

T he first head coach I was to hire was for football. I'd never heard of Bo Schembechler. And from the mail I received after I hired him, a few hundred others hadn't either. Looking back over my association of 25 years and more with Bo, it wasn't exactly a walk in the park, but it was obviously the most important and rewarding appointment I was to make in my 20 years as athletic director. Here is how it began:

When Bump Elliott and I decided in the summer of 1968 that this would be his last year as coach and he would become Michigan's first associate athletic director, I began to collect opinions on who we should consider to take over the football program. Those whose opinions mattered most in my search included George Allen,

Bennie Oosterbaan, Marcus Plant, Sonny Werblin, Elliott, and Bob Shaw, who was an assistant to Elliott. Over several months I would consider a half dozen prospects, but for some reason the name *Schembechler* kept cropping up.

The first time I heard Schembechler's name was from Plant, our respected faculty representative. He had a daughter at Miami University in Ohio where Bo was coaching. Plant pointed out that he had a 40-17-3 record and had never had a losing season. In addition, he had been an assistant to Woody Hayes at Ohio State and to Ara Parseghian at Northwestern. With that history he had to know what the Big Ten was all about. A Big Ten background was a plus with me.

Bump and I talked with Shaw, who had coached in high school in Ohio and knew Schembechler. His most telling remarks were that he was "really organized," but had a bad temper. At that point Bo was one of several on my short list. Nonetheless, he was obscure, and even many of those who had heard of him still weren't sure how to pronounce his name. Broadcasters would regularly trip over the long German name, spitting out something like *SHEM-bleh-ker*. Newspaper reporters would inadvertently type *Bob* instead of *Bo*, and reporters (before the age of portable computers) found themselves spelling out each letter of his name while dictating their stories back to the office. Years later, fans and foes could easily pronounce SHEM-beck-lur, but many probably didn't know his first name was Glenn, not Bo.

Yet even though Schembechler's name was far from widely known, I was worried about the news media getting wind of his visit for an interview at Christmas time in 1968. So we registered him at the Ambassador Hotel on South State Street in Ann Arbor under a different name — then couldn't remember it. Assistant athletic director for business, Dave Strack, and I had to utilize a bit of Sherlockian deduction while searching the registration book to find him. I remember Strack saying he believed it was *Mr. Barberton*, because that was Bo's hometown in Ohio. But it turned out we had registered him as *Mr. Shems* from Oxford, Ohio. We went through the entire hotel registry to find someone from Oxford and that's how we located Bo.

Actually, *Glenn E. Schembechler* probably would have gone unnoticed by most media types who might have been snooping through hotel registers. Everyone was looking to find out who we were going to hire. Newspaper and radio people were all over town during the two weeks before Christmas because I had said we were going to have somebody in place by the holiday.

There was one diligent reporter who knew how to investigate, Pete Waldmeir of *The Detroit News*, the longtime city-side columnist who was then a sports columnist. Waldmeir had done the same registry sleuthing the night before, not only at the Ambassador, but at other hotels in the area.

Pete figured he'd find a name he knew by going over the registers. When he spotted Oxford, Ohio, he put *Shems* and the city together, then called Miami University and couldn't locate Schembechler. So he figured he had it, which he did, and *The Detroit News* had the story first. All the newspaper and radio people thought I'd tipped off Waldmeir because Pete had covered track when I was track coach and we had become friends, as we are to this day. But I had not tipped him off. In fact, I was probably as much worried about him as anyone because he was a very good investigative reporter and had been to town several times during that week, hoping I would say something that would give him some ideas. I never did.

Elliott was in on Schembechler's visit, having agreed to an associate A.D. job with the condition he be allowed to coach the 1968 team. His replacement would take over for the 1969 season. The two of us, plus Strack and Plant, talked with Schembechler before taking him to the Ambassador.

Bump Elliott was always a good coach. He never had a chance with the outdated facilities. He did a remarkable job as athletic director at the University of Iowa for more than 20 years.

I had already spent eight months considering who we should hire to take over the football coaching job at Michigan. I probably had 50 head and assistant coaches on the list and another fifty letters and wires recommending people.

For all athletic directors, the appointment of a football coach might be considered the most important they have to make. Football is the life-blood of most athletic departments. I regarded this search very seriously.

I had no intention of hiring an assistant coach for the job. You simply cannot take an assistant from another institution into a vast program like Michigan's and expect success. I've seen many examples of assistant coaches going to high-powered positions and failing because it was just an overwhelming situation. An assistant's responsibilities are limited. Someone who has never organized a staff or directed recruiting or had to worry about Big Ten and NCAA rules simply would be too preoccupied to do the best job of coaching. So we were after a head coach.

I started calling around. Allen, who made winning with veterans his trademark while coach of the National Football League's Washington Redskins, gave me three or four names. One of them was Ben Martin of Air Force, who told me he planned to retire in five years and felt it wouldn't be fair to take such a job. I always thought that was a decent thing to do. Allen mentioned a couple of pro coaches, which I didn't want any part of, and the last person he mentioned was Schembechler. Allen was the second person to drop that name, but I knew little about Schembechler and didn't put him at the top of the list. I decided the one person I was going to attempt to get was Penn State coach Joe Paterno. Paterno was a big name even though he had been head coach there for only three years. He had done a remarkable job after stepping up from an assistant's role to replace Rip Engle.

Penn State was going to play in a bowl game in January 1969 and it was in early December of 1968 I set up a meeting with Joe. I met him in Pittsburgh and we spent three hours in a hotel talking. When he left, I felt there was a 50-50 chance he would come to Michigan. A week later he called me and said he didn't think he could make a decision until after the bowl game. I told him, "Joe, I can't wait a month for you to decide." Then Paterno said, "I don't think, really, I should leave Penn State anyhow."

"I'm sorry to hear that," I replied, "but I understand it and wonder if you'd do me a favor and not mention this because this is my first football appointment as athletic director and I don't need that kind of publicity."

He told me not to worry and he didn't mention it for 22 years. He never used it to get a raise and never mentioned it for publicity. But in 1990 we were at the College Football Hall of Fame dinner at the Waldorf Astoria in New York where I was getting a minor award and Joe was the featured speaker. He turned to me and said, "Canham, can I tell the story now?" I said go ahead. And he told the story about how he almost came to Michigan. I've wondered what would have happened had he done so.

Joe Paterno and I at a Football Hall of Fame dinner in 1969, a year after he decided to stay at Penn State.

Ironically, 22 years earlier, I had gone to the same Waldorf Astoria for another Hall of Fame dinner and a guy named Schembechler cropped up in conversation. The person who brought him up, though, spoke of his qualifications but couldn't recall his name. Elliott and I had started off to New York together, but I stopped off in Pittsburgh and hooked up with him again later. Together we went to a New York celebrity hot spot, Toots Shor's restaurant, to meet Bill Mazer, an ABC commentator with a highly-rated talk show in the Big Apple. Mazer was in a group I had run around with at Michigan when we were students. In fact, my father-in-law, Walter J. Norris, a businessman in Grand Rapids, Mich., helped him get his first radio job with WOOD in Grand Rapids in 1941. He was "Bill Todd" on that station.

Elliott and I were sitting at the bar talking with Toots Shor when Mazer walked in. Shor asked why we were all there.

"We're out here for the banquet," I said, "but we're really looking for a football coach. Have you got any ideas?"

"I don't," said Shor, "but that fella over there does," and he called over Sonny Werblin, owner and general manager of the NFL's New York Jets, who were soon to see their brash quarterback, Joe Namath, lead them to a Super Bowl upset over the Baltimore Colts.

We talked for a while and I asked him if he knew anybody who met our criteria. Werblin said, "Well, I don't know his name, but there's a guy coaching at Miami of Ohio — and that's a good school for coaches, as you know. This guy, I don't know what his name is, but I look at his movies and he's a very good coach in fundamentals and he's got a pretty good record." Werblin also mentioned one or two others.

Well, that was the third time Schembechler had come up in conversation. It registered at the back of my mind, but the night was young and would become more interesting. Soon, other famous people started drifting into the restaurant. There was Earl Wilson, the Broadway columnist; Bob Considine, the sports and back-page syndicated columnist; comedian Marty Allen, the guy with the big mop of black hair; and Jacqueline Susann, who had just written *The Valley of the Dolls*. She spotted Mazer and made a beeline toward our group in the bar. A few nights earlier she had been on his talk show. Bill introduced Bump and me to Susann and the other celebrities and she asked us to join their table in the dining area. So Bump and I spent the next three hours sitting in a group far removed from football, but it was one of the most fascinating evenings either of us had ever spent. Wilson, from Ohio, knew Woody Hayes and we had trouble getting him to talk of anyone else.

We returned to Ann Arbor and related our stories to Plant, Strack, and others. Eventually, the tips about Schembechler would take priority over the tales of our celebrity schmoozing. I asked Elliott to call the man from Barberton and ask him if he would visit Ann Arbor. Schembechler came, talking not just with me but also with Oosterbaan, with whom I consulted a good deal concerning football matters.

I was impressed with Schembechler after 15 minutes. He was exactly what I was looking for, someone who was very self-assured, tough, and had head coaching experience, as well as a midwest background. At our first interview I asked him if he would take the job if it was offered and he said yes.

"Well, give me a couple of days and I'll get back to you," I said. "I'll call you."

It took more than two days because I still had other commitments to follow up on. But when I called Bo, confirmed the job offer, and asked him when he could come up and go over the details with me, he said, "Right now." That happened to be the day before Christmas, so he came to Ann Arbor on Christmas Day. I knew then he really wanted the job and that he was extremely committed to coaching. I wasn't wrong.

Van Patrick, the late Detroit sportscaster and longtime play-by-play announcer for the NFL's Detroit Lions, somehow found out, probably from Waldmeir, I had selected Bo and called Larry Paladino at *The Associated Press* in Detroit.

"I'll give you the story if you give me credit," Patrick said. And so the story moved on the *AP* wires, including the broadcast wire to other radio and TV stations throughout Michigan. Everything was attributed to Patrick. Waldmeir had the scoop first, however. Of course, the story was quickly corroborated and the reactions set in: "Bo, who?" "Shlumblecker who?"

I received a lot of criticism when I hired Bo because, I think, some people wanted a Michigan man. But there were few Michigan men out coaching except for Bob Hollway, who was with the Minnesota Vikings of the NFL, J.T. White at Penn State, and two on Bump's staff,

The December 1968 press conference announcing Bo Schembechler as the Michigan football coach. We all look pretty serious.

Frank Maloney and George Mans. I knew, though, we needed a head coach with midwest experience.

My mail was not flattering. One person told me the guy I hired sounded like "a butcher from a German village." And I received several letters expressing resentment that I would hire someone closely associated with Woody Hayes, the irascible coach at archrival Ohio State. Bo had been on Woody's staff. Few people knew about my business background because I never publicized it while I was coaching track. All the critics knew was that I had been the track coach and, "what would a track coach know about football and hiring people?" Although I may have been bothered somewhat by the criticism, I had confidence in my choice, which history showed certainly was a good one.

So what were we going to pay this future College Football Hall of Famer? I offered him $21,000. In those days Bump was making $19,000 and I think Schembechler was making $18,000 at Miami. But we were projecting a deficit, and he said "salary wasn't important" because it was a good opportunity for him. I took him seriously.

So he got $21,000 — more than Fritz Crisler, Oosterbaan, or Elliott ever got — and the next week he brought his staff up during the Christmas vacation break because he only wanted to keep Maloney, Mans and Lou Lee from Bump's staff. The assistants Schembechler brought were: Jerry Hanlon, Dick Hunter, Jim Young, Larry Smith, Chuck Stobart, and Gary Moeller. We paid the assistants from $11,000 to $14,000 a year, sizable increases from what they got at Miami, but a far cry from what coaches get nowadays.

Bo's starting salary was $21,000 — but he got a new cap and head set.

The day I met Bo's assistants there was no heat in any of the buildings because of the holiday break and school being shut down due to a fuel shortage. So we all went over to Colonial Lanes on Industrial Highway nearby and talked in the Pin Room lounge. They asked what sort of contract we were going to be able to give them and I said, "No contract. You've got the same tenure I have. I think we have about five years. If you guys don't succeed, we're all going to be out of here."

All the time Schembechler was coaching at Michigan he operated without a contract and had only my word that he had a revolving five-year agreement. There was never a time when I had any concern about that, and I don't think Bo did either. Our relationship over the next 20 years, including mine with his staff, was one of complete cooperation and we got salaries up where they belonged, too.

Unfortunately for Bo, that handshake deal and our honor-bound un-written contract made him vulnerable to a handshake deal later with Domino's Pizza founder Tom Monaghan, owner of baseball's Detroit Tigers. That prompted Schembechler to leave Michigan to become president of the Tigers. After a few years, though, Monaghan fired him preceding his selling the club to pizza rival Mike Ilitch of Little Caesar's.

Bo had Michigan in a Bowl every year and the Rose Bowl most often. He always was outstanding at the press conferences.

Bo went to court for termination pay. He never had a contract with Monaghan except some scribbled information on a dinner napkin, which he used later as evidence in the lawsuit against Monaghan. He had been promised 10 years of employment. Just as I had promised him employment and had never broken my word, he didn't expect Monaghan to break his. I don't know how that played out in court because agreements were sealed, but I do know that the lack of a contract at Michigan — the handshake agreement we had — was what he used as a reason for not insisting on a written contract with Monaghan.

Like everyone else, Schembechler was enchanted with Michigan Stadium — and totally disenchanted with our other facilities for football. The first thing we did was figure out where we could put some meeting rooms. We built a suite of rooms under the baseball stadium stands which were pretty sad. But at the same time they were a hundred percent better than anything Elliott ever had, as it beat the hallways of Yost Field House to death.

Because of the poor facilities, Bump really didn't have much of a chance to compete on a level playing field with the other Big Ten schools. We had antiquated locker rooms that Yost had used on the second floor of the fieldhouse and team meeting rooms, as mentioned, were in the hallways. And the night before a game, instead of going to a hotel to get away from the campus noise, the football team was put up on the second floor of the golf course on double-decker cots, not very good cots at that, and there was no air-conditioning.

One cold Friday evening prior to a game the heating system went out at the golf course. Bump had to get some buses from the university in the middle of the night, take the team over to Ypsilanti and put them up over there. That's hardly the way to get ready for a Big Ten football game.

No wonder he jumped at the opportunity to be the associate athletic director, effective in 1969. When I made that appointment, though, people thought Elliott had been fired. That was not the case. I knew Bump was a pretty solid coach and a great recruiter and if we helped him and gave him some facilities and got him some better assistants, I had the feeling that Michigan would do very well. While Elliott would not admit it, his greatest weakness was in hiring. He never seemed to have the great assistants that, in my opinion, would have given him an unmatched record at Michigan. The Wolverines finished with an 8-2 record in 1968, and Michigan doesn't fire people who win eight games — or didn't until 1995 when Moeller "resigned."

While Schembechler didn't inherit nice facilities, he did have the benefit of quality upper class players coming back and a fine freshman class recruited by Elliott. Those players were in for a rude awakening in the spring of 1969 because Elliott and Schembechler were complete opposites. The players worked twice as hard as they had been used to working and were not quite able to comprehend this bombastic, tough drill sergeant named "Bo." My son-in-law, Don Eaton, was in Schembechler's first class. He tells now of the rude awakening the players had.

In the end, though, the players showed they could adjust to the coaching differences. Michigan concluded the regular season by handing Ohio State a 24-12 loss at Michigan Stadium in one of the all-time biggest upsets by the Wolverines. They wound up in Pasadena at the Rose

When Jim Young left to coach at Purdue, Gary Moeller became Bo's No. 1 assistant.

Bowl, where Schembechler would suffer a heart attack the night before the game. Young took interim control in a 10-3 loss to Southern California. That season, though, took me off the hook about my selection of the little-known Ohio guy with the long name. Some thought the track coach would survive.

In retrospect, it seems doubtful that a coach like Schembechler, or any coach, could be appointed today the way he was picked for Michigan. With gender equity and discrimination laws, most jobs have to be posted long in advance and run laboriously through committees that often don't have a clue about what is really needed. In the Schembechler case, I merely touched base with President Robben Fleming, who was always supportive of my appointments. And then I discussed the matter with Plant and went over the plans we had with the Board in Control of Intercollegiate Athletics. When the board approved our recommendation, the job was offered.

We did not bring people in to be interviewed by the board and therefore we could keep our months-long search relatively free from scrutiny. That, in my opinion, is extremely important. Most coaches do not want to be considered for jobs if it's going to be in the paper or on radio or television. They simply refuse to talk to anyone unless absolute secrecy is provided. Imagine the publicity had we tried to bring Allen or Paterno to the campus and put them in front of a board of selection. Paterno simply wouldn't have come and there would have been no opportunity to talk with him at all. And imagine the scrutiny that would have accompanied any public deliberations over Bo Schembechler, a guy who was not a household name. The criticism, even guffaws, from influential alumni could have stymied the selection before I was able to pull the trigger. Who knows how Michigan's football program would have fared from 1969 until now?

In the summer of 1969 restaurateur Win Schuler had a picnic for the Michigan and Michigan State staffs. The highlight was to be a donkey race between Bo and Michigan State's coach Duffy Daugherty. The donkeys just stood there and wouldn't move. The race was declared a draw.

◆◆◆

Chapter **8**

Marketing Michigan

◆————————————————————————

Coffee Cups and Slippery Rock

W hen I sat in Fritz Crisler's office that July 1, 1968, and looked out on Ferry Field, I wondered, "What have I done?" I had intended to quit coaching when Fritz left, to go out on South State St. and run my company, School-Tech Inc. I just couldn't see working for another athletic director after 20 years as track coach under Fritz.

In our last conversation he had mentioned casually that we were facing a $250,000 deficit for the 1968-69 school year. The first thing I did that day as the new athletic director was talk to Norma Bentley, the department's do-everything secretary, about the situation. She confirmed it.

The deficit, though, wasn't the biggest problem I saw when I sat down with department confidants Bennie Oosterbaan, Dave Strack and Bump Elliott. It was image. We had not been

"A $250,000 deficit? You must be kidding!"

consistent winners in football and our attendance was averaging in the 60-thousands. For some games against opponents like Northwestern only half the seats were filled, not a pleasant sight. With a half-empty stadium, proper financing is impossible.

On top of that, intrastate rival Michigan State, under the athletic directorship of Biggie Munn and with the popular football coach Duffy Daugherty, had captured the interest and imagination of the public in the state. Duffy charmed the media and it showed. Radio station WJR was broadcasting MSU games, not Michigan games. MSU also had a radio network that went into every small town in the state. In addition, a comparison of column inches in the state's newspapers showed the reverse of what was to come during the next 25 years. We had run an early survey of the Sunday papers and found MSU was getting twice our exposure.

Elliott and I agreed 1968 would be his last as football coach before he would step into the associate athletic director's job. Will Perry, who had been assistant sports editor for the *Grand Rapids Press*, was taking over directorship of the sports information department. At the same time, basketball coach Strack was becoming my right-hand man as business manager. We all knew what had to be done: change our image and fill the stadium *right now.*

First on the agenda was sell football tickets, lots of them, because there were plenty of empty seats in the 101,001-seat stadium. I had been exposed to advertising all my life through my father and I understood direct mail through my own company. We set out on a course of direct mail promotion and advertising not tried before by any institution.

We printed 400,000 ticket applications. The ticket department had formerly mailed fewer than 100,000. In the mailing envelope they had put a postcard for requesting individual game tickets and a card for each away game. Also included was a card for season tickets and other notices of policy, parking and the like. When you opened the envelope, it was like confetti falling out on the desk. To make it simpler we decided on a full-color self-mailer. It was much cheaper. By reducing the printing and eliminating the work of stuffing envelopes, Michigan could reach 400,000 people rather than 100,000, for the same money. We purchased mailing lists of high-income individuals and people who had bought new cars in 1967. We figured they had transportation to the

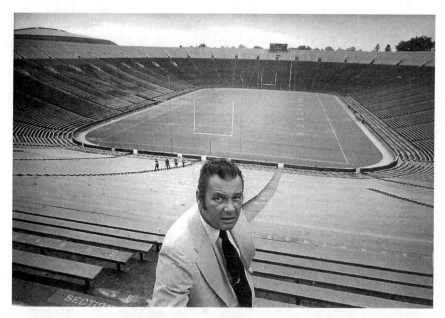

First priority: fannies in the seats — all 101,001 of them.

game and probably enough money for tickets, programs, and hot dogs.

Frank Deford, then with *Sports Illustrated*, some time later wrote, "The Michigan ticket application looks like a promotion for a Florida land development." That reaction suited us fine. We were out to attract enough attention to let people know we had football tickets for sale. It worked because our mailing was more attractive than basic white envelopes. We were in full color with an oversized flier and pictures — when it hit the desk it attracted attention. Just unfold it and there were souvenir offers and the ticket application. Ticket sales went up 14 percent. People who bought tickets got their money's worth. Coming off a poor season in 1967, Bumps's final team in 1968 went 8-2 my first year. We were off to a great start.

Included in the flier were two pages of premium offers: coffee cups with the Michigan helmet on them, pennants, playing cards, jackets, T-shirts, sweatsocks. All displayed Michigan logos. Perry sold the Automobile Club of Michigan a $5,000 full-page ad promoting tailgate picnics and AAA insurance. The company also had a tailgate cookbook for sale. It sold plenty with that first flier, and the $5,000 helped with our postage. We figured if people didn't buy football tickets they might buy coffee cups.

I had seen tailgating at Stanford and knew we should promote it here. Making a family day of a football game by including a tailgate picnic might encourage more women to become interested in coming to Ann Arbor. Tailgating was in its infancy. Many schools copied our tailgate promotions and our use of premiums to pay for the ticket mailing.

What could be finer than alfresco dining in the parking lot?
We promoted tailgating to attract the women and kids.

Eventually it became commonplace.

With the ad sale and souvenir sales from the first flier we more than recouped the cost of sending out the 400,000 brochures. With the ability to put ticket applications on people's desks essentially at no cost, we knew we'd be able to sell an awful lot of football tickets that hadn't been sold before. And that's what happened. A few years later we mailed 1.7 million ticket applications and sold out the stadium. Every mailing was profitable because of the ancillary benefits from coffee cups, T-shirts, and soon, 60 other products. We were in the souvenir and premium business big time.

Today Michigan is given credit for instituting souvenir and premium sales and for pioneering the licensing of logos and products. I'm not sure that's totally true, but what we did do and how it began at Michigan is an interesting story.

In the '60s when I was coaching track we would compete most springs in California against Stanford, Air Force, and UCLA.

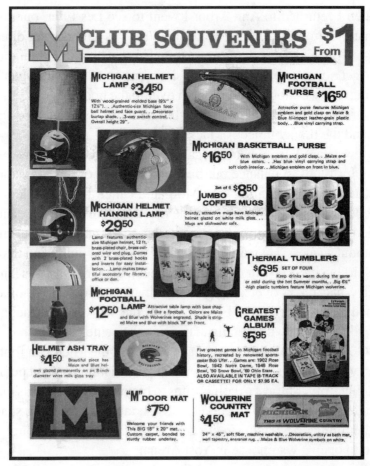

From 1968, a page or two of licensed premiums were in all ticket applications for all sports. No one had tried that before. It worked, and today all schools use the idea.

Occasionally, if we had a good team, we'd face Southern California. During one trip to UCLA I went to the bookstores and saw rack after rack of not only pennants but sweatshirts with UCLA insignias.

I went to see John Wooden, the all-time great basketball coach, at the request of our basketball coach, Bill Perigo, who had played professional basketball with Wooden in Indiana. John introduced me to athletic director J.D. Morgan, who later became a good friend. I mentioned that I assumed the athletic department was involved in the buying and selling of the sweatshirts. He said the bookstores had complete rights to the sweatshirts and pennants.

When I returned to Ann Arbor I went to see Les Etter, our sports information director. There was no such thing as a marketing director in those days; Les was the closest thing to that. I said I thought we should get some sweatshirts and T-shirts made with "Michigan" on them, but that we shouldn't turn them over to the bookstore. "Let's sell them ourselves," I said. Les agreed but he never was much of a promoter and the thought died for lack of a second.

A few years later when I became athletic director and we were looking for funds to balance our budget, I thought of the bookstore at UCLA and my conversation with Morgan. I called J.D. and asked him if the bookstores were still getting the revenue. "Yes," he said, and he had tried and tried to get some of it diverted to the athletic department, but without success. He warned me that if we were going to go into the sweatshirt business on our own, to keep the bookstores at arm's length.

Perry had taken over as sports information director. We quickly designed several logos: the block M with the Wolverine through the center, the block M with Michigan through the center, and the block M with "Go Blue." In addition, we made copies of the Michigan football helmet, which was nationally known and very distinctive, and put it on everything from ashtrays to coffee cups to playing cards, T-shirts, neckties, ladies' handkerchiefs, scarves, gloves, table lamps, lamp shades, and other things. The items in our first ticket mailing sold enough that we had to open a warehouse in Yost Arena.

We were putting Michigan ticket applications in a customer's mail box at no charge — the sale of coffee cups paid our printing and mailing costs and even made a profit. Each mailing found us designing more logos and coming up with more products to put them on.

This went on for several years before we realized we could license, register and copyright the logos to make their use restricted by others. It was Pete Rozelle, the commissioner of the National Football League, who told me we should copyright our block M and all the logos we had designed. I knew we could copyright the logos, helmet design and variations on the M, but doubted we could copyright the basic block M. I was wrong. We had no trouble protecting everything we applied for. Licensing wasn't far behind. Then in 1975 *Sports Illustrated* wrote a story about marketing at the University of Michigan. We were soon inundated with requests from schools for more information on what we were doing.

Thirty-some schools visited the campus to see how we had paid for our ticket applications by selling coffee cups. Perry had started the licensing program. As soon as we began to license our products, every school in the nation did as well. Lawsuits sprang up from some manufacturers and retailers claiming "prior usage" rights — but we won them all, as did other institutions. I'm not sure we were the first school to license products, but we were the first to be recognized in the area and were highly publicized for doing it. In that sense, Michigan was an

In 1975 seven pages in Sports Illustrated *told the nation about Michigan's methods. More than 30 schools descended on Ann Arbor to see what we were doing.*

innovator and a pioneer in premium and souvenir sales, plus licensing.

In an effort to stop the flood of people coming to Ann Arbor to see what we were doing, and the mail and phone inquiries, we began to run seminars in all parts of the country on marketing and promotion and business management. We'd usually run two on the East Coast; one large one in Ann Arbor; one in the South, often Texas; and two on the West Coast, one in Washington or Oregon, and the other at Disneyland in Anaheim, Calif. To this day I receive letters from young people who attended those seminars saying how valuable they were.

It's amazing that the Ohio State-Michigan game in Ann Arbor hadn't had a capacity crowd in more than 12 years. Michigan State was our only consistent sellout. Michigan *at* Ohio State, however, always saw standing-room only. In July of 1969, Schembechler's first year as coach, we still had 25,000 seats left in Michigan Stadium for the Ohio State

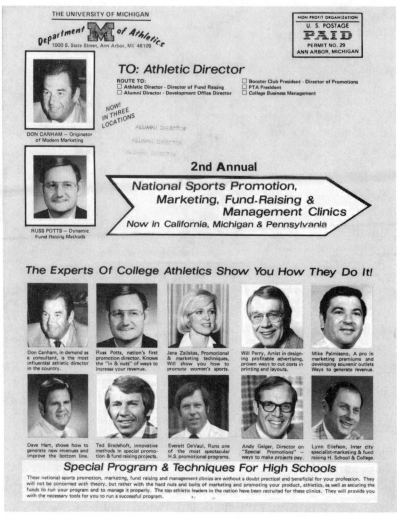

And the block "M" at the upper left is copyrighted.
One of our marketing seminar flyers: We always
sold out in California, Michigan, and Pennsylvania.

game. So we advertised in Ohio — Columbus, Toledo, and other major cities. Coach Woody Hayes had the "team of the century," quarterback Rex Kern and company. In three weeks we sold 23,000 tickets in Ohio and insured a sellout. Since Ohio fans couldn't get football tickets in Columbus, they trooped into Ann Arbor to see their team play. Michigan won the game and a trip to the Rose Bowl. The following spring we mailed our season ticket applications to all of those Ohio people and sold thousands. At least they could see a Michigan-Ohio State game every other year. To date they have never given them up. Game day in Ann Arbor sees a traffic jam on the roads from Ohio. We even picked up a Toledo radio station to broadcast all our games.

Advertising in Ohio newspapers was so successful that the next season we placed full-page ads in the regional editions of *Sports Illustrated*, AAA's magazine, *Motor News, Newsweek* and the magazine sections of *The Detroit News* and the *Detroit Free Press*; always with a few coffee cups, T-shirts and bumper stickers for sale to pay for the ticket application ad.

An important strategy gone largely unnoticed is the way we slanted everything to appeal to the woman of the house. "She controls the weekend," a friend, Art Lichtman at the University of Oregon, once told me when I asked how he made track and field a sellout situation at

Sold out: With ticket manager Al Renfrew, looking at the results of another Ohio State sellout. It's happened each game since 1969.

Oregon. Art was so right, and we did all we could to promote U-M football games as family events — tailgate picnics, bands, photos in our brochures of women and children walking into the stadium, campus tours. We even had the Budweiser Clydesdale horses come in to attract kids. We assumed men already knew we had a place of business at the corner of Main Street and Stadium. Others followed our lead like it was a new invention. Today Michigan and most other schools have as many or more women and children spectators as men.

Television, of course, has now shown off the game and its pageantry, and that has helped the major institutions. Whether it has helped attendance at smaller schools is still being debated. Most evidence indicates TV has had a negative effect on small school attendance.

One thing the situation taught me was not to talk about our won-lost record to sell tickets. It just wasn't there the first year. So we built our whole campaign around the spectacle of college football: tailgate picnics, safety, bands, campus exposure for the kids, three plays a minute, and anything else we could think of. Few schools can say we're No.1 and we were one of those that couldn't just then.

While promoting track and field meets in New York, Detroit and Ann Arbor in the '50s and '60s, I quickly learned that whenever there's an announced sellout the ticket demand starts to heat up. Sellouts at least create the illusion the event is worth seeing. That's not always true, as some Super Bowl and World Series games prove.

Will Perry: He always had an idea and never got enough credit.

With 40,000 empty seats for football games it must have appeared we didn't have a great product. So we started a campaign to sell $2 tickets to high school students and we organized huge band days to put "fannies in the seats." Product or not, soon we had sellouts — but thousands of fans paid only $2, and 10,000 seats often contained kids with horns who got in free. Each year, from 1970 on, we had to reduce the number of $2 tickets and eliminate some of the high school bands until, in the mid-'70s, we went to full-price sellouts. Band days and the cut-rate tickets disappeared. It was a sad state of affairs because those occupying the cheap seats were exactly the people we needed to create Michigan fans for the future.

The 100,000 football crowd became commonplace at Michigan. When we reached 130 consecutive crowds of 100,000-plus early in the 1996 season it was with a yawn. People have learned to expect it, but few seem to absorb its significance. Other schools still get excited over their capacity crowds of 57,000, but we have had 100,000-plus sell-outs for years.

Sports Illustrated, in an issue early in the 1995 season, wrote: "Michigan drew only 100,802, which was 1,699 short of capacity for its 24-7 victory over Memphis last Saturday, the smallest crowd to attend a game at Michigan Stadium since 1980." It might be asked, how did Memphis State ever get on the Michigan schedule in the first place? But, in any case, it illustrates that many have forgotten the days when the stadium was half empty, how hard it was to fill it, and how important a decent schedule is.

Our major target in the marketing plan was television. Crisler had hated TV from its inception because he honestly felt television was the greatest competitor the universities had at the gate. I think most of us felt there was a good possibility the smaller schools would be hurt by television, but major schools might use the exposure to promote their programs. That turned out to be the case. At that time, however, the NCAA TV plan gave protection to the small school by limiting the number of times the majors could appear.

Crisler would not allow ABC, the network doing NCAA telecasts, to use a ground camera on the field. He would not permit removal of seats in the end zones to provide space for TV cameras. Although there were plenty of seats that easily could have been sacrificed for that purpose, he just didn't want to encourage television broadcasting in Michigan Stadium. The cameras were only allowed in the press box.

I launched our change of policy by calling Bill Flemming, a Michigan alumnus who teamed with Chris Schenkel in telecasting college football. I wanted Flemming to inform ABC Sports president Roone Arledge that we would cooperate in any way to facilitate the televising of games from Ann Arbor. Arledge called immediately. From later experience I learned he seldom received or made calls. A year later I was on the NCAA TV committee and ABC knew it was welcome in Ann Arbor.

The NCAA limited schools to two TV appearances each year.

Sometimes a team would show up on the screen just once, and three times was unusual. Michigan wasn't getting its limit at home, often only the Ohio State game. When the Wolverines played Purdue, for instance, the game might be telecast from West Lafayette, Ind., because cameras were welcomed in Purdue's Ross-Ade Stadium by Athletic Director Red Mackey. But with the new attitude at Michigan, ABC in short order began to televise Wolverines games from Ann Arbor. It was a great setting — the largest stadium in the country — and there were good camera locations that never had been utilized. We let them on the field and in the end zone and even built them a booth on the press box photo deck.

"Canham is willing." Michigan alumnus Bill Flemming carried the message to ABC's Roone Arledge.

To enhance our new image we also had to update facilities and improve maintenance. Crisler was certainly a great administrator, but he had, at the end of his career, an aversion to maintenance and new construction. In fairness to him there were money problems as we simply had too many empty seats in the stadium. The situation was critical. The baseball stadium had a leaky roof. The running tracks, both indoor and outdoor, were 10 years behind the times. Everyone else was going to synthetic tracks and we were still running on cinders. Crisler Arena had taken our financial reserves and our student fees.

Michigan Stadium was our biggest renovation problem. Weeds grew up between the seats during the summer. The stadium concrete had spalled and chipped and in some locations was actually hazardous to walk on after years without maintenance. In my time we spent $8 million on stadium renovation, a million or more of that on rest rooms for women since they were now coming to games with the kids.

Stadium scoreboards, too, were bad. In my first summer the plant engineers told me the scoreboards were rusted and hazardous and had to be replaced immediately. We hired a contractor to replace them, although where I'd find the money to pay the bill was a problem we had to ignore. Luckily our first marketing program paid for them with the

Ohio State revenue boost alone. Initially there was concern that new footings would have to be put in because the new scoreboards were so much heavier than the old. But Fielding H. Yost, being an engineer, had overbuilt everything for the original stadium

ABC started to appear regularly. They even got cameras on the field and in the end zone. On TV days 10,000 band kids made it look like a sellout.

and his double scoreboard footings were suitable. Work was completed a day before the first game. Electricians worked all night to get the new boards working. It was my first major crisis. Game day I was afraid to ask if they worked.

As for the seats, numbers were so worn out that in some sections they had to be marked in chalk prior to each game. When the seats were fiber glass-covered and re-numbered, contrary to some opinions we did not paint narrower seats so as to squeeze in more spectators. I still hear that charge, but they remain 15 inches on center.

Two actions got me in trouble with the faculty and perhaps with the administration as we tried to change our image: I had the fence around the stadium painted yellow, and I used a helicopter to fly over Tiger Stadium in Detroit during the 1968 World Series to promote ticket sales. These things might not seem so bad, but in 1968 in some circles at conservative Michigan they were frowned upon. The yellow fence was considered garish and it wasn't thought proper to have helicopters trailing U-M advertisements. Blame Strack for the fence! One day he and I were taking a walk around the stadium, bordered then by a gray wall, with no landscaping and a gray fence.

"This place doesn't look like a first-class stadium," I said, and remarked that something dramatic needed to be done.

"Well, what do you think about painting the fence red, white and blue?" Strack responded.

Although he was being facetious, it got me thinking. "No, let's paint it either blue or maize," I said.

"I vote for yellow," Strack said. The fence was painted maize — bright yellow.

Well, you'd think we had set off a bomb on the 50-yard line.

How could we be so irreverent with the great Michigan Stadium?

Dave Strack: Blame the yellow fence on Dave.

If the student newspaper, the *Michigan Daily* had not agreed with what we did, we might have had real repercussions. But one student reporter wrote, "It looks better than the Ohio State gray or the Michigan State green or Wisconsin red. It looks neat!" So we changed our image quickly and in time the controversy passed. Years later (and I should have done it earlier) we repainted the fence Michigan blue. Some people wrote in saying they preferred the maize. Who can win them all?

The other somewhat innocuous episode that wasn't well received involved a promotion I did with J.L. Hudson Co., the huge department store chain. Hudson's was selling Michigan football tickets for us in its billing mailings. Lou Cromwell, marketing director of Hudson's, had a helicopter fly over Tiger Stadium during the 1968 World Series pulling a banner that read, "Buy Michigan Football Tickets." TV cameras panning the sky immediately picked up the ad and soon from coast to coast Michigan was a topic of conversation. The promotions showed that U-M was off on a different, aggressive marketing track. The helicopter did just what we hoped it would do, call attention to the University of Michigan. But not everyone was enthusiastic. In those days it was not considered dignified for universities to advertise. Today it all sounds pretty tame.

In our quest for a new identity and new money, we utilized for parking every inch of appropriate property under athletic control! As more and more football tickets were sold, more parking had to be found.

Enjoy a Fall Saturday Afternoon at Michigan

You may be impressed by Band Day; its 14,000 musicians offering a panorama of brilliant colors... or the spectacle of Homecoming... or the pure entertainment of Michigan's famed Marching Band—Whatever the reasons, a Saturday afternoon in Michigan Stadium is really something the entire family can share.

Each year thousands of new fans watch Michigan football and they come back because there is more than just championship teams to cheer. The unique atmosphere of college life commands the day.

First, Michigan Stadium is easy to reach and parking is ideal (note picture above of vast areas for cars). The fun actually begins hours before kickoff with a tailgate picnic. The band entertains before the game and at halftime, then presents a mini-concert afterwards.

This season seven home games feature the best in college football. Stanford, Baylor, Missouri and Ohio State will try to break the Wolverines' 35-game unbeaten streak in Michigan Stadium. Why not join the Michigan crowd for a Saturday you won't forget.

It was like finding money, parking on the golf course. Yost would die first. We advertised "Parking is only a chip shot to your seat."

Parking around Crisler Arena, adjacent to the football stadium, never had been sold for football. Most of it was complimentary to faculty, business people, and season ticket holders, and the property wasn't developed as it is today. Most of the lots were gravel and the southeast lot was grass. And there never had been parking on the Michigan Golf Course across the street from the stadium. We began parking 3,000 to 5,000 cars each game on the golf course and that was like finding money.

Another early improvement was putting artificial turf in the stadium. In 1968 at the last home game of the season, Michigan played Wisconsin in the rain. I watched from the press box and couldn't distinguish the numbers on the muddied players' jerseys. I heard that Tennessee had installed artificial turf in its stadium. The Houston Astrodome also had artificial turf, but as far as I knew no college facility other than Tennessee had installed it. I contacted the Volunteers' athletic director, Bob Woodruff, who raved about the turf.

Although Monsanto Co. had developed Astroturf, 3-M had produced a surface called Tartan Turf and that is what Tennessee had put down. Both companies tried to woo Michigan, but we settled on Tartan Turf. In our opinion, 3-M had the better product, which later proved to be the case. Through our own engineering department we had developed an underpad, so we felt we had the best artificial surface available. I still think it was and would not have returned to grass, as happened after I left.

The project received considerable publicity and when we had Football Press Day in 1969 the turf had just been installed. We watched as newspaper reporters and fans crawled around on their hands and knees feeling the artificial turf. The only warning we gave was, "Don't chew gum," because that was the one thing we weren't sure we could get out of the turf. (Later we found that freezing the gum with ice cubes made it possible to chip it out.)

The opening game was against Vanderbilt. Cheerleaders threw miniature rubber footballs commemorating the game up into the crowd — we weren't sure how good Schembechler's first team would be so we had backup entertainment. When things went bad on the field, the balls came out of the stands. That was our last football giveaway.

Although U-M's athletic facilities were among the best in the country, they weren't utilized enough. Soon we were presenting attractions such as the Harlem Globetrotters in Crisler Arena and art fairs and flower shows in the track building. We even brought boxing to Crisler Arena, and Muhammed Ali fights on the big screen TV there were popular. We tried a country and western show in the arena, although it wasn't a big success. Other concerts went over well, including an appearance by Elvis Presley not long before his death.

We hit the jackpot when the Detroit Lions played an exhibition game against the Baltimore Colts at Michigan Stadium. For years Russ Thomas, general manager of the Lions, had asked about putting on an exhibition game in the stadium. The practice was to pay the host school 15 percent for such use. I told Thomas the game could be held there if the Lions split the gate with Michigan. U-M would pay the visiting team a flat fee. Everything else, concessions, parking and ticket sales, would be divided equally between the Lions and the Michigan athletic department. We didn't do anything for 15 percent.

Thomas and Lions' owner William Clay Ford, himself a former U-M tennis player, talked it over with me a few times and finally agreed to try it. Detroit had drawn only 16,000 people for its exhibition game against the Colts the previous year. I guaranteed the Lions at least 35,000 spectators although I wasn't at all sure of it. Thomas and I talked with Colts' owner Carroll Rosenblum on the phone and told him the Colts would be guaranteed $50,000. He refused that offer but said the Colts would agree to do it for $75,000. A hold-up, I felt.

Between the signing of the deal and the game a year later, the Colts won the Super Bowl. Additionally, George Plimpton decided to use *that* game to film the movie based on his book, *Paper Lion*. The publicity took off as we stirred up excitement surrounding the prospect of the movie company being there and the Super Bowl champions coming in. Supplementing it were mass mailings by us and by the Lions.

The game drew 92,000 people, a record for an exhibition, and Michigan split the profits with the Lions — more than $600,000 after the Baltimore guarantee. The crowd was not a typical Michigan crowd. Many were seeing the stadium for the first time, so we put ticket applications on all sideline seats and weren't surprised at our sales from that experiment.

On game day I was standing in the tunnel and in came Rosenblum and his son. Rosenblum stopped in his tracks when he saw the crowd. "Where is this SOB Canham?" he said. "We aren't playing for any $75,000 with a house like this!"

He didn't know me from a bale of hay. "I think he's up there with Bill Ford," I said, and pointed to the press box. I figured further dealings with Rosenblum were the problem of the Lions, not Michigan.

The Wolverines still got half the gross, more than $360,000, but I don't know what the Lions may have worked out to salve Rosenblum's bruised wallet. I used that money to build the first football building at Ferry Field. Unfortunately, Rosenblum drowned in the ocean a few years later. Before his untimely death he offered me a job with the Los Angeles Rams and laughed about the incident.

Another large, and hugely successful, promotion was the Slippery Rock-Shippensburg State football game in 1979 featuring two small college teams from Pennsylvania. For years when the scores of Slippery Rock games were announced at Michigan Stadium, the crowd would let out a cheer if Slippery Rock was the winner and a groan if it lost. It was one of those quirky traditions — like Whiskey, the little dog that pushed a soccer ball with his nose from one goal line to the other at halftimes — that punctuated the whole experience of a Wolverines football Saturday in Ann Arbor.

I was standing on the photo deck at one of the games and Steve Filipiak, the announcer, gave the Shippensburg-Slippery Rock results. He dramatized the final score, saying something like, "In the last seconds, Slippery Rock pulled the game from the fire with a touchdown." The crowd went bananas. I turned to Perry and said, "Monday let's see if we can transfer next year's game here and show people that small-college football could be marketed."

So the next year Michigan did just that, bringing in the two Pennsylvania teams on a Saturday when the Wolverines weren't using the stadium. The teams were guaranteed the same money they would have made by playing a home game in their own stadium. U-M also paid their expenses, brought in their bands, and had a carnival. We hired the San Diego Chicken to make an appearance and the Budweiser Clydesdales were featured as well. The game drew 62,000 people and was covered by ABC-TV's *Wide World of Sports*, as well as national radio. It was one big picnic. And profitable for all.

I thought it might encourage other major institutions to do the same in an effort to help small-college football, but apparently it didn't. Subsequently I brought Slippery Rock back to play Detroit's Wayne State. I planned to bring Grambling up, and to that end had talks with the southern school's legendary coach, Eddie Robinson, but it didn't happen.

Seven Exciting Saturdays at Michigan ...(And) Each One a Special Event

STANFORD

Sept. 20
Stanford always a rugged foe for 'M' and this year will be no exception. Air-minded Cardinals with 38 lettermen back have dangerous flanker Tony Hill and two top quarterbacks ready.

BAYLOR

Sept. 27
Baylor's Southwest Conference champions went to Cotton Bowl last year and have 14 starters returning. Real challenge for 'M'. High School Band Day makes this one of season's highlights.

MISSOURI

Oct. 4
Missouri was last team to defeat 'M' in Michigan Stadium and Tigers have the talent to do it again. Top rusher and regular QB plus rugged defense all return.

NORTHWESTERN

Oct. 18
Northwestern looks for solid season with 13 regulars back. Tailback Jim Pooler, league's 5th top rusher, leads attack for Coach John Pont.

INDIANA

Oct. 25
Indiana has 45 lettermen and 17 starters from team that nearly upset 'M'. QB Terry Jones led Big 10 in passing as soph. It's Homecoming Saturday.

PURDUE

Nov. 8
Rugged Purdue, led by fullback Mike Pruitt (6 yd. average) always battles 'M' to wire. Coach Alex Agase has 13 starters back.

OHIO STATE

Nov. 22
Ohio State with Heisman Trophy winner Archie Griffin and QB Cornelius Greene visits Michigan Stadium and this one again figures to decide a championship and bowl bid. Kickoff is 1 p.m.

The roar of the crowd: we made our ads as vivid as possible, short of building in the sounds of the stadium. This one depicts high school band day, always a hit. Unfortunately, every one of those several thousand musicians took up a 15-inch space that was increasingly in demand by paying customers. Goodbye band day.

Robinson wanted to play Air Force or another team of that caliber, and the right opponent couldn't be found. Had we brought Grambling in with its great band we would likely have equaled the Slippery Rock crowd and perhaps surpassed it. Eddie would have taken home a hat full of money.

During all this time my right-hand marketing man was Perry, who certainly was the right person at the right time when I went looking for a sports information director to replace the departing Etter. Perry had gone to Michigan and played baseball for Fisher. He did not earn a letter, but Fisher in those days only gave out 13 or 14 letters, compared with coaches today who award three times that many. Had Perry played for any other baseball coach he surely would have been an "M" man. His son, Steve, played for Michigan and lettered, and signed a contract with the Dodgers. Eventually the M-Club awarded Will Perry an honorary letter.

I decided to hire Perry a half hour after I met him. He had interviewed me for his newspaper when my appointment was made. Other than Dave Diles, he was the only interviewer who had done any research whatsoever on my background. I was not a household word; as a track coach I certainly hadn't grabbed headlines so it was unusual for reporters to know my background. Will was at Michigan when I was coaching track so I knew a little about him. But his intelligent questions during the newspaper interview got my attention and we hit it off personally. Knowing that Etter was leaving, I had been thinking of a replacement. A few days later I offered the sports information job to Will. We discussed salary and he persuaded me to up my offer from $12,000 to $13,000, not much more than he was making at the *Grand Rapids Press*. But we were broke.

The block M with the Wolverine on it was Perry's idea. He had a student draw the Wolverine and Perry combined it with the block M and had the design copyrighted. We developed other logos with the "M." The Wolverines would be lost now without the revenue they generate year after year. Perry administered all the licensing from the beginning. Most of the world-famous insignias and logos now providing Michigan with $6 million yearly were designed by Will and me on a kitchen table more than 25 years ago.

We found that virtually everyone in the country was using the

University of Michigan shield. Although it had nothing to do with the athletic department, we immediately developed a royalty program to include the shield. Royalties from the shield go to the university itself. But just about everything else funnels money to the athletic department, even the music for the "Let's Go Blue!" cheer when used by private enterprises in promotional materials. At one point 67 different items were earning royalty money for U-M athletics. It's in the hundreds today, I'd guess.

For a few years we licensed and collected royalties ourselves. Later we were approached by a man named Steve Crosland from California who was starting a licensing company using UCLA

We designed several variations on the block M, then applied for copyrights on all. The licensing fees now provide Michigan with millions each year — $6,000,000 in 1995.

souvenirs. We both thought Michigan could do just as well or better than UCLA, and we were right. During the first year or two our revenue from the licensing arrangement with Crosland was between $100,000 and $200,000. After the first three years that amount grew dramatically. Crosland marketed in Europe and Japan as well as the U.S. Now the revenue to the athletic department is in the millions each year.

In our effort to market Michigan we also changed the way sports information was distributed. I vividly recall sitting in TV sportscaster Al Ackerman's office at Channel 7 in Detroit one day before we went on the air. He showed me hundreds of press releases he had received in the last couple weeks. The stack was two feet high. Most of them never were opened. Will had seen that sort of thing too, so we pitched our mimeo machine. When he had an important story, Perry got on the phone to key sports editors and writers throughout the state and contacted the radio and TV outlets. He didn't forget the wire services, either, because he knew they would transmit the news to all the smaller outlets he didn't have time to call. Then we installed call-in phones accessible 24 hours a day with updated scores, interviews with coaches, and other information. The number of calls from the press and radio people was spectacular. We had started the move to the electronic age. Michigan today is on the Internet.

Perry's football and basketball programs won awards and he put together first-class media guides. He was one of the first SIDs, along

with Russ Potts of Maryland, to realize they were really marketers and PR people, as well as information sources. After several years I knew Perry would be far more valuable to the department as an assistant athletic director. He initially turned down the offer because he enjoyed the media people so much and was popular with them. It was a few years before he finally accepted the new position.

Perry and I in the press box in 1995. Someone else worries about crowd control now.

Perry's last project was the Margaret Dow Towsley Sports Museum in Schembechler Hall. He designed the displays, put everything together, and came up with an exhibition well worth seeing. When I look back at all those who have contributed, I think it is Will Perry who did the most with the least amount of credit in making Michigan Michigan.

◆◆◆

Chapter **9**

Scheduling Notre Dame

◆————————————————————

Million-Dollar Gates

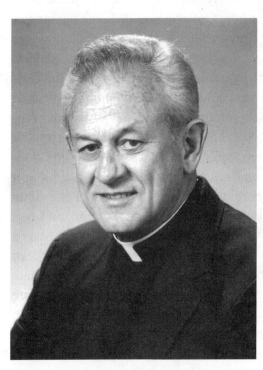

Father Edmund Joyce of Notre Dame

T he marketing of Michigan didn't stop at coffee cups and pennants and colorful ticket brochures. Unless we generated more revenue from football ticket sales, none of our plans for change could be fulfilled. It was essential to get a more attractive football schedule than we had, so Dave Strack, Bump Elliott, and I sat down early in 1969 and tried to figure how we could enhance it.

We had some great names on our schedule, including Duke, Vanderbilt, Navy, Virginia, Missouri, and even California, but those were not teams that caught the imagination of fans or fired their desire to buy season tickets. Season tickets are a must. Since they're paid for up front, they are weather-proof. Rain or shine the money is in the bank.

We knew we had to get a team that had a magic name. Strange as it seems now, at that time we didn't even sell out Michigan Stadium for the Ohio State game. Obviously, when we played Baylor or Northwestern or Indiana or some of the teams named above, we didn't have much leverage to motivate season buyers. You can't fool the sophisticated fans. You can promote and promote, but unless you have something worthwhile to offer, you're wasting your time and money.

The first school we thought of was Alabama because Coach "Bear" Bryant was then at the height of his career. He was such a national figure that if he changed hats it would make headlines. I called Bear and I also asked my friend from South Carolina, Weems Baskin, to talk to him. Bryant didn't know me from Adam, but Weems had worked with him and they were close friends. So Weems set it up for us to meet in New York at the time of the College Hall of Fame banquet at the Waldorf Astoria in December of 1970.

Bryant kept saying, "Oh yes, I think we'd be interested in playing Michigan on a home and home agreement." But I never had the feeling he really wanted to because he could have done anything he wanted with the Alabama schedule. In the end he told me (this was after Schembechler had had two good years) that he just didn't want to play a team as tough as Michigan so early in the season during the non-conference part of the schedule. That made us feel pretty good, but it didn't solve our scheduling problem. We then turned to Penn State where Joe Paterno had been on the job for five or six years and was extremely successful. Paterno went back and forth with us. Penn State's athletic director seemed to indicate that we could get together, but in the end we did not. One obstacle with both Alabama and Penn State was that our Big Ten schedule dictated our having only the first three weeks open. During this period, however, I had gone to a banquet in Detroit and sat next to Ed "Moose" Krause, the famed and popular athletic director at Notre Dame. He turned to me and said, "Don, Michigan and Notre Dame should be playing football."

"Well, why not?" I said. "Let's see what we can do."

I had always admired Notre Dame. They play anyone, and Krause was one of the most trusted men in all sports. Rev. Edmund Joyce, the executive vice president and chairman of the faculty athletics board, was a national leader I had come to know through the NCAA committees. I didn't harbor prejudice against the Notre Dame Irish as both Fielding Yost and Fritz Crisler had. Yost felt animosity toward their legendary coach, Knute Rockne, and Crisler couldn't be in the same room as Coach Frank Leahy. In addition, Fritz always thought you would divide the family by playing Notre Dame. "Our Catholic students will be sitting in the Michigan stadium cheering for the Irish," Crisler would say. That sounds slightly preposterous today, but it reflects the view held by Crisler and many others prior to our country having had a Catholic president.

Edward Krause: his suggestion started the series.

A few days later Father Joyce called me and asked if I'd be willing to drive to South Bend and have lunch with him. I said I would and that I'd bring Strack. So Dave and I had lunch in Morris Hall at Notre Dame and we discussed the possibilities with Father Joyce. Over the next year we made the trip often.

I told him we'd like to play Notre Dame, but with each school keeping its own gate receipts, not a split gate arrangement as was common. Notre Dame had only 50-some thousand seats. I knew if we played Notre Dame in Ann Arbor we'd fill our 101,000 seats with no difficulty, plus it would insure more season ticket sales. We even contemplated putting a premium price on the game. We were talking about an extremely lucrative weekend. At Notre Dame, however, we were talking half as many spectators and not as good a gate split as we generally received at most Big Ten schools. Joyce was irritated and I think surprised I made that type of proposal, but one must remember we were fighting to balance our budget during this period of negotiations and wanted to change the way contracts were written.

Dave and I had previously decided to negotiate this "own gate" contract with Alabama and Penn State so we were prepared with pretty good figures to present to Notre Dame. The idea offered advantages for both institutions. It could use the same contract to its advantage with other schools the Irish played — bring in Tulane, for instance, on a flat guarantee, not a split of the gate. We wanted to use the Notre Dame contract for new non-conference schools we scheduled and put an end to paying some visiting schools what we paid Ohio State or Illinois. Duke, for example, was not a draw like a Big Ten team but took 50 percent of our total gate at home. Revenues from Big Ten games, by regulation, had to be shared equally and all schools were all in favor of that. It just seemed a little unnecessary to us that we should share our huge gate with schools not in our family.

Father Joyce and I always met at the Friday press parties after our series started. Here we were before a Michigan-Notre Dame game in Ann Arbor.

Father Joyce rejected our proposal out of hand and Dave and I left. A few days later I wrote Father Joyce a letter outlining what I had in mind because I didn't think I had done a very good job of presenting it initially. First of all, I pointed out, a Notre Dame-Michigan game would certainly be televised nationally to the tune of — even back then — close to a million dollars. Notre Dame and Michigan would split television revenues, which were not part of the gate, so Notre Dame could keep approximately $500,000 for every televised game played at either place. Michigan's share of television, however, would be only $50,000 because we were bound by contract to share it 10 ways with the Big Ten schools. I don't think Father Joyce realized that situation until my letter.

Second, I emphasized that Notre Dame could use the Michigan contract (each school keeping its own gate) in negotiations with other teams with whom they had a home and home arrangement. Notre Dame's most recent game at Tulane, for example, had had a very poor turnout and made little money; but when Tulane came back to South Bend, Notre Dame had to share the gate on a sellout. For another variation, if it played someone with a one-shot deal it could set a flat fee, not 50 percent of the gate. And the third thing I pointed out was that a Notre Dame football ticket was always far more expensive than a Michigan ticket. For the Michigan game it could put any price on the ticket it wanted.

A few days later I heard from Father Joyce, who asked if Strack and I could come to South Bend again. We met at Morris Hall with him, Krause, and several others, including business manager Joe O'Brien and Public Relations Director Roger Valdiserri. One reason the agreement took so long was that we were talking *only* about a long-term contract; we were not interested in a two- or four-game series. I think Notre Dame policy at that time was more cautious, so that was one of the hangups. Moose and I had no difficulty with this, but I'm not sure Father Joyce wanted to tie Notre Dame to Michigan over a long-term period. Finally, we agreed on the details and made the first known contract where two majors kept their home gate.

Then we had to figure out open dates for both schools. That was no easy task because most football schedules are made 10 years in advance and the Big Ten provided only the three early weekends in the season, prior to the start of Big Ten games, to play outside institutions. Scheduling was not about to stand in our way, however, because we knew it was going to be a bonanza for Michigan to have Notre Dame coming into that stadium every other fall. Besides, if you're going to be a national champion you'd better play the best — at least that was our feeling in early 1970.

So our marketing of the Michigan football team was on schedule, possibly ahead of schedule. In 1969 we had installed artificial turf in Michigan Stadium and had taken out all of the box seats, the poorest seats in the house that ringed the stadium at ground level, and increased the stadium capacity from 101,001 to 101,701. (The "one" was put on the attendance by Fritz and he always said, "That seat's for me." I left it there; and when I look up at the board and see the total number of seats with the one tacked on the end I realize that seat is still Fritz's.)

Also in 1969, Schembechler and company upset a great Ohio State team and Michigan was in the Rose Bowl for the first time since 1964.

We certainly were on our way, we felt, and then Bo had a heart attack prior to the Rose Bowl game. But following his surgery and full recovery we were back in the Rose Bowl in 1971. And for the next 10 years Michigan was rated in the top 10 in the nation in the final college football polls. No other institution during that time duplicated that feat. We had eight Big Ten championships in football during that period. It was truly a golden era for us. Adding Notre Dame to our schedule was to ensure a tremendous spectator demand for years to come.

While the Notre Dame contracts were negotiated in the early '70s, it was not until 1978 the first game was played, at South Bend. On the eve of the game at a huge press conference Krause said, "When we look back 25 years from today we will probably see that Michigan won half of the games and Notre Dame won half of the games." Michigan did win the first game, 28-14, and lost the second game in Ann Arbor, 12-10. Moose's prediction was off to a great start.

The significance of the Notre Dame series was threefold:

First, once we confirmed the announcement we automatically established the concept of each school keeping its own gate. The contract we used at the signing of Notre Dame is the same contract that is used to this day. We did, however, provide for expenses of $100,000 for the visiting team. Nonconference schools came into Ann Arbor for $300,000 and $400,000 guarantees — considerably less than a 50 percent share of the gate, yet more than they made in most other games.

The second significance was it guaranteed a national appearance on television every year, and that has been borne out in the 20-some years from the date of the signing.

Third, the contract provided us with continuous sellout crowds from the first Notre Dame game at Ann Arbor in 1979. At Michigan a similar situation to the Ohio State sellout situation occurred. People who wanted to see a Notre Dame game started to buy Michigan season tickets. With a 55,000-seat stadium, thousands and thousands of fans didn't have a chance to see Notre Dame play at home. To illustrate the popularity of the series, in 1980 in Ann Arbor the first pure $1 million gate in college football history occurred. One million dollars in ticket sales were generated and it did *not* include television, concessions, or parking. And each school keeping its own gate helped our budget.

Joe Falls wrote the following column in 1992:

Joe
FALLS

U-M discovers a $2-million pot o' gold at the end of this Irish rainbow

ANN ARBOR — How big is this Michigan-Notre Dame game? It is the biggest regular-season money game in the history of college football — a payday worth almost $2 million at the gate . . . and Michigan gets to keep almost all of it.

And to think, they used to sell tickets for a buck apiece around here. They've come a long way, Mr. Yost.

According to ticket manager Steve Lambright, it breaks down this way:

- 73,000 tickets at $22 apiece: $1,606,000.
- 20,000 student tickets at $10 apiece: $200,000.
- 7,000 faculty and staff tickets at $17.60 apiece: $123,200.
- Total: $1,929,200.

And, of course, this doesn't count parking, concessions and programs, which will put the final figure well over $2 million. Who says the college game isn't big business?

Oh, I forgot. If you'd like to sit under the press box, out of the rain, it is $2 extra. This is called the "Blue Section" and is reserved for the bluest of the Blue backers. They've got just a couple of hundred of these seats, and they go for $24. (But you get a sense these people can afford them).

Any way you look it, this illustrates that the U-M football program is the most dynamic thing that has happened in sports in the past 15 years.

Think about it . . . crowds of 100,000 or more for 97 consecutive games, dating to 1975.

Nowhere else in the country has this happened.

The credit goes to the old athletic director, Don Canham. He orchestrated this whole thing,

When he got the idea in the 1970s of playing Notre Dame on a regular basis, he proposed a home-team keep-all setup. His reasoning was that this would benefit the Irish as well as the Wolverines because, though there are fewer seats in Notre Dame Stadium (59,000), they could charge more for them.

"I didn't care if they charged 50 bucks apiece — I knew they could get it," Canham said.

In time, they agreed to increase the expenses to $300,000.

The deal actually started at a banquet where Canham sat with Moose Krause, the Notre Dame athletic director, and told him that the two schools should get together and play each other. Krause liked the idea and proposed it to Fr. Joyce.

Between 1,000 and 1,500 will get in free. These are mostly university officials, recruits from all sports, and of course, President James Duderstadt, who probably wishes he were paying for his tickets after all the problems his school is having with the recent government audit into U-M's federally funded expense claims.

Right or wrong, they count the rest of us — writers, broadcasters, etc. — as part of the regular crowd. With ushers and volunteers, that brings the final count up to the customary 106,000.

Michigan puts everything in the bank except $300,000 in expenses for Notre Dame. It is literally a home-team-keep-all setup, the only one of its kind in the country.

The Irish are given 6,000 tickets, but at the top price of $22.

Where Notre Dame benefits is that this is a nationally televised game, and the Irish get 50 percent of the income. Michigan, as a member of the Big Ten, gets only 10 percent. But the Wolverines do share in other games involving Big Ten teams.

All of which results from the vision and effort of Canham, the man who marketed Michigan football into the largest moneymaker in college sports.

— The Detroit News

Today the Michigan-Notre Dame game, and for that matter any sellout in Michigan Stadium, provides more than $2 million in ticket sales. So that hole in the ground that Yost dug still provides the majority of the revenue to conduct all sports for both men and women, without using general fund money from the university.

At Father Joyce's retirement dinner in 1986.

The most memorable retirement party of my time was for Father Joyce. Father Theodore M. Hesburgh , Notre Dame's president, had invited 70 or more people to a formal eight-course retirement dinner for his famed vice president, a complete surprise for him. Each invitee had to have had some memorable experience with Joyce. Among them were his gardener, his barber, and many from his storied athletic career. Joyce sat at each table for one course of the dinner so he talked with everyone. The only speakers were Hesburgh and Joyce, but many presented Joyce with mementos. I gave him a plaque from Michigan and said the picture we used was from his "high school yearbook" — not so, but it got a laugh. In the background is Chuck Neinas, a close friend of Joyce's.

◆◆◆

Chapter **10**

The News Media

◆──────────────────────────

ABC on the Sidelines

F ritz Crisler was admired by the press during his time at Michigan, but he didn't return the sentiment. Writers and broadcasters were simply *there*. For Crisler, they had no bearing one way or the other on U-M's athletic accomplishments or, presumably, on the interest people took in the university's teams and the attendance that went along with it.

ABC-Televisions's top crew — the announcing team of Bob Griese and Keith Jackson, the best in the business for many years.

Well-known journalists from Crisler's era included Grantland Rice, H.G. Salsinger of *The Detroit News*, Arthur Daly of the *New York Times*, and Braven Dyer of the *Los Angeles Times*. And there were others, like Wilfred Smith of the *Chicago Tri-*

bune and John Carmichael of the *Chicago Daily News*, to name a few.

Throw broadcasters into the mix, such as Harry Wismer, Ted Heusing and Bill Stern, and you had some mighty influential people willing to hand over free publicity to Michigan football and other sports programs.

From coast to coast they publicized the Wolverines. Great fans of Fielding Yost and then of Crisler, they first put Michigan on the national stage in the '20s, '30s, and '40s.

Dyer of the *Los Angeles Times* was a great track and field fan and was famous for his "leads" to events he covered. One of his best concerned Jesse Owens. The University of Southern California had won the NCAA championships in 1936, beating Ohio State, and Owens, 60 to 40 and 1/5 points. The Ohio State 1/5-point came from a pole vaulter named Whitey Wonsowitz when he tied for fifth place with five others to divide the 1 point. Owens had won four events and scored the other 40 points for Ohio. Dyer wrote, "Ohio would be the NCAA champion if they had only come to town with one more Jesse Owens or 350 more Whitey Wonsowitzes."

There were no "media" in those days, just the "press," with radio sports broadcasters lumped in with print journalists. When I enrolled at Michigan in the late '30s, television was an experimental gadget. It wouldn't become significant for another decade or more.

Crisler often told his coaches, "You do not need the press if you're winning; if you're losing, they aren't going to save your job." That summed up his philosophy on the subject. When I replaced him as athletic director in 1968, the media climate couldn't be called hostile. However, by that time Michigan State, under its affable athletic director Biggie Munn, was enjoying much kinder coverage than Michigan under Crisler. I knew immediately I had a two-pronged problem. One, I was not a popular choice to succeed Crisler. I think the average Michigan alumnus was saying something to the effect of, "Who the hell is this track coach to take Fritz Crisler's place?" And two, I realized we had to conduct a massive public relations campaign. Some revolutionary actions were necessary to make people understand that Michigan athletics was now under new management and developing new policies.

One of my first appointments was a Michigan man, Will Perry, as sports information director. Perry was a sports columnist with the *Grand Rapids Press*, a good writer, good reporter and old-fashioned, hard-nosed copy editor. He impressed me at once when he came down to interview me after I was appointed A.D.

Les Etter had been the sports information director for many years. Etter and I were close friends and I respected him. I think he would have stayed on had I asked him, but I could see he was tired and wanted to do other things. He was writing children's books and painting, and I understood his decision to retire. It wasn't a bitter one, I was sure. Some thought I fired him, but that was not so.

Perry and I sat down immediately to map strategy for changing Michigan's public relations course. First on the agenda was to do ev-erything possible to get WJR radio in De-troit to cover U-M in football and basket-ball rather than con-tinue with Michigan State. That might be hard, especially since Bob Rey-nolds, the leading radio sports-caster in the Detroit market, was a long-time Michigan State friend. We need-ed WJR and its 50,000 watts.

Jim Brandstatter played for Bo, now is a top WJR color man.

Perry and I contacted some leading Michigan alumni, such as Jack Tompkins, vice president of American Airlines, and Doc Robinson, Lou Hide, Bill Mazer Sr., and several others in the Detroit area. They spread the word to those who advertised on Michigan State broadcasts that U-M alumni controlled many corporations in the area and wanted coverage switched to Michigan on WJR. General Motors and Ford were our top targets, as we had contacts there.

It wasn't an easy task, but Tompkins, Robinson, and others hounded the management of WJR and eventually got results. The station did drop Michigan State and picked up Michigan in 1976. A major factor helping us was that Coach Bump Elliott's 1968 football team had a good season and beat Michigan State. Then came a 1969 championship and a Rose Bowl trip in 1970, Bo Schembechler's first year as coach. That suggested Michigan's upswinging grid fortunes were for real. Bo then lost few games in the '70s.

Mill Marsh with Elmer Swanson and me, watching baseball practice in 1949.

TV changed how games are reported in the press. The need for straight game stories in the newspapers has diminished because fans now can watch football, basketball, and so many other sports events on live television. Columnists in the TV age have more opportunities to jump in with opinion pieces. Some, but not all, do it well. I've always been impressed with columnists and sports writers who can sit down and, five or six days a week all year, come up with an original idea for a story — plus a punch line.

For that reason I never told a reporter, "No comment," regardless of the situation. I may not have revealed everything I knew, but I always tried to give them *something* to write about because it was their livelihood. I learned in my days as a coach and as an official in several organizations that, if treated fairly, reporters would be fair. They always were with me, at least.

I had dealings with so many writers and broadcasters it's hard to remember them all. But some were unforgettable. Perhaps first on the list is Mill Marsh, the *Ann Arbor News* sports reporter during my days as an athlete and a coach. Always a humorist, Mill called one of his

Wayne DeNeff

children "Swampy."

"How would *you* like to go through life with the name, 'Swampy Marsh?'" I asked him.

He answered, "I don't."

Mill's light view of life carried over into his approach to intercollegiate athletics and Michigan. He never took them very seriously. And if the phrase, "It's only a game," were attributed to anybody, it should be attributed to Marsh.

Two other fine reporters from the *Ann Arbor News* who stand out in my mind are Dave Tefft and Wayne DeNeff. Both found it hard to criticize amateur athletics and athletes. I think both men probably wrote more nice columns about Michigan, its coaching staff and its administration, than any local reporters since. Today they'd be considered "homers."

Detroit's dailies, *The News* , the *Free Press* and, until its demise, the *Times*, provided extensive Michigan sports coverage. Looking back to the '60s, I'd say that Tommy Devine of the *Free Press* was the first investigative reporter I encountered. I can recall him being booed at football and basketball games when he walked into the arena because of some column he had written that wasn't all hearts and flowers. Compared with some these days, Devine's columns weren't very hard on anyone.

George Puscas

Another *Free Press* writer, in the '40s when the paper had seven or eight staffers who were expected to cover everything, was John Sabo. And still another, who later became sports editor, was Sabo's brother-in-law, George Puscas. He was always a favorite of mine.

Some other outstanding columnists and writers who worked for the *Free Press* in the '40s and '50s were Lyle Smith and Hal Middlesworth, who went on to become public relations directors of football's Detroit Lions and baseball's Detroit Tigers, respectively. Among the current crop who have done an outstanding job for decades are Curt Sylvester, Charlie Vincent, and Jack Saylor.

As for *The News*, Salsinger, Sam Greene and his son, Doc Greene, were class acts, as were Pete Waldmeir, Joe Falls, Lynn Henning, Jack

Doug Mintline

Berry, Bill Halls, Watson Spoelstra, Larry Middlemas and Jerry Green. Spoelstra, Falls, and Halls (*AP*) plus Berry and Sylvester (*UPI*) started out at wire services.

Bob Murphy and Edgar Hayes from the *Times* were gentlemen. Murphy in particular was a sentimental columnist who could see nothing wrong with anything Michigan did. He idolized Ben Oosterbaan.

As for the wires, Harry Atkins succeeded Larry Paladino at *The Associated Press* in 1979 and has been the Michigan sports editor there since. Both wrote countless U-M sports stories seen coast to coast, as did versatile Rich Shook of *United Press International* for some 15 years. Now, though, UPI relies on stringers.

Some of the old-timers who were significant but now long gone include Doug Mintline, *Flint Journal*; Mike Sturm, *Bay City Times;* Wendy Foltz, *Battle Creek Enquirer;* Clank Stoeppels, *Grand Rapids Press;* and Bob Hoerner, *Lansing State Journal.*

Among other fine writers who covered Michigan for years, many who still do, are: Jack Moss, *Kalamazoo Gazette*; Dean Howe, *Flint Journal*; Bob Becker, *Grand Rapids Press;* Dave Mathews, *Lansing State Journal*; Jim Buckley, *Saginaw News;* Bill Brenton, *Monroe Evening News;* Don Winger, *Midland Daily News;* Jim Hoenig, *Adrian Telegram;* Chuck Klonke and Bernie Kennedy, *Macomb Daily;* and Jim Taylor, *Toledo Blade.*

Vince Doyle

I grew up with sports television and radio and knew well most of the personalities who contributed to Michigan lore. Two who were always on the job and always positive about us were Vince Doyle, WWJ Radio, and Pete Sark, WFDF Flint. They were the most competent radio broadcasters around. They always had a tape recorder and missed very few stories. And they created more

Pete Sark

than their share, too.

We used radio call-in shows extensively when we were trying to change the way we did things. Interesting radio contributors in the '60s and '70s were the weather shows. We convinced them to plug the Michigan football games on weekends, especially if the Saturday was going to be a nice day. Some still do that.

Joe Falls kept telling me to improve the hot dog fare in the press box. I just told him to "pack a lunch."

I probably was closer to Waldmeir and Falls than any others. On more than one occasion I watched them sit at a typewriter in my office and put together a column for their next day's edition. How they came up with the stories and punch lines on the spur of the moment amazed me.

It wasn't until the '60s that TV was much of an ingredient in the publicity blender. The early batch of sports anchors were mainly Al Ackerman, Ray Lane, Don Kremer, Paul Williams, Van Patrick, and Dave Diles. Diles was a former *AP* writer who went on to national prominence on *ABC Football Scoreboard* shows. Since then he has written many books from his home in

Al Ackerman

North Carolina. He is a great talent.

A new breed of TV sportscasters came along in the '70s and '80s at Detroit stations, such as Jay Berry, Don Shane, Eli Zaret, Fred

Dave Diles

Pete Waldmeir

Bill Bonds, tough interviewer for anyone trying to be evasive, broke more than his share of stories. Here on Channel 7 in 1980.

McLeod, Steve Garagiola, Dave Lew Allen, Larry Adderley, and former U-M player Jim Brandstatter, people who were always fair in their coverage of Michigan.

Of those I spent time with, I would have to say Diles, the late J.P. McCarthy, and Bill Bonds were the best interviewers. All three listened to what one had to say and most of the time they built their next question on the answer given to the one before. Too often interviewers don't seem to hear a word the guest says, but not Diles, McCarthy, and Bonds. All three are Detroit legends, the late McCarthy as a WJR radio morning show host and Bonds as a controversial news anchor with WXYZ, Channel 7 and WJBK, Channel 2. Bonds now is doing a morning radio show.

J.P. McCarthy: Well-informed on any subject, remarkable on athletics. He never had an enemy I knew of. On WJR in 1986.

For play-by-play, Bob Ufer, former U-M track star turned outstanding pro-Michigan football commentator on WJR, clearly stands out in my mind, as does the play-by-play football work of Frank Beckmann, Dale Conquest of WWJ, and Larry Henry for WJR and WWJ basketball.

Even Dick Vitale, the former University of Detroit and Detroit Pistons basketball coach-cum-national TV basketball analyst, had a part in U-M's broadcast history. When he was coach of the Pistons and Michigan was conducting seminars on athletics marketing and promotion around the country, I booked Vitale as a luncheon speaker at a seminar in Crisler Arena. I had heard him talk when he was at U. of D. Few knew then of Vitale, who would become a bullet-talking, phrase-inventing national icon for the sport of basketball. Subsequent to the invitation, which would pay Vitale something like $400, he was fired by the Pistons and was at the bottom of his world. He called me on the Tuesday before the Friday luncheon speech and asked if I wanted him to withdraw.

"Of course I don't," I responded. "You're still Dick Vitale, aren't you? That's who's booked in here."

Sure enough, Vitale

This must be a pre-game interview with Dick Vitale and Bill Frieder, because Bill still has his coat and tie on and his hair is combed.

gave one hell of a speech, getting a standing ovation, and he's had a sentimental feeling for the University of Michigan ever since. In his telecasting, to this day, he usually speaks well of Michigan. We've gotten good public relations in many strange ways. That was one.

Due to Michigan's up-front relationship with the media people, we avoided some stories that might have been embarrassing. I remember once when Paladino, at the request of his office, was sniffing into a story in the early '70s about the chances of a strike by black athletes. This was something that was happening at a few schools around the country. Michigan, dating back to my days as a trackman at U-M, had always been color-blind and there was no movement for any such revolt. Some of the activist leaders already had met with me and I knew of their plans to shut down the university. But they said they had no quarrel with the athletic department and wanted me to know it. I knew we were going to be OK, and we were. After Larry talked with me and some others, he did not raise the issue or write the story. That was an example of the advantage of always leveling with the press. "No comment" was not the way to do it.

One of the greatest sources of coverage, of course, has always been the student newspaper, the *Michigan Daily*, which manages to deliver top-notch sports editors and reporters year after year. Many of the names seen in newspapers throughout Michigan and elsewhere are reporters who got their start at the *Daily*. We always tried to help them.

In an effort to spread our coverage primarily among the alumni, we encouraged and subsidized to an extent two specialty publications that gave us good coverage, too. None was slicker or more tailored to U-M fans than *GO BLUE!* magazine and its successor, *aMaize 'N Blue*. Unfortunately, the publishers, Tom LeDuc out of Seattle with *GO BLUE!* and Robert Oxley with *aMaize 'N Blue*, couldn't sustain them for more than a few years. The magazines were noted for the fine photography of Joe Arcure, John Hillary, Joe Sell, and Barry Rankin, including color centerfolds.

Later, Ron Cameron published *Sports Fans' Journal* for four years and I was among the columnists.

John Humenik took Perry's place for a year when Will moved to the assistant director's job from sports information. Then Bruce Madej got the job and found the formula for a publication to benefit the athletic department. Bruce started the *Wolverine*, a tabloid, much cheaper to produce than a slick magazine like *Go Blue!* It is self-supporting with subscriptions and ads. The NCAA no longer allows the department to subsidize house publications as once was possible. Bruce's venture has been of tremendous help to the department. In addition, Madej now has Michigan athletics on the Internet.

On the national scene were some recent TV broadcasters who have become household names. Keith Jackson and Bob Griese, the ABC team, belong at the top of the list. Griese, the former Purdue quarterback, sent his son to Michigan where he's a quarterback for the Wolverines. Jackson is the best around on play-by-play. I'd rather have him on a game than anyone.

I served on the NCAA TV committee for 12 years, longer than anyone else, and it gave me a chance to know all those involved in the business of broadcasting college football. During my time, Chris Schenkle and Bill Flemming, a Michigan man, were a combination that was hard to beat.

Bud Wilkinson, Ara Parseghian and Frank Broyles immediately come to mind as former coaches who successfully made the transition to telecasting and were always welcomed at Michigan. I always thought Broyles was the best color man of all — at least, I learned more about the game and its complexities from Frank than from anyone else.

Broyles was a major contributor to our early coaches' show success. Elliott had never had a regular TV coach show. When we were trying to start one for Bo, with Bob Lipson producing and Adderly on air with Schembechler, advertisers were hard to come by. Few

Ara Parseghian, one of the former coaches who turned to broadcasting.

knew Bo and no one knew how much success he would have.

At dinner with Broyles one night he told how he started his football show at Arkansas. It was the first time I'd heard of "roll-overs." By selling a calling card-size ad with just company name and address for $2,000 for the season, one could flash roll-overs on the screen — 20 to 30 advertisers in a 30-second spot. The roll-over ad had a heading, "These businesses support Michigan football." For 11 weeks of television exposure for just $2,000 we had all the advertisers we needed, and Lipson was on the air with *Michigan Re-*

Frank Broyles, A.D. at Arkansas, helped get the Michigan Replay *show financed.*

play. His Michigan football show later with Brandstatter grew to be the most successful coaches' show in the country and is seen in many markets. Coach Lloyd Carr is now in Bo and Gary Moeller's old hot seat.

Other radio personalities, many of whom didn't specialize in sports, enjoyed Michigan athletics and regularly gave us plugs. Joe Donovan has done an extensive football scoreboard show on WWJ after Michigan games for many years. Warren Pierce of WJR did pregame and halftime interviews each week; he was great. Sonny Eliot always contributed to the enthusiasm with comments on his own TV and radio weather shows. Jimmy Launce, fired by WJR in 1996, was always in Michigan's corner with his huge audience as well.

Not too many women on television have covered Michigan sports, but there have been a few; among them, Detroit TV sports reporters Anne Doyle (Vince's daughter) and Gail Gardner.

Substance often has taken a back seat to gimmicks and highlights for some recent TV and radio sportscasters, like WDIV's former anchor Bernie Smilovitz. His style was not my ideal. It remains to be seen whether the new generation can equal its predecessors in integrity and ability, but it could happen. Now, though, there are so many sports attractions competing against each other it is difficult to get air time or newspaper space for anything except scores and auto racing.

I couldn't begin to list all the important beat writers and sportscasters who have come onto the scene in the last decade, but most have big shoes to fill. Many of their predecessors were capable, fair, and made no effort to sensationalize. Our press boxes were packed with them and, whether they were from large or small newspapers or stations, they deserve credit for much of Michigan's success.

On balance I can't think of more than three or four people in the media who weren't first class — a pretty fair percentage of thousands who covered Michigan.

◆◆◆

Chapter **11**

Bob Ufer, Voice of Meechigan

◆ ━━━━━━━━━━━━━━━━━━━━━━━━━

More Than a Broadcaster

A man known to Michigan sports fans as a radio broadcaster played a significant role in the athletic success of the university. But it was as a broadcaster that he was involved in its resurgence as a national power in the 1970s and 1980s. Of course I'm referring to Bob Ufer.

Bob and I were teammates on the Michigan track team during the early '40s. His considerable influence upon my life began in 1946 when

he urged Ken Doherty, Michigan's track coach, to hire me as an assistant coach following my discharge from the Air Force. "Urged" may be an understatement; he *insisted* — or so I've heard. He followed up with a similar campaign more than two decades later. In 1968, Bob, along with Marcus Plant, the Michigan faculty representative, contacted several regents, the Board in Control, and some members of the selection committee asking them to consider me as the director of athletics. I

never asked President Robben Fleming if Ufer had also spoken with
him on the matter, but it wouldn't surprise me if he had. Ufer covered
all the bases in everything he did.

Although he wasn't a complex man, Bob was much more than an

*The Mercerberg Academy, Pennsylvania, flash, in the clear and
headed for the goal line. Bob, as a half back, set the state of Pennsylvania prep scoring record in 1938. He played frosh football
when he came to Michigan a year later.*

ex-track athlete and a broadcaster. I probably knew him better than
anyone else from 1940 until his death from prostate cancer in 1981.
When anyone tells a story about Ufer it's probably one I've already
heard. In fact, I might have been there; I saw him at least weekly. He
served on my board of directors at School-Tech Inc. from 1960 to 1981
and he was the insurance man for my family and for the company. For
more than 30 years he was a tremendous recruiter for the athletic department. More important, he was a friend.

Ufer got his start in the broadcast booth by happenstance. In 1942
the athletic department's publicity director, Fred Delano, needed a spotter for a Michigan football game that was to be covered by network
broadcaster Bill Stern. Because Ufer had been around the campus and
was already doing some local radio broadcasting, Delano asked him if

Bill Stern and Bob Ufer, 1942: One Saturday afternoon the network pro needed a spotter. Ufer was on his way.

he'd be interested. Bob was delighted just to meet Stern and did an excellent job for him. Stern used him on other Michigan games when he came to town and Ufer's infectious enthusiasm led Stern to take him to some of the away games for which Stern was doing the play-by-play. Ufer was enchanted with play-by-play and in 1945, when WPAG became Ann Arbor's first radio station, he auditioned for the position of sports director. Ted Baughn, the station manager, was equally taken with Bob's enthusiastic style and hired him.

Bob started out doing a 15-minute daily sports show from 4:15 to 4:30 for $35 a week. A minor problem was the controversy he immediately created by ridiculing Michigan State and Ohio State on the air. Alumni of those schools quickly wrote to the station protesting that a guy like Ufer would be allowed to broadcast. Baughn tried to calm them down, without much luck, and finally threw up his hands because letters in favor of Ufer outnumbered those against.

In the fall of 1945 Bob did his first local broadcast of Michigan football on WPAG. He had to drop one of his favorite activities, broadcasting the Friday night football games of Ann Arbor High School. His replacement was Bill Flemming who, as a student, was doing some broadcasting on WUOM, the university's radio station. Flemming went on to great success on *ABC Sports* doing NCAA football for many years.

It wasn't until Bo Schembechler became the coach at Michigan that Ufer really took off. He was so excited about the immediate success Schembechler was having with the 1969 football team that he became even more partisan. He called Bo "George Patton" and Woody Hayes "Dr. Strange Hayes" or "Adolph Hitler." Purdue was the "Luftwaffe" because it threw the bull so much. He had a nickname, and usually not a very complimentary one, for all of the opponents. One of his classic descriptions popped up time and time again after he first used it in 1969: defensive back and kick returner Barry Pierson, he said, was "going down that mod sod like a penguin with a hot herring in his cummerbund." Listeners heard that with every hot tailback or kick retriever who ever ran down the artificial turf.

Ufer was a unique broadcaster who wore his emotions on his sleeve, but even during times of crisis his sense of humor was present. In private he was extremely kind and considerate. He spent a lot of his time worrying about whether he had hurt someone's feelings, which he seldom did. An astute businessman, he became a millionaire early in his career. He left a thriving business to his children who, incidentally, have expanded it considerably. He'd be proud.

Joe Falls, sports writer for *The Detroit News*, knew Bob well and described him thus: "Those of you who never have heard of Ufer have missed the warmest, kindest, friendliest man to broadcast a football game. He was as wild as a whirlwind on Saturday afternoons, a tornado, a hurricane, a tidal wave, he would sweep over you with his flowery rhetoric, but away from the mike he was a pussycat, a quiet, dignified man, who raised six children and sent them all to college. He loved Michigan and didn't care who knew it." Joe might have added that Bob's enthusiasm knew no bounds and right up until his death one of the most important things in his life was sitting in Michigan Stadium announcing a "Meeechigan" football game.

Ufer's original broadcasts of Michigan football on WPAG barely cleared the city limits. His fame spread because people carried pocket radios in the stands. Throughout the stadium you could hear him broadcasting from that small Ann Arbor station. People who had never heard

"He was as wild as a whirlwind on Saturday afternoons, a tornado, a hurricane, a tidal wave...." Joe Falls, The Detroit News

of Ufer discovered him when they came to a Michigan game.

It wasn't long after I became athletic director that WJR began to discuss with Bob his leaving WPAG and going to WJR. Incredible as it seems, Ufer was concerned about his loyalty to WPAG and whether it was right for him to leave. Those he talked to, namely Phil Diamond, the former German professor, and me — and probably his children —

urged him to make the move. In the mid-'70s when he finally did decide to go, he came to my office with the contract and I was astounded at how little WJR agreed to pay him that first year. In retrospect, one could hardly blame them; they had no assurance he'd be the success on 50,000 watts he was on little WPAG. Would Ufer sound as good in Detroit or Grand Rapids as he did in Ann Arbor? WJR reached across the state and deep into Ohio, a different audience from that in Washtenaw County. The rest is history, as they say, because Ufer became a sensation and increased the ratings for the broadcast dramatically. I assume WJR finally paid Bob what he deserved, although we never discussed his salary after the first year. The fact is, he really didn't care about the pay; all he wanted was to sit in that booth at the stadium and cover Michigan football.

Ufer changed the way sports broadcasting was conducted in Detroit. He was a "homer" with a capital H, the likes of which no one had ever heard before. Most broadcasters who do a team on a regular basis naturally become attached to the team. But in those days listeners generally found broadcasters trying to be impartial, or close to it, on the air. Ufer was the opposite. He'd start his broadcast by letting everyone know just where he stood. At one time we had seven different stations, plus WJR, doing our broadcasts, all Michigan stations except one from Toledo. I listened with interest as the other announcers began to mimic Ufer's enthusiasm and partisanship. Once they'd seen his success, they worried less about appearing neutral.

Bob created many fans for Michigan football during his 40 years of broadcasting and he promoted Michigan's athletic success in another way: He helped many coaches in various sports with recruiting. Time after time in my years as track coach my assistant, Elmer Swanson, and I would turn Ufer loose on a promising track man to help sell him on Michigan. Bob's historical knowledge and perspective of the athletic program was second to none, and even before he became famous as an announcer he'd been well-known as a former Michigan athlete. Ufer had held an American record in the 400-yard dash, bound to impress any young track man. He helped us for the 20 years I coached track, and he always pitched in to recruit football talent for Bump Elliott, and later for Bo Schembechler. On weekends during the recruiting season Ufer would talk with young recruits from all parts of the country, always reciting some of his Michigan poetry and stories. You couldn't count the number of athletes he recruited with his sheer enthusiasm.

Bob's greatest asset was his sense of humor. An early example involved a green herringbone suit I had worn to college in 1938. I'd paid $18.95 for that suit at Richman Brothers in Chicago. When I graduated four years later I sold it to Ufer for $12. "A perfect fit," he said. Five years later in March of 1946, when I was hired as the assistant track coach at Michigan, he was the first one in my office. He had on the green herringbone suit, now a little threadbare but kept all those years to show me he'd really snagged a bargain for his $12. I can still see the grin on his face when I recognized that green herringbone.

During the time I was athletic director and Schembechler was the football coach, Ufer, usually at noon on Thursday, would tape a pre-game show in Bo's office. Following the taping, he'd come downstairs to my office to recite his halftime and game-ending poem or an editorial (often changed depending on how the game went). Sometimes I would say to him after I'd heard his poem, "Uf, you can't say that on the air; it just sounds dumb." Or I might say, "Gee, I like it; that's pretty good." Regardless of my opinion, his own version usually went on the air unedited. All of his shows were pro-Michigan no matter what happened on the field, and without doubt he was the best P.R. man Michigan ever had.

One of my prize possessions is a 9-foot sailfish that hangs on the wall behind my desk. Bob caught that fish off the Baja Peninsula and had it sent to me, all because of an off-hand remark

Catch of the day: too big to stuff in the mailbox.

I made. School-Tech was building new offices about that time. Ufer and I were on the board discussing the construction. Bob was to leave on a fishing trip to Mexico a day later. I mentioned he might consider catching a fish to hang behind my desk. Some weeks later a shipping box the size of a grand piano arrived from Mexico. It was the sailfish.

The shipping charge alone was $400 and I have no idea how much it cost him to have it mounted and prepared for shipping. That was Ufer, however. I'd imagined a minor three- or four-foot fish behind a desk and ended up with a wall-covering whopper.

What he did for others in his charitable work reveals something of Bob Ufer's character. On more than one occasion I helped him climb into a Santa Claus suit, padded him with pillows and helped load his car with Christmas presents. Off he would go a day before Christmas with a list of needy children in the inner city. With the pillows, he made a pretty good-looking Santa Claus.

The toughest times with Ufer came in the early fall in 1981. Knowing the cancer was consuming him, he would walk into my office and say, "I hope I have one more game left; I hope I can make the Wisconsin game," or "I hope I can make the Purdue game," or "I have to make the Ohio game." And once, feeling his very worst, he came in the office, looked at me with a big grin and across the front of his teeth someone had painted with nail polish, "Go Blue." Ufer's humor lasted his lifetime.

That fall when he was so ill, we often talked. I knew what treatments he was taking and I think we both knew how futile it was. Even in his darkest hours he never showed he felt sorry for himself. Not once did he say, "Why me?" Occasionally he would express great optimism. He was going to make it, he'd say. At one point he left the country for treatment and returned hopeful. In fact, he had made a video tape for the doctors treating him, to be shown to other cancer patients. On top of all his other fine qualities, Ufer had courage. He died Oct. 26, 1981, at age 60.

On my own 60th birthday, he organized a surprise party and gave me a walking cane with a horn attached and an autographed picture of Dick Vitale, then the non-stop talking coach of the University of Detroit. I never had heard much of Vitale, but later on we became friends.

Friends and strangers alike packed the First Congregational Church on State St. near the U-M Diagonal for Ufer's funeral. One of his sons, Bob Jr., said those who pay respects to his father's grave should listen carefully, "for through the trees in the wind you just might hear 'The Victors' playing."

Organist Michele Johns played that great Louis Elbel fight song when the some 500 persons filed from the church after the Rev. Terrance Smith had concluded the ceremony. Five hours later, the marching band that Ufer loved so much opened a memorial service before 2,000 at Crisler Arena with Michigan's alma mater, "The Yellow and Blue" and closed it with "The Victors."

Ufer was buried next to Fielding Yost.

"Those who mourn his passing can find solace in the knowledge that part of Ufer remains in everyone who has ever heard his broadcasts," wrote the *Michigan Daily.* "That is his legacy."

But, for those who knew him well, the legacy of this many-faceted, generous man extends far beyond the broadcast booth.

Ufer in his radio booth in Michigan Stadium, where his voice will always echo every time the Wolverines take the field.

◆◆◆

Al Kaline and William Clay Ford, first class guys.

Jesse Owens, an old friend, returned to Ann Arbor in the late '70s.

Chris Schenkle, ABC long-time play by play star, in 1990.

Pete Rozelle, NFL — he helped us license our products in 1969. Here in 1984.

Bennie Goodman, not a great fan, but cheering for Michigan in the press box in 1982.

The Wistert brothers — all made All-American, all wore No. 11.

George Allen, L.A. Rams — an early business partner, at the Rose Bowl, 1987.

Woody Hayes — more than a great coach, an authority on military history.

Tom Harmon, Michigan's greatest football player in 1987. He was a pretty fair golfer, too.

Red Berenson — as player and coach, his teams won NCAA Championships. Here in 1995.

Bob Ufer and President Gerald Ford at a Crisler Arena rally — but Ufer didn't get him elected.

President Robben Fleming with Ron Johnson in 1968, Fleming's first year, Ron's last.

President Harlan Hatcher at 95 years of age — in the press box in 1995.

Fritz Crisler in 1982 — I've no idea where the Ohio banner came from, or where we were.

Governor G. Mennen Williams with Scotty in the press box in 1982.

President Allan Smith, probably telling me I need a hair cut, in 1986.

Chapter **12**

Life Among the Presidents

◆————————————————————————

A Mistake or Two

Mass confusion resulted when, in the late 1980s, the Presidents' Commission of the NCAA mandated that presidents must take control of athletics on their campuses. Some presidents confused *control* with *management*. Michigan was one of those institutions.

At most universities the president had always had control of the athletic program but left the actual management up to the faculty-dominated Boards in Control of Intercollegiate Athletics. The chain of responsibility was clear: the presidents appointed the athletic directors (or recommended them), and appointed or approved the faculty, student and alumni members of the board. More often than not they had administrative officers sitting on the board. Of course, athletic admission requirements are the prerogative of

President Robben Fleming
Everyone's favorite.

presidents, not athletic departments. In addition, university by-laws are specific as to rules of conduct for *all* students, athletes included. How much more presidential control was needed?

Competent presidents are not trying to manage day-by-day operations of athletic departments — the controls mentioned above are still in place as they have been for decades. Where management from the president's office has occurred, programs have started to slide and problems seem to have multiplied.

Michigan's Board in Control had a long run during which, for the most part, it really was in control. In 1915 the board was reconstituted and Ralph Aigler from the Law School was appointed by the regents as chairman. It was then that faculty control debuted in earnest. All the presidents for the next 73 years — or, until 1990 — felt comfortable giving the athletic department, with faculty supervision, authority to do what it thought was right. And it worked. That's why, even though disagreements came up from time to time and occasional questions arose about whether the president should have the board's authority, the system didn't change. Michigan led the nation in administration and others copied her system.

Those seven-plus decades of common-sense leadership ended in 1988 when James Duderstadt assumed the presidency of the university. In 1990, just after athletic director Bo Schembechler left Michigan to become president of the Detroit Tigers, the predicted problems began. President Duderstadt reconstituted the Board in Control by removing three alumni members. It was clear athletic authority would now come from the president's office. It was a terrible mistake in the eyes of people who saw the future ramifications.

Early in the Duderstadt presidency there was an incident that indicated this administrative change. Red Berenson, the hockey coach, had suspended a player who was involved in a fight at a sorority house. The suspension was not a light one and the athlete missed several games. After a time, Red felt the player should be reinstated.

I was not athletic director at the time, but from an outsider's point of view I thought the penalty adequate. Duderstadt, however, immediately announced he was going to continue the athlete's suspension because he didn't think Berenson's penalty was severe enough. This was done not with a call to the coach, but with a press release. It was incredible, a president interfering with team discipline, and it hadn't happened at Michigan before.

The player's father immediately had his lawyer call Duderstadt to say he was filing suit for double jeopardy. Duderstadt quickly announced, again to the press, that he had reviewed the incident and decided to allow the athlete to compete. It was obvious then that a new era of athletic management had emerged.

In 1995 several things occurred that illustrate the mistake of taking control of the athletic department away from the faculty, alumni and students who serve on the Board in Control of Athletics. The first widely-publicized incident concerned football coach Gary Moeller.

Moeller had gotten drunk and made a fool of himself at a restaurant in the Detroit suburb of Southfield, where he had gone for dinner with his wife. We all knew there was something wrong; those of us who knew Gary realized the incident was completely out of character. Neither he nor his wife were much more than light social drinkers. I had attended more than a few banquets and cocktail parties with Moeller. Never, in 24 years, had I seen him have too much to drink. Often he didn't drink at all.

The incident was complicated when Southfield police allowed the release of audio tapes to broadcast outlets and newspapers, along with transcripts of police reports, an unethical move prior to any indictment. The news media seized the story and played it to the hilt. What should have and could have been handled in a dignified way became a national story, even featured in *Sports Illustrated*. Gary needed defending.

A few days after the incident, athletic director Joe Roberson called me. His first words were, "Don, I'm going to let Gary Moeller go."

I was stunned because Moeller had not had a hearing and hadn't been convicted of anything except perhaps by some sensation-mongering disk jockeys — who, of course, never had a drink in their lives. "Wait a minute, wait a minute," I said. "Don't fire anyone. Drag your feet, appoint a study committee, do anything. Because, Joe, I have been through these things and they have a

Joe Roberson

way of looking completely different after a week or so. Talk to Gary, at least."

"I have at great length," Joe replied. "I gave him several alternatives but didn't fire him. He didn't like the alternatives and said he would resign first."

I have no idea what the alternatives were, but they probably involved a suspension or a one-year leave of absence.

President
James Duderstadt

Joe got a little more specific. "Don, I *have* to let him go," he said.

After telling me Moeller would be leaving, Roberson said, "I'm going to put Lloyd Carr in charge as an interim coach and start immediately on a search for a new coach for next fall."

I've always opposed *interim* in anything. I think it undermines the continuity you might have had. Nothing really gets done because any decisions made will be thought of as temporary. I advised Joe not to hire Carr as interim coach.

He replied, however, "I'm going to do that." It was his right and later proved to be a successful move. But the interim tag may haunt Carr and Michigan in years to come.

Interim coaches have a tough time recruiting for the future. Recruiting was extremely difficult in 1995 — a critical year for the football program — because of that adjective.

I wasn't opposed to Carr as coach. As a matter of fact, when I was consultant in 1990 at the University of Wisconsin, I suggested Carr as the number one choice to be the Badgers' head coach, if the university wanted to make its selection from assistant coach ranks. If they were considering an established head coach, both Chuck Neinas, executive director of the College Football Association, and I had recommended to athletic director Pat Richter that he hire Don Nehlen, head coach at West Virginia. Nehlen was offered the job but said no. Finally it went to Barry Alvarez, an assistant under Lou Holtz at Notre Dame, whom Neinas had recommended. Incidentally, Donna Shalala, President

Clinton's Secretary of Health and Human Services, was the chancellor at Wisconsin then.

Gary then resigned, rather than accept the "alternatives." I wasn't sure who had brought on the resignation, the regents or Duderstadt, but I didn't feel Joe could do it on his own and still don't. He says otherwise. A fair guess is that Joe, after talking with Moeller, touched base with Duderstadt to tell him Gary resigned. I do know Duderstadt told the regents of the decision and that he approved the "resignation."

Not long afterward, due to the Freedom of Information Act, correspondence surfaced regarding Moeller being given $400,000 in severance pay, something never announced but uncovered by the news media. Roberson was out front, taking blame for the severance pay issue. The administration still maintained that Moeller had resigned. It was a preposterous situation.

The regents wanted to know, publicly, who authorized the $400,000 payment. Again Roberson took the initial blame. The Board in Control knew nothing about it; if the regents hadn't authorized it, it was clearly a decision from the president's office. No athletic director could do that on his own. The logical question was: if Moeller resigned, why was he given any severance pay at all? And why $400,000?

During this time an announcement was made that Nike was paying the athletic department millions for the right to "design uniforms and provide equipment" — and to use the Nike swoosh on those Michigan uniforms. Many alumni and several regents were up in arms.

So it was not a very good spring. The Board in Control quickly was blamed for the multiple problems, but the regents eventually learned the board had not discussed or voted on any of the controversial issues. It's hard to imagine faculty, alumni, and students on the board approving of the those actions that had been OKed by the university administration. Their authority had been taken away in 1990.

Carr subsequently took over the football team and, in a remarkable performance in a terrible situation, proved far more competent than anyone, including me, had imagined. After four games it was obvious this guy was a coach. He had organized and delegated. He had put a team on the field that had been torn apart by what the players regarded as the unjustified firing of their coach — the man who had recruited

Gary Moeller (l) and Lloyd Carr

them, the man for whom they'd played and who they all liked and respected. In addition, Carr said all the right things at every press conference and handled every emergency with dignity.

The Varsity M Club and others who knew what Michigan athletics and tradition were all about immediately moved to take away the *interim* label. That action was urgent. We were hearing that other universities were taking advantage of Carr's interim status. The word was out that U-M had an unpredictable president and that "athletes would be wasting their time by visiting the University of Michigan" during the late fall of 1995 with an interim coach.

After the seventh game Michigan didn't have many recruits signed up for visits. Former coach Bo Schembechler, in conversation with Penn State coach Joe Paterno on the Monday following that game, learned Paterno's Nittany Lions already had a full commitment of recruits for visits. Michigan had few. The great athletes were already committed. Ohio State was on the verge of securing the nation's top class. Only time could tell how well Carr and his staff overcame the late start in the recruiting wars. The concern of some was that in 1995 we did not get a great freshman class; and if you have two ordinary classes in a row you're not going to win championships in the Big Ten. Carr, however, felt the 1996 class was quite good.

It wasn't until Nov. 13, 1995 — the Monday after the Purdue game, the 10th game on our schedule — that Carr was appointed head coach minus the interim tag. Roberson made the announcement, finally with Duderstadt's approval. It was something Joe had tried to get done for weeks. The appointment had to come from the president to the regents.

The permanent appointment came as a direct result of some regents deciding that if an appointment wasn't made at once they would take the matter into their own hands. They realized how popular Carr was and what an outstanding job he had done. The announcement was received with almost universal support. Two weeks later Carr's Wolverines upset a previously undefeated Ohio State team, knocking the second-ranked Buckeyes out of a conference championship and putting Northwestern in the Rose Bowl.

It was obvious that Duderstadt, even at the end, did not understand the tradition that is Michigan. And he never appreciated the importance of faculty control of intercollegiate athletics at this university or others. An example of his vacuous sense of Michigan's athletic tradition was evidenced by Duderstadt's response to an uninformed comment on a WXYZ-TV show from Detroit the day before Carr's full-time appointment. Moderator Chuck Stokes said something like, "In Don Canham's regime he had more power than the president." Amazingly, Duderstadt agreed with him. The insult was not to me or to the athletic program, but to presidents who preceded him: Robben Fleming, Allan Smith and Harold Shapiro. And to the Board of Regents and the Board in Control of Intercollegiate Athletics during my time there. It is incomprehensible that any employee of the University of Michigan — faculty or administrator and certainly not an athletic director — could wield more authority than that granted by the president and regents.

Similar comments had been made about my A.D. predecessors, Fielding Yost and Fritz Crisler. In truth, from the time of Yost through my administration, athletic directors worked closely with the presidents through the Board in Control. Duderstadt apparently didn't realize I never made a decision with any impact whatsoever without having a vote from that faculty-led body, plus approval from the president. Past presidents simply let the athletic directors make decisions they were qualified to make, just as they allowed deans to run their own departments and schools.

Fortunately, for most of this century Michigan didn't have to worry much about presidents who felt the need to manage athletics. Presidents Alexander Ruthven, Harlan Hatcher, Smith, Fleming and Shapiro were solidly behind faculty control. Athletic directors, beginning with Charlie Baird, followed by Phil Bartelme, Yost, Crisler, me, and Schembechler, conducted athletics through the Board in Control of Intercollegiate Athletics.

Fleming was the new president in 1968 when I became athletic director and we worked together to further define the role of the board and to increase the authority it had over the athletic program. In my case, the board was a tremendous buffer as well as a sounding board. Both Crisler and I were accused of running it with an iron hand. Although it was said the board seldom voted against anything we presented to it, that was probably true only because seldom did either Crisler or I submit unreasonable proposals.

In almost every case board members were highly intelligent and could analyze the direction in which we were trying to take the athletic program. I can remember only two times when the board argued against a proposal I had made. Looking back, I realize the board was right in one case. In the other they sided with me on a split vote, but I respect those who voted their conscience.

The matter in which I was wrong involved the location of the Track and Tennis Building. I wanted it in a different part of the athletic campus. The board thought it should be down at the west end of Ferry Field. In my mind now, there's no question that is where it should be.

In the other case, I felt Michigan should join the College Football Association. The group included 100 of the major Division I football-playing schools. But it didn't include schools from the Big Ten or the Pac-10. We had everything to gain and nothing to lose by joining. It would not have affected how Michigan conducted intercollegiate athletics and might have saved the NCAA television program. The CFA made some proposals that were good for intercollegiate athletics in general and football in particular. Later they were adopted by the NCAA, culminating in the NCAA reorganization into divisions in 1996.

There were other times, of course, when the board and I disagreed. But in any case, neither Crisler nor I ever pressured the board and we never made a major decision without its approval. We talked over everything with that body.

I often discussed major athletic problems with the presidents, from Fleming to Shapiro. Crisler and President Hatcher had a solid relationship, with Fritz continually touching base with Harlan and Ruthven on whatever he was doing. A conversation I had with Hatcher in 1995 confirmed this. There was only one time, he said, when he had to make a major decision that wasn't passed to him through the Board in

Control and eventually on to the regents; that was after President John F. Kennedy was assassinated in 1963, when Hatcher intervened and canceled the game with Ohio State.

Fritz himself had explained the situation to me years after it happened. After the assassination he had talked to the president's brother, Attorney General Bobby Kennedy, or at least with his office. It was Kennedy's feeling his brother would have wanted football games to be played following the assassination. Many schools, of course, did, and the press also reported that opinion. Crisler and Dick Larkin, Ohio State's athletic director, then announced they would play the game.

Hatcher was appalled we would think of playing a football game after the death of our nation's president, and of course he was right. He called Fritz and told him that despite what the athletic directors had decided he did not want the game played. Crisler complied, although he didn't agree. Obviously there was no time to discuss it with the board, but I think both Hatcher and Crisler would have presented it to the board had there been time.

While athletic director, I served under three presidents: Fleming, Smith and Shapiro. Never did any of them overrule the Board in Control. At no time during my tenure were they embarrassed by board actions, or at least they never mentioned it to me. Several incidents stand out where Fleming and Shapiro demonstrated their confidence in the board.

Presidents Allan Smith and Harold Shapiro
Both understood athletics.

Fleming was the most popular president among the faculty during my 50-plus years at Michigan. He was a mediator by profession and always listened to all sides of an issue. Time and again he'd have people leaving the room satisfied that a solution had been arrived at fairly. A specific instance of this happened in 1960 when the Detroit Lions were playing their National Football League games in Tiger Stadium, with an eye on the great Michigan Stadium. Meanwhile, one of their division rivals, the Chicago Bears, was trying to get its games moved from Soldier Field to Dyche Stadium on the Northwestern campus.

I had talked with Russ Thomas, general manager of the Lions, and he said there were discussions among NFL owners about trying to move onto campuses in some areas. Michigan and Northwestern weren't the only targets. Michigan State in East Lansing also was considered as a potential site, and a group was soliciting funds to establish a professional team in Columbus, Ohio, the home of Ohio State. Still another group — and this was long before the Baltimore Colts went to Indianapolis — hoped to establish a pro team in Indiana and play their games on alternate Sundays in Lafayette and Bloomington in the home stadiums of Purdue and Indiana.

Athletic directors Ed Weaver of Ohio State, Bill Orwig of Indiana,

and I began a campaign among all the athletic directors to get the Bears' proposal for Dyche rejected. A majority, 8 to 2, supported our position. The Big Ten faculties had to confirm the decision.

As Marcus Plant, our faculty representative, and I walked through the airport in Chicago on a Thursday morning on our way for Marc to cast Michigan's vote, he was paged. It was President Fleming, who wondered if Marc would vote in favor of the Bears playing at Northwestern's field.

Ed Weaver

In fairness to Fleming, he did not know the pro threat to other schools. It was my fault for not apprising him of the consequences for Michigan and other schools by that vote. In any case, Plant told Fleming he was sorry but he couldn't comply with his request because the board at the Monday night meeting had voted unanimously to reject the Bears' request. The pro facilities vote was the most important vote in Big Ten history.

Fleming merely said, "Marc, I didn't know that," and that was the end of it. It was a beautiful example of a president backing up a faculty board despite pressure from some of his peers. Fleming was consistent in his support of intercollegiate athletics as conducted at Michigan during the dozen years we served together.

Another example of his support came when I hired Schembechler as football coach. Fleming and I were sitting together at a banquet. "Bob," I said, "we're going to have to look for a new football coach this week."

"How do you plan to proceed?" he replied.

I told him I thought recommendation by the subcommittee of the Board in Control, plus a vote by the entire board, would be the most expedient way to do it. The choice would then go to him and the regents for final approval.

"Well, that's fine with me. Just keep me informed," he said.

He didn't consider interfering with the board or appointing another search committee, not always the approach at other schools at the time. We selected Schembechler without difficulty and the board that served during that time can forever be pleased with its decision.

Shapiro, Fleming's replacement, on more than one occasion also demonstrated confidence in the faculty's control of the athletic program. I discovered once that Brian Eisner, our tennis coach, had used two ineligible players in a match against Northwestern. It wasn't a capital offense, but it was serious enough to bother me. The players were good students, but they simply hadn't been cleared by the board's eligibility committee to compete. Under NCAA and Big Ten rules that is a serious infraction.

I took the case to the board. It voted, with one or two dissents, to suspend Eisner for three months without pay. Eisner decided to see a lawyer and threatened to sue the athletic department, the university, and me for his return to coaching and his pay.

Up until then we had discussed the matter privately, but the threat of the suit made it a public issue and there was some pressure. Shapiro called a meeting in his office of several university lawyers and administrators, eight or nine people in all. Shapiro went around the room and asked each to express his view of the situation. Most said, "Let's stay out of trouble. Let's reinstate and pay him."

They were worried we might lose the case. My recollection is that only Dick Kennedy, a vice president, supported the position taken by me and the board. I was disappointed in the reactions of those in the room and felt it was a lost cause. After everyone had spoken, Shapiro looked at us and said, "I've heard all of the arguments on this situation, but I'm afraid I must agree with the Board in Control of Intercollegiate Athletics and Don Canham in this case. The meeting is adjourned." It was a positive endorsement of faculty control.

A few years following my retirement, football and basketball scholarships were cut and coaching staffs were reduced at the request of the NCAA Presidents' Council. It was said to be an economy measure. It's hard for me to understand the wisdom of that action at the major institutions. First, the coaches are our best academic counselors. They know where the kids are almost hourly. Second, those two sports — football and basketball — at most institutions generate the funds that support the entire athletic program for men and women. If Oldsmobile is in trouble, General Motors doesn't cut back on the production of Chevrolets to conserve funds.

Frankly, Michigan would not be Michigan and would not have had its tremendous successes in intercollegiate athletics both on and off the playing field had it not been for some giants — faculty, alumni and students — who served on the Board in Control. Michigan was fortunate to have Aigler as the faculty representative prior to my 20 years as athletic director, and then to have Plant during most of my term.

There have been moves in the past to integrate the athletic department finances within the university. But whenever it was about to happen someone always woke up to the realization that Michigan's great athletic campus, probably the best in the world, was built with the athletic department having autonomy and faculty control. All the buildings on the athletic campus were built with athletic department funds. None was built, or even had its utilities provided, by the university general fund.

Although periodically there were moves to change the administration of intercollegiate athletics — the structure that has allowed Michigan athletics to become so prosperous and successful — they never before materialized. In 1990 the Duderstadt administration ended that golden Maize and Blue era, at least temporarily.

◆◆◆

Chapter *13*

Life Among the Coaches

◆───────────────────────────────

Individuals All

For half a century I competed for, coached with, or hired some of America's most notable coaches in many sports. They all had two things in common: the ability to focus on what was important, and a certain toughness combined with fairness that endeared them to their athletes. The more I study coaches the more I realize the great ones also were actors, but that they had the respect of those who competed for them. Some wouldn't win a popularity contest, but all were sincere. Athletes are not easily fooled.

Michigan has had remarkable good fortune in having had, in so many instances, the right coach at the right time. It's a big reason for Mich-igan's out-standing reputation in athletics. The teams of Fielding Yost, Fritz Crisler, Harry Kipke, and Bo Schembechler in football won more than 90 percent of all

Cliff Keen   *Ray Fisher*
Two of my favorites.

games Michigan has ever played. Matt Mann in swimming, Cliff Keen in wrestling, Ray Fisher in baseball, Charlie Hoyt in track, Dave Strack in basketball, Bill Murphy in tennis, Vic Heyliger in hockey, and Newt Loken in gymnastics were some of the first giants in the Michigan program. These were the ones who had the major impact on their sports.

My favorites from the early '40s were Keen and Fisher. I shared an office with them when I became track coach in 1948 but knew them both when I was a student and an assistant coach. An office with Keen and Fisher was an education.

Ray Fisher — he knew pitching.

Ray was a New England Yankee and former major league baseball player, one of the players on the 1919 Chicago White Sox team who wasn't involved in the "Black Sox" gambling scandal. Fisher never had a filing system for correspondence. He'd get a letter in the morning, give it to the secretary, answer it, crumple the letter — and the copy of the answer he wrote — and throw them in the wastebasket. I never saw him file anything. If you opened his desk drawers you'd find rule books and schedules, nothing else.

Keen, who was a lawyer but didn't practice much before becoming a coach, sat in another corner of the 15-by-20-foot office we shared. He was an excellent technician without even knowing he was being technical. I can recall him demonstrating holds and escapes with his athletes whenever one would come into our office, which was often. He'd explain why he made a certain move and why it gave him leverage and how he wouldn't have made it if the student moved the other way. I probably learned more from Cliff than anyone else in my life on how to approach coaching from a logical standpoint. I can also demonstrate some pretty complicated "escapes," too.

Keen's wrestling squads won 13 Big Ten conference championships and finished second twice. Other years they at least were in the top half of the standings. His dual meet record was 276-88-11. Eighty-one of his athletes won conference titles and 11 were national champs. While establishing the Michigan wrestling program, putting it among the finest in the country, Keen's fame spread. He was on the U.S. Olympic Committee from 1928 to 1952 and was manager of the U.S. wrestling team in London for the 1948 Olympics.

Keen also was a president of the National Wrestling Association and chairman of its rules committee. He was the coach at Michigan when he received his law degree from the university in 1933. During World War II he became a commander in the Navy.

As a collegian at Oklahoma State, Keen was an undefeated wrestler and earned a title in the National Invitational Championship meet. He won the Olympic trials in 1924, but was sidelined by a broken rib for the games themselves — an episode he never mentioned to me.

When I became athletic director in 1968, Keen was nearing retirement age. He told me that would be his last year. I appealed, saying he couldn't quit on me in my first year as A.D. because everyone would think we didn't get along. We both laughed and Keen said, "How long do I have to stay?"

"You can't leave for at least a year or two," I said.

Keen grinned. "Well, I guess I just have to get you started right." So he remained as coach the next three years and we remained close friends for 25 more years, until his death.

As for Fisher, one of my favorite experiences with the old baseball coach involves a January coaches' meeting in Chicago. Each year we would go there by train for the annual get-together, sometimes rooming together. He hated to pay single rates. In 1951 we were to meet on Friday to go to Chicago as we had done before. This particular Friday I went home and learned there'd been a call to my wife, Marilyn, from Ray's wife, Alice, asking where I was. Alice had told her I'd missed the train and Ray had gone to Chicago alone.

I called Alice and told her the meetings weren't until the following week — her husband had gone to Chicago a week early. She said only,

"Oh, my goodness." The following Monday, Ray came into the office and never said a word about Chicago. He had gone there on Friday and returned Saturday, I guess. I often wondered what his expense voucher looked like. The next Friday he met me at the train station and we traveled to Chicago and stayed together with absolutely no mention of his trip a week before.

Fisher had a reputation for frugality, although he was quite well-to-do and had made two or three different fortunes in the stock market. But on trips to Chicago he always ate in the hotel coffee shop, shunning any fancy restaurants.

Ray had college baseball figured out long before most others. He realized the game was 90 percent pitching. If you had a great college pitcher or two you could fill in with football players and every walk-on who showed up and you'd still win more than your share of games. I watched him do that during his entire career. He spent little time on recruiting, just coaching.

He was a masterful coach and teacher and many major leaguers attested to his great teaching ability. He spent hour after hour in the pitching cage in Yost Field House while my track team worked around the outside the cages. I would see him teaching some pitching technique over and over and over. His teams won 637 games from 1921 to 1958. They finished first or tied for first in the Big Ten 14 times and won the NCAA championship in 1953. And if you go back over the box scores of Michigan's games under Fisher for some 30 years you'll find he always had good pitchers. Don Lund succeeded him and continued the dynasty. He won a Big Ten and national title as well.

Matt Mann was one of the most colorful of U-M's great coaches. Born in Yorkshire, England, in 1884, he would eventually make numerous contributions worldwide to the development of swimming. Competing for the Leeds Swimming Club, Mann, at age 9, was the boys' swimming champion of England. When he was 16 he became the British Empire freestyle champion. At 21 he migrated to Canada, then to the United States, and competed in many national championships before coaching in Buffalo, N.Y., with outstanding success. Then it was on to the University of Syracuse, where he revolutionized swimming techniques by changing the teaching methods. It brought him immediate national attention.

In 1910 his Brookline High School team in Massachusetts broke the world record in the 200-yard relay and several of his swimmers went on to earn national interscholastic championships in various events. He stayed at Brookline for five years and also coached at both Harvard University and the Naval Academy in Annapolis part-time.

After guiding Brookline to back-to-back national prep titles, in 1916 Mann moved to the New York Athletic Club to take one of the most prestigious swimming jobs in the nation. Additionally, he coached Yale University swimmers three times a week and developed champions in both places. Mann's Yale teams never lost a meet.

In 1919 Mann became swimming coach at the Detroit Athletic Club. During his time there he started Camp Chickopy for Boys in the Canadian wilderness. It exists to this day, run by his daughter and her husband, "Buck" Dawson. Mann became coach at Michigan in 1925 and soon developed a host of world and Olympic champions. He made the Wolverines one of the nation's top three swimming powers, along with Yale and Ohio State, three schools that dominated swimming for decades.

A remarkable Mann statistic is that from 1927 to 1945, 19 consecutive years, his Wolverines finished either first or second in the NCAA championships. From 1926 to 1948, his teams won 16 Big Ten titles and in the other years never were below second place.

The original Matt Mann swimming pool at Michigan is covered over and is now the Cliff Keen Arena in tribute to the wrestling

Matt Mann revolutionized swimming in the U.S. and made Michigan a national power.

legend. The new Matt Mann pool is located in the Canham Natatorium.

Gus Stager replaced Mann as men's swimming coach in 1954 and

Gus Stager
He retired too early.

coached until 1979, then returned briefly in 1982. Michigan remained a power in swimming and won additional national championships. Gus was a great coach and one of the most popular coaches with his swimmers I ever knew. He also was one of my coaching peers who retired far too early for Michigan.

Swimming always was one of my favorite sports, although I never was much of a swimmer. After a few bad years following Stager's retirement, Jon Urbanchek (men) and Jim Richardson (women) have taken Michigan to the top with their programs, comparable to the Big Ten dominance Indiana had under men's coach Jim Counsilman (1958-90). They are worthy successors to Mann and Stager.

Swimming couldn't be mentioned without including two great diving coaches, both U-M legends: Dick Kimball, the Olympic coach who brought world-renowned attention to the U-M program, and Bruce Harlan, who was killed in a summer diving exhibition in the 1960s. We had made several instructional films together the summer he died. Harlan's motor skills were incredible and he became both a national diving champion and national trampoline champion. He won the Olympic springboard diving championship in 1948 and earned a silver medal in platform diving that year. He was very young when he died, leaving a widow with two young children.

Bennie Oosterbaan, Don Weir, and I raised educational funds for the Harlan children. Bruce was so well-liked and had such a contagious personality that we just mentioned his name and people wanted to help his family. Memory tells me we raised more than $27,000 in a matter of days, enough for the children's schooling. His family, though, had another tragedy to come. Harlan's young son died before he could use the education funds, killed in a horseback riding accident out west where the family had moved.

When the new swimming facility was named the Don Canham Natatorium, someone asked me why it was named after me: I wasn't much of a swimmer. Well, I said, Yost couldn't skate and we named Yost Ice Arena after him, and I'll guarantee you Keen never played volleyball in the Cliff Keen Arena. President Robben Fleming and the regents never asked me if I could swim.

Loken didn't have a building named after him, but he's still a Michigan legend. Crisler hired Newt to popularize gymnastics, which he did. There are others, of course, who contributed a great deal to Michigan lore without brick and mortar memorials, but Newt was the pioneer in gymnastics and deserves permanent recognition. Loken spent 36 seasons as U-M's gymnastics coach, leaving a superb record few can match. Twice he was named national coach of the year when his teams won the NCAA championship. When trampoline became a competitive event, he produced two national team championships in that sport as well. Additionally, his teams won 12 Big Ten titles. Only Illinois has won more. Loken's Wolverines won 250 dual meets, losing only 72 and tying one. That's a .776 winning percentage, an unheard-of accomplishment. His athletes won 71 individual conference titles and 21 NCAA crowns.

Like Fisher, Keen, Mann, and many others mentioned in these chapters, Loken was inducted into the University of Michigan's Hall of Honor. He has been honored by numerous other organizations for his contributions to gymnastics. Before he became a coach, Loken was a fine athlete in his own right at the University of Minnesota. Twice he was Big Ten all-around gymnastics champion and he was team captain. He also was an outstanding cheerleader and nationally known for his books on cheerleading.

Newt Loken made Michigan a gymnastic power in the '70s and '80s.

Loken also produced instructional films on cheerleading and trampoline and, at one time, Michigan and Loken were the focal point of cheerleading in the U.S. Although now in his late 70s, Loken is still

Loken — still going strong, leading cheers into his 70s.

leading pep rallies and emceeing various fund-raising events and alumni meetings for the university. How does he do it? He's as old as I am.

Long before my time, Michigan had won far more than its share of Big Ten track and field championships. Keene Fitzpatrick, who coached from 1896 until 1910, established Michigan as a power. He won .923 percent of his meets. The longest-serving coach until my tenure was the great Stephen Farrell, who coached for 16 years with a meet victory record of .758. He also guided U-M to the NCAA championship in 1928, a pretty fair accomplishment in view of Michigan's climate. Charlie Hoyt (1930-39) and Ken Doherty (1940-48) kept the winning reputation intact.

My coaches were Hoyt and Doherty. Hoyt was a master motivator. One always felt what he said was the gospel truth. I remember my

Keene Fitzpatrick

Stephen Farrell

sophomore year when I had performed quite well in the indoor Big Ten championships, much to my surprise and his as well. After the meet he took my hand and said, "You're going to be a great champion some day." I don't think he really meant that, but for three years that confidence he had in me was my motivation. I think of that handshake and that statement, made in the University of Chicago fieldhouse in 1939, to this day. His ability to reach each person with an arm on the shoulder, a handshake, or just sound advice was truly genius.

Hoyt left Michigan to go to Yale. Doherty left to go to the University of Pennsylvania. It was his departure that opened the door for me to become head coach two years after I had become Ken's assistant. I succeeded Doherty in 1949 and my teams went on to win 12 Big Ten titles before I became athletic director in 1968.

Bill Murphy (1949-69) must be given credit for starting Michigan on the road to tennis greatness. U-M won numerous titles in his 20 years. Before he was a coach, he played for the University of Chicago. He and his twin brother Chet, who later coached at California, were prominent players nationally before they became coaches. He left my first year as athletic director and eventually coached at the University of Arizona.

Charlie Hoyt, the motivator second to none. He taught me the importance of a compliment.

Brian Eisner succeeded Murphy as Michigan's tennis coach in 1970 and his teams have won 18 Big Ten titles since then. The Wolverines, by 1996, had won 36 Big Ten championships. When the new tennis complex is completed on South State Street, I think we'll see Michigan's domination of Big Ten tennis continue.

Three coaches made exceptional contributions in ice hockey at Michigan. Vic Heyliger first established U-M as a great hockey school. He came from Illinois and quickly turned the Wolverines into a national power with six NCAA championships: 1948, '51, '52, '53, '55, and '56. He was the one who brought Michigan hockey into the national limelight.

Vic Heyliger

Al Renfrew, his successor in 1958, saw his 1964 Wolverines win the NCAA and Big Ten titles, and the 1968 squad also won the national championship. His 1961, '62, and '69 teams won conference crowns. His greatest contribution, though, was not in hockey but in management. Al left the ice rink for a hot seat as ticket manager. He was outstanding in that position.

When we suddenly began selling millions of tickets in football and basketball, the system that had been used in Don Weir's ticket office was of another era, with manual adding machines and the tickets tallied by hand. When Weir decided to retire, Renfrew, who had occasionally helped with road game ticket distribution, told me he was thinking about retiring from hockey and would like to become ticket manager.

I knew Renfrew was honest, bright, and could roll with the punches, which one must do in that job. Al became a sensational ticket manager. Renfrew introduced computerization to the ticket department, copied later at many other schools and institutions. Today the Michigan ticket department owes a debt of gratitude to Renfrew for his vision and devotion. He has a pretty good sense of humor, too.

Of course, the third hockey legend is Red Berenson, the next coach to keep the Michigan hockey tradition alive. Berenson, captain of the 1962 Wolverines, was always a coach I wanted at Michigan. In fact, I tried to hire him twice when he was managing the St. Louis Blues of the NHL, following a distinguished career as a player. The third time I approached him proved successful.

I always worried about pro coaches moving to college coaching. I vividly recall saying to Red during his first days on the job, "The only concern I have is that you've been in the professional league all your life and you just simply have to know and follow Big Ten and NCAA rules. And you really probably don't know rule one."

He agreed and said, "Give me the rule books." So I gave him rule books for both the Big Ten and NCAA and by the time he took on his duties at Michigan in the fall of 1984 he scored the highest of all the coaches on a written test I gave on rules. I never worried again. His great intelligence, charm, and coaching ability are going to leave Michigan with a rich heritage in that sport — something that became evident when his Wolverines won the NCAA hockey championship in 1996. Stay tuned.

Red Berenson — he knew Big Ten and NCAA rules and followed them.

Due to retirements I had to replace every Michigan coach, and I appointed all of the initial coaches in women's sports. They were to become the legends of the future. Bo Schembechler, John Orr, Bill Frieder, Berenson, Bud Middaugh, Eisner, Ron Warhurst, Urbanchek, and Jack Harvey quickly became Big Ten

Carol Hutchins

coaching greats. On the women's side I hired Sandy Vong in volleyball, who coached the first Big Ten championship team for women; Red Simmons, the track and field legend; plus Jim Henry, whose team won Michigan's first women's track championship. A notable appointment was Carol Hutchins in softball, who moved her sport to the national scene after winning several Big Ten championships and back-to-back College World Series appearances in 1995 and 1996. Also, Jim Richardson had his women swimmers in second place in the NCAA and to date they have

Jim Richardson
Women's swimming

Jon Urbancheck
Men's swimming

Dick Kimball
Diving

won 10 consecutive Big Ten titles, a phenomenal record.

The toughest situation I had with any coach occurred in 1982 when Schembechler was approached by Texas A&M to coach football there. When Bo told me about it I didn't worry, as everyone knew A&M was usually one step ahead of the sheriff. I did, however, know they would be talking "big money," so I met with President Harold Shapiro at his home the night before Bo was to make a decision and said I'd like to give Bo a $25,000 raise, which would put him over $100,000 and make him the highest-paid coach in the Big Ten. I thought he deserved it. He would be making twice what some Big Ten coaches were making.

I told the president I thought we ought to give him that much, but that if we did he would exceed the president's income. Shapiro, a pragmatic man, said it didn't bother him at all. The head of the U-M hospital already made more than Shapiro. The raise would also put Schembechler's salary ahead of mine.

I went to Schembechler's house at 8 a.m. the next day to offer him the raise, pending review by the Board in Control of Intercollegiate Athletics, which we both knew would approve the action.

He seemed quite satisfied with that and said, "You know I don't want to leave Michigan. I said, "I know you don't," and with that I left.

I was confident he would not accept the Texas A&M job. I had talked to two of his assistants who were just astounded he would even discuss the job, feeling the way he did about the Southwest Conference. Half the schools were on probation for cheating at the time and the other half went on probation at some time during the next few years, including Texas A&M.

Bo had constantly talked about ethics and to my knowledge at that point was above board in recruiting and every other aspect of coaching. So, it was surprising to me he spent that entire day in his house letting people speculate as to what he was going to do at a press conference that had been called for 7 p.m..

I had to leave my office because the athletic department was over-run with media people and my phone was ringing off the hook. Joe Falls and Lynn Henning of *The Detroit News* were the only two people who figured where I might be and they sat with me most of the afternoon talking about one thing or another. They, too, were amazed Schembechler would give the Texas A&M job a second thought, knowing the way they operated athletics at that university and in that conference. The money was so huge it was tough to turn down, I guess.

Schembechler, of course, did turn the job down. I figure he never seriously considered it. The thing that bothered me more was to take place that evening. At the press conference, Tom Monaghan, founder and owner of Domino's Pizza based in Ann Arbor, presented Schembechler with a pizza store in, of all places, Columbus, Ohio, home of Ohio State. It really was a bush gesture. The store never made money, but Monaghan made it clear to the public that his gift was an effort to keep Schembechler at Michigan.

Why Bo let Monaghan be part of that evening I'll never know, nor forget. Monaghan and I had never been very close. In fact, we had been just barely civil to each other ever since I had refused to give him a key to Crisler Arena so he could go in and exercise in the basketball weight training room at 7 a.m. before anything was open. Schembechler later ended up in court with him, as everyone knows, over a salary dispute when Bo was fired from the Detroit Tiger presidency.

In retrospect, however, over a 20-year period my relationship with Bo was good. He always supported me publicly and privately, as far as I know. And I always did everything I could to help him and the football program because without a healthy football program an athletic department doesn't have a chance to succeed. Appointing Bo was obviously my most important selection. I see him often now and he has developed a pretty fair sense of humor.

I realized early that coaches often leave suddenly. For that reason I always had a list of people I would consider as replacements for any of

Fred Snowden, Rudy Tomjonovich, and Johnny Orr. Fred was Michigan's first black full-time coach.

the head coaches. At one point, for instance, had Schembechler left I might have appointed Bill McCartney, who subsequently left for the University of Colorado. At another point I would have called on Don Nehlen, who wound up at the University of West Virginia.

In basketball, too, I always had an assistant coach I liked, a sound coach who would be loyal and could step up to the top job. Loyalty always has been high on my list in dealing with people. So when Dave Strack moved into the assistant athletic director's job my first year, it was no problem moving Orr from assistant to head coach. That's an appointment I never regretted. And, in addition to his coaching talents, Orr was a funny guy who could have been a standup comedian.

At one point I had Fred Snowden at the top of my list as Orr's

Don Nehlen was always high on my list.

replacement should John leave, but Snowden left first and went to Arizona as head coach. Then as John's assistant we hired Frieder, the high school coach from Flint, Mich. He succeeded Orr when John went to Iowa State.

Frieder is one who never got the respect he deserved during his time at Michigan. He always was one of my favorites and if I had remained as Michigan's athletic director I'm quite certain he would still be Michigan's basketball coach. No coach ever worked harder or took care of details better than Frieder.

When Orr came to me and said, "I'd like to hire Bill Frieder from Flint," I had never heard of him, even though his high school team had taken the Class A Michigan championship. When I asked where he had played,

Orr replied, "Nowhere." Bill was nervous when we met, but I could see he really wanted the job. He was pretty serious, and I felt his personality would provide balance with Orr's. John was always loose and carefree.

It was obvious that Frieder slept little and I would see him at the office nights and weekends when he was an assistant. After he succeeded Orr he was a non-stop recruiter who took care of the details on the job like Schembechler always did in football. His outstand-

Bill Frieder — Not one who would make the pages of Gentleman's Quarterly

ing record at Michigan was no accident.

Frieder, however, was always over-sensitive. It wasn't an image thing. You only had to look at his clothes and often disheveled hair to realize he didn't care much about his image. My guess is that his never having played major college basketball caused him some insecurity. He constantly came to my office justifying something he had done that I knew nothing about. I recall several midnight visits to my home to explain some negative newspaper or radio story that I'd paid no attention to. But Bill always did.

One morning in January 1982 Bill came into my office looking like he'd been up all night, and probably he had. His team had lost another tough one the night before. He sat there a moment and then said, "Don, I think I should resign." That was a surprise and I could see he was serious. I looked at him a moment and then said, "Get the hell out of here. I'm the only one who decides who coaches around here, and I'm too busy to change coaches." He just smiled, got up and left the office. An hour later I dictated a letter to him and had my secretary hand-deliver it. I knew him pretty well and realized he needed more reinforcement than I had given him that morning. I was sorry to see him leave Michigan for Arizona State but we have kept in touch. Thirteen years after sending him that letter, I got it back with a nice note from him. Bill's letter to me is a keeper as well.

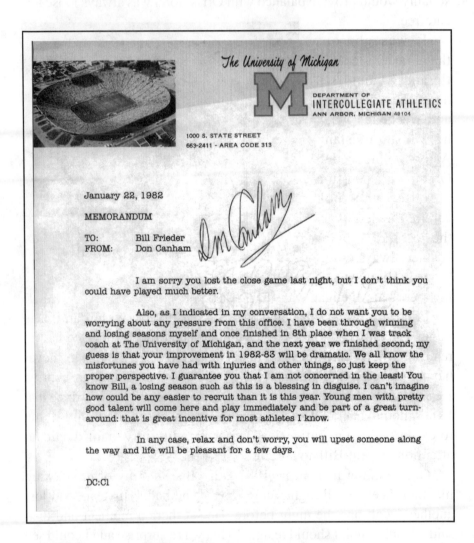

The University of Michigan

M DEPARTMENT OF
INTERCOLLEGIATE ATHLETICS
ANN ARBOR, MICHIGAN 48104

1000 S. STATE STREET
663-2411 - AREA CODE 313

January 22, 1982

MEMORANDUM

TO: Bill Frieder
FROM: Don Canham

     I am sorry you lost the close game last night, but I don't think you could have played much better.

     Also, as I indicated in my conversation, I do not want you to be worrying about any pressure from this office. I have been through winning and losing seasons myself and once finished in 8th place when I was track coach at The University of Michigan, and the next year we finished second; my guess is that your improvement in 1982-83 will be dramatic. We all know the misfortunes you have had with injuries and other things, so just keep the proper perspective. I guarantee you that I am not concerned in the least! You know Bill, a losing season such as this is a blessing in disguise. I can't imagine how could be any easier to recruit than it is this year. Young men with pretty good talent will come here and play immediately and be part of a great turn-around: that is great incentive for most athletes I know.

     In any case, relax and don't worry, you will upset someone along the way and life will be pleasant for a few days.

DC:Cl

When I think of basketball coaches, this story comes to mind: once when I was returning from a Big Ten meeting in Chicago I stopped into the Camelot, a restaurant in Allen Park on Southfield Road owned by my friend, Jim Cunningham. I'd told Marilyn where I was going and she had a message waiting for me saying Orr had called and it was urgent I talk to him immediately. So I called Orr at home and, out of the blue, he said, "Don, I'm leaving Michigan and going to Iowa State."

I was stunned. "You have to be kidding," I told him. "Don't do anything, I'll be right over to see you. Who the hell goes to Iowa State from Michigan?"

"It's too late," Orr said. "They're sending a private jet to pick me up. They really want me." John liked attention and money.

I realized it was hopeless. Just then, Cunningham walked in the door. I grabbed his arm and told him the news. Cunningham didn't believe it either. I said I knew only one reason why Orr would leave Michigan to go to Iowa State and that's money. I was correct. They paid him an awful lot of money to be their basketball coach, and I think he felt it was time to move in any case. They were never sorry, either.

Some days later I found out that after I left the restaurant, Cunningham called J.P. McCarthy, the noted morning show host on Detroit radio station WJR, and told him what he'd just learned about Orr. McCarthy knew Orr quite well, though, and since he hadn't heard from Orr or from Will Perry, the sports information director, or from me, he assumed it wasn't true — only to watch and listen as others beat him to the story.

McCarthy said later that he thought the call was "from some nut." He'd missed a scoop because Cunningham wasn't very convincing and J.P., of course, always heard from his share of nuts.

Orr became a success at Iowa State and was very popular in Ames. And Frieder became a great success at Michigan after starting out with a talent-poor team, only to leave when Schembechler became athletic director. Bo and Frieder never got along and I was not surprised to see him leave when Schembechler became A.D.

Bill was removed as coach just before the NCAA tournament in 1989. That was a result of his pre-tournament announcement that he intended to leave after the NCAAs to coach at Arizona State. Frieder was relieved of his coaching duties because Schembechler figured he wasn't a "Michigan man" anymore and shouldn't be coaching the team in the tournament. Consequently, Steve Fisher stepped up from his assistant's post and guided the team all the way to the NCAA championship. Bill never forgave Schembechler.

Frieder was one of the most loyal employees I ever had. He's still a close friend. He has also proven he was a much better basketball coach than some critics said he was during his years at Michigan. For some reason it seemed to hurt his reputation that he was such a great recruiter. Some said he should win because his players were so good. (Fisher has heard the same nonsense.) That was a factor in his deciding to leave Michigan, although the major factor was constant disagreements with Schembechler.

Frieder had called me in Florida the night before making his announcement. He said he had to accept then and there because Billy Tubbs of Oklahoma would take the job if Frieder didn't announce his intentions. He had no thought that Schembechler would not let him coach in the NCAAs. I did — and mentioned it to Bill that night.

In track and field, the Wolverines have had excellent coaches, with Jack Harvey in track and Ron Warhurst in cross country. They have won their share. Warhurst is a great distance coach. Harvey is a master of motivation. Both men are extremely popular with the athletes. Those appointments I don't regret.

After Stager's retirement in 1979, Michigan's swimming program faltered until I hired Urbanchek in 1982. A former U-M swimmer and a Hungarian refugee, Urbanchek was a successful club coach on the west coast and internationally successful when he came aboard. I hired Richardson in 1985 to take over the women's swimming program. Both are now national figures and Michigan again is a national swimming power.

Our fortunes in swimming began to improve dramatically after we built the new natatorium in 1987. I knew that with those two coaches we would begin to dominate the Big Ten and probably win the NCAA championship quite early. In 1995 the men's team did win the NCAA title and the women finished second. When Tom Dolan and Eric Namesnik of Michigan finished 1-2 in the 400-meter individual medley at the 1996 Olympics in Atlanta, they were featured in *Sports Illustrated* with a "Go Blue!" headline. It's just the beginning, in my opinion.

In baseball, Middaugh succeeded Moby Benedict, who had taken over from Lund when Don left to become farm director of the Detroit Tigers. Middaugh had been the coach at Miami of Ohio where he had an outstanding record. He came highly recommended by Jon Falk, the equipment manager for football (and a baseball fan) who came up from Miami of Ohio shortly after Schembechler. Everyone I consulted recommended Middaugh and I hired him after an hour's meeting. He was impressive.

Of all the coaches I knew in all sports over some 50 years, Middaugh was as good as any. I watched him care-

fully build a program into one that was always nationally ranked. One couldn't find an empty seat at Michigan baseball games during his time. We won championship after championship, six in all, and Michigan appeared at the College World Series in Omaha year after year.

He had a remarkable talent for selecting players. He brought to Michigan many young men who were qualified in the classroom and personally, as well as being great baseball players. Barry Larkin, Jim Abbott, Chris Sabo, Hal

Bud Middaugh

Morris, and Scott Kamienicki are just some of the superb players he developed who went on to star in the majors.

However, there was a problem, the kind with which Michigan rarely is connected. The program violated NCAA rules, not just a few, but many. Some were minor, but some were serious and Middaugh was fired in 1990. I don't know if he deserved to be fired or not. I never did see the list of complaints against him and never was consulted as to the violations. I do know he was treated deplorably and hauled into court on an embezzlement charge. He was crucified in the newspapers and by public announcements from the university. One would think he had committed murder.

My first encounter with the situation occurred in the football press box when Jack Weidenbach, then acting athletic director, came up to me and said, "We caught Bud Middaugh embezzling $19,000." (The published figure turned out to be much higher than that.)

Stunned, I said, "What?" and then was interrupted. I didn't see Weidenbach again that day. A few days later the headline in the *Ann Arbor News* said Middaugh was being "indicted for embezzlement."

The charge stemmed from Middaugh's handling of the football program sales at Michigan Stadium, it was said.

Bob DeCarolis, who carried the title of business manager, was the person who first raised the issue of the "alleged shortages" involving football program sales, which were nose-diving under Middaugh. Had DeCarolis tried to find out why income was down — or checked his correspondence from me sent years ago, or called me — he might have understood why sales really declined: At every game someone was passing out 25,000 free small-sized newsprint programs outside the stadium. Our $2 program sales started down. Middaugh's case was thrown out of court almost immediately by the judge. There was no embezzlement and the worst that had happened was that he broke some NCAA rules, something less than embezzlement. After the ruling, little was heard from his accusers.

The damage, though, had been done and the publicity was irreversible. Middaugh had been fired and embarrassed with no concern given to him, his wife or his children. Middaugh's life was ruined over false charges and anyone connected with the lawsuit should be ashamed. It was a sad chapter in Michigan's history. There never has been an adequate retraction.

To this day we refer to the great Michigan family — of which Gary Moeller also was a member.

Chapter 14

The Black Athletes

They Changed the Formula

Among the most dramatic changes in intercollegiate athletics took place following World War II. Except in the South, black athletes began to be widely recruited by virtually every major school. Before the war it was unusual for teams to have more than one or two black athletes, and most of those were in track and field. Few were in Big Ten football and none in basketball.

At Michigan in football, no black athlete earned a letter under Fielding Yost, who coached from 1901 to 1923 and from 1925 to 1928. In fact, he did not allow blacks (who were referred to then as Negroes or "coloreds") to even try out for the team. Yost made no apologies or explanations.

When he became athletic director in 1921, though, his reputation depended on how successful all the teams were. His opinions might not have changed, but his

William DeHart Hubbard, recruited by Fielding Yost

approach did. Yost actively recruited a black athlete, the great William DeHart Hubbard, for the track team. After all, other schools were using black athletes in track. Michigan wouldn't be making waves and might need to recruit blacks just to keep pace. Why not Hubbard, who was long jumping just inches short of the world record and running the 100-yard dash in under 10 seconds at Walnut Hills High School in Cincinnati, Ohio?

John Behee's 1974 book, *Hail to the Victors,* a history of black athletes at Michigan, told of the unique way in which Hubbard, with Yost's sanction, went to Michigan on a full scholarship. Behee said a U-M alumnus, Lon Barringer, was aware of Hubbard's talents, both in athletics and academics, because he read the Cincinnati papers while living in neighboring West Virginia. He figured Hubbard, an A-minus-average high school student over four years, would be good Michigan material — if Barringer's good friend and fellow West Virginian, Fielding H. Yost, was receptive.

"Yost was willing to approve almost anything to enhance the athletic glory of Michigan," Behee wrote. "The alumni could not object too strongly to one black, not when it looked like Hubbard would be a world-beater." Yost enthusiastically endorsed the idea and told Barringer to go ahead.

The plan, though, was a bit unusual. The *Cincinnati Enquirer* was running a subscription contest. The 10 area high school students who collected the most new subscriptions would get $3,000 college scholarships to attend the school of their choice. In 1921 such a sum would easily put a kid through four years of college (although today it would barely pay for books and fees.)

Barringer told Hubbard that if he would attend Michigan, every effort would be made to help him win the subscription contest. How could Hubbard pass up that offer? Consequently, nearly every U-M alumnus in the country got a letter from Barringer on the subject, and many subscribed to the *Enquirer.*

Even Branch Rickey, then owner of the St. Louis Cardinals baseball team and the man credited with bringing Jackie Robinson to the Brooklyn Dodgers to break the baseball color barrier, subscribed. So did the U-M library, many people in Ann Arbor and Detroit, and plenty in Cincinnati. Needless to say, Hubbard was among the contest's winners and in September of that year he enrolled at Michigan.

"It would seem than an athlete with this combination of superb athletic talent and good scholarship should have been besieged by alumni and coaches of numerous colleges," Behee wrote. "Such was not the case. Michigan faced little opposition."

He then quoted Hubbard as saying, "It wasn't very fashionable for blacks to attend college. Very few of my boyhood playmates and high school chums went past high school. I was the only black on the Michigan track team those four years and rarely competed against others, even in national meets." In Hubbard's U-M class there were eight blacks among 1,456 graduates.

In no time Hubbard was tying or setting records in dashes and jumping events. He wound up being named to *Spaulding's Guide* All-America track team in 1922. The long jump pit at U-M's Ferry field, meanwhile, was extended two feet from its former 25 feet, 1 1/2 inches. In the Midwest sectionals that year, held at Ferry Field, he won the long jump but ended up second in the 100-meter sprint. Next came a meet at Harvard at which a final determination would be made in selection of athletes for the U.S. Olympic team.

"Forget the 100 meters and concentrate on winning the long jump," Behee quotes Coach Steve Farrell as saying. "If you spread yourself too thin you might not win anything." Sure enough, Hubbard made the team as a long jumper and joined three other black track athletes from the U.S. at the Olympics in Paris.

At the games Hubbard fouled on his first qualifying jump, injuring his heel. But he ignored the pain on the second leap, earning a berth in the finals. On his sixth and final trip down the runway in the finals he was in stride, gained speed, hit the take-off board well, and landed 24 feet, 5 1/8 inches away — to become the first black American to win a gold medal in an individual Olympic event.

One would think Yost might have learned something from that achievement, besides the swell of pride he must have had for having agreed to accept Hubbard. But, as he would show a decade later, it must not have affected his judgment.

In 1934, when black athlete Willis Ward was among the stars of the track and football teams and Harry Kipke was the football coach, Yost apparently acceded to a request from his good friend W.S. (Bill)

Alexander, football coach at Georgia Tech, that Ward not be used in the Wolverines' game against the Yellow Jackets. Yost, it should be noted, was the son of a Confederate Civil War soldier.

"I don't believe you can afford to use colored players as it has never been done in the case of games with teams from this section," wrote Dan McGugin, football coach at Vanderbilt, to his brother-in-law, Yost, in May 1934.

Willis Ward: Great athlete, great lawyer, outstanding judge

After sitting out the game against Tech, Michigan's only victory in a 1-7 season, Ward was upset to the point of telling Kipke in a letter that he planned to quit the team. Friends were taking up a collection to help pay for Ward's senior year in college, should he quit football.

Kipke, who had worked hard talking Yost into letting the Detroiter Ward come to the university to play football, was only carrying out orders from athletic director Yost in the Tech incident. He tried to explain to Ward that his quitting would eliminate future opportunities for others of his race at Michigan and Kipke said he never again would stick his chin out for a black athlete.

Ward related this story to me in 1971. He said at the time it hurt him to make the decision, but he had felt the future of the black athlete at Michigan would be enhanced if he stayed with the squad, so he did.

This was a time also when Ralph Aigler, our faculty representative, was not the man he should have been. Aigler, a professor of law and chairman of the Board in Control of Intercollegiate Athletics, ducked the question when letters began to come in protesting the decision by Yost and the athletic department to direct Kipke not to use Ward against Georgia Tech. Yost used the old saw about athletic participation being a privilege, not a right, and said Michigan should take into account the feelings of Georgia Tech. No mention was made of the feelings of Willis Ward and his friends.

It also was a disappointing time for Alexander Ruthven, the president of U-M, who had made the commitment that under no circumstances would he interfere with decisions made by the athletic director and the Board in Control. He stuck to that policy, but it seems an exception might have been made in this case.

There were even threats of disruptions at football games over the decision. Yost hired detectives and police to ward off trouble. The news media severely criticized Michigan in editorials and front-page stories. National magazines reported the discrimination and compared it with that leveled against the Jews. Yost didn't have to worry about his contemporaries calling him racist amidst all the fuss. His contemporaries thought just like he did. It was the students, always at the forefront of a more open society, who were the "problem."

The commissioner of the Big Ten, John L. Griffith, sympathized with Yost in a November 1934 letter to him, quoted by Behee: "You were telling me up at Minneapolis about the radical students' organization that stirred up the rumpus about Ward in the Georgia Tech game. Can you, without too much trouble, advise me whether or not there are any other liberal clubs in Michigan?"

Ward had not been made captain of the track or football teams, honors for which he was deservedly qualified, but he was more upset about being held out of the Georgia Tech game. Ward's post-Michigan career would be spent mostly in Detroit courtrooms, where he was a judge. And while he was a judge and I was the track coach and then athletic director, I used him as a track official at U-M meets and also at the NCAA Indoor Track and Field Championships, which started in Detroit in 1965. I got to know Willis quite well in his later years and saw him often. He sat with me from time to time in the press box at Michigan games. Until his death, he was often there when Michigan had a home track meet. Track, he said, was always his favorite sport.

Just after Hubbard and just in front of Ward, two other black track stars went to Michigan, Booker Brooks and Thomas "Eddie" Tolan. Tolan, a Detroit Cass Tech High School product who stood just 5 feet 6 inches tall, was the leading 200-meter runner in the nation in 1932

Booker Brooks
One of the pioneers

Eddie Tolan, the 1932 Olympic
champion at 100- and 200-meters
He was only 5'6" tall.

while a Wolverine.

At the time of the 1932 Olympics in Los Angeles, no American had won the 100-meter sprint in 12 years — but Tolan did it in a photo finish with Ralph Metcalfe, each timed at 10.3 seconds, setting Olympic and world records. In the 200, Tolan won by two yards over his nearest rival.

The contributions of Hubbard, Tolan, Brooks and Ward called attention to the fact that Michigan was an institution where the black athlete was welcome. Since their day, Michigan probably has had more outstanding black athletes than anyone else in the Big Ten and perhaps even the nation.

Much of what I know about the history of the black athlete at Michigan, even though my own experiences date back to the late '30s, came from Behee. I was the athletic director while he was writing his book and I've read one of the few remaining copies several times. The sad part of the matter was that the book had limited exposure. It was published by Behee himself and distributed by Alberts Book Store in Ann Arbor.

To my knowledge, discrimination in athletics at Michigan was not a major problem during my time as an athlete. That was probably because there were so few blacks on our teams. However, when I was on the U-M track team in the late '30s and early '40s, there were always three or four blacks who lettered, among them high jumper Wesley Allen and decathlete Bill Watson, who was elected captain in 1939.

Watson, a great athlete who lettered in 1937, '38 and '39, was my friend up until his death. He came from Saginaw. He high-jumped over 6 feet 5 inches, long-jumped 25 feet, and was the national decathlon champion, as well as three-time Big Ten outdoor champion in three different events. He won the conference indoor shot put title three times, setting records twice. In his senior year he scored 20 points in the NCAA championships, scoring in four different events. If World War II hadn't come along, Watson probably would have been the Olympic decathlon champion in 1940.

Bill Watson, my roommate on an interesting trip to St. Louis

Following his graduation, Watson went to work for the Detroit Police Department and wound up with some mental problems. Ward took him in and tried to help him. But when Bill came into Willis' bedroom one night with a gun, Ward had to turn him out. A few months later, Watson was killed in a shoot-out with some other police officers after pulling a gun on them during a street fight.

There's one Watson story I recall with humor. In 1939 Bill and I traveled back together on the train from a track meet in California, heading for the national Amateur Athletic Union championships in

St. Louis, Mo. We had been given expense money for room and meals and Bill thought we'd save some money if we stayed at an acquaintance's place. So when we got off the train we were picked up in a dilapidated old car and taken into the inner city. Bill knew someone in this particular "house" and we were given a room on the second floor. As it turned out, it was a house of ill repute and customers came and went all night long downstairs and stomped up the stairs to use the bedrooms next to ours. We spent half the night looking out the window watching the clients coming in. Not surprisingly, I couldn't get off the ground as a high jumper the next day. Bill was tremendous, though, posting some of his best performances that day. The coach never asked where we stayed.

It is still hard for me to believe that in 1940 Allen and Watson rode the service elevators with the employees at the Sherman Hotel in Chicago when we competed in the Windy City. I roomed with Watson one semester and one summer and always roomed on the road with Allen. And as I look back I'm amazed at how they accepted that indignity and how few coaches at that time tried to do anything about it. It is also incomprehensible that, until 1948, there was a gentlemen's agreement among basketball coaches in the Big Ten that no black athlete would be used in intercollegiate competition. I used to ride in those freight elevators with Watson and Allen, and some other white teammates did, too.

After I became assistant track coach in 1946, the next great track athlete was Charles Fonville, who broke the world record in the shot put. He was to become one of my closest friends until his death in 1994. Fonville was also an outstanding basketball and football player, but he declined to compete in those sports. He was a Detroit lawyer.

When I was track coach, the team when traveling would usually eat in the hotel's private room. I recall once being asked to have the black athletes eat outside the hotel. It happened at the Windemere Hotel on Chicago's south side, if one can believe it, but in that day the Windemere was a white retirement center. Obviously, we said no.

One of my vivid memories goes back to a great black hurdler named Van Bruner, who had scored high in the NCAA championships. We were invited to compete in the Arkansas Relays, where Johnny Morris was the track coach and Otis Douglas the athletic director. I had known

Douglas when he was at New York University. I asked him and Morris about how Bruner would be treated if we brought him down. Arkansas was not known for liberal views. Both Douglas and Morris said we would have no difficulty even though he was the first black ever in the meet. It was their belief that it was time for that track meet to be integrated. Because Morris insisted, we were treated extremely well, not only in the dormitories, but in the restaurant at the hotel where we were staying. Van integrated Arkansas, at least.

On another occasion just after the war when we were having a dual meet with Abilene Christian College, the opposite situation came up. There was no problem at the college, even though it had no black athletes, but the city of Abilene was not ready to integrate. The difficulty arose when the athletes wanted to go to a movie and management asked the blacks to sit in the balcony, not down on the first floor with the white athletes. They, of course, refused and told me about it when they came back to the dormitory. My assistant, Elmer Swanson, and I marched down to the theater and raised such a disturbance they quickly changed the "rules." Elmer was loud and very effective.

Times began to change in earnest at Michigan and other Big Ten schools during and just after World War II. Fritz Crisler, then the athletic director, opened up football for such standout black players as Bob Mann, Lenny Ford, Julius Franks and others.

Crisler's teams of 1946 and 1947 were the first in U-M history to field more than one black starter, Gene Derricotte, an offensive and defensive halfback, and two ends Mann and Ford. The team won the Big Ten championship in 1947 when it went undefeated, 10-0, including a 49-0 Rose Bowl triumph over Southern California in Crisler's last year as coach. Crisler was named national coach of the year.

It wasn't until 1952 that basketball finally became integrated at Michigan, when John Codwell Jr. and Donald Eaddy played. Codwell's father, a doctor and a Michigan graduate, had written to Coach Ernie McCoy asking if his son would be allowed to play. The answer was yes, and Codwell wound up lettering three years.

"There were surprisingly few problems," Codwell said in Behee's book. "Being a pioneer was pleasing and we were determined to do well so others could play."

In all, six blacks lettered in basketball at Michigan in the '50s.

Perry and Charles Harris. Harris was the first black athletic administrator.

Then, in the '60s, Cazzie Russell, Bill Buntin and Oliver Darden ushered in a new era, helping Coach Dave Strack's teams to three Big Ten titles, a third-place finish in the 1964 NCAA tourney, and a runner-up finish the next two years.

I hired the first black coach of a Wolverine team, Ken Burnley, as track assistant in 1968. He would have become the head coach if he had stayed, but he went into administration and in 1996 was a superintendent of schools in Colorado and a finalist to direct the U.S. Olympic Association.

Over the next 20 years Michigan hired the first black head coach, Jim Henry, who midway through the '90s still was the U-M women's track and field coach and was doing very well. The first black basketball coach was Fred Snowden, who had an impressive record at Detroit's Northwestern High School. He later became the head coach at the University of Arizona. The first black administrator was Charles Harris, who was my assistant until he became the A.D. at Pennsylvania and then Arizona State.

Richard Cephas, who ran track for me from 1959 through 1961, said I wasn't necessarily the kind of guy an athlete could sit with at dinner making casual conversation. But, he said, "If blacks were forced to stay in a crummy hotel, everybody was going to stay there ... I've got a lot of respect for [Canham] on that score."

Burnley, recalling the theater where I demanded *all* my athletes

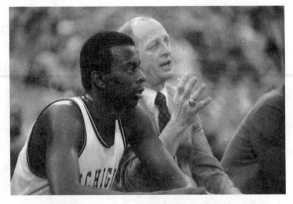

Phil Hubbard and Johnny Orr

be allowed to watch together, told Behee: "It really makes you feel good when you see a guy stand up for you like that. I've heard stories of incidents occurring before I came to Michigan where Canham stood up for the blacks without question or hesitation. The athletes felt he was one of the first coaches to really give them a square deal."

Willis Ward: His favorite sport was track, his best event was the high jump.

In the late 1960s and early '70s, race relations were tense at campuses all over the country, including in athletic departments. But in my tenure as athletic director there never was a significant incident involving race and there hasn't been since.

"I think Michigan was a bit ahead of other schools in race relations," said Marshall Dickerson, one of my track men in the early '60s, quoted by Behee.

It may have been a long time coming, but when the gates opened up, thanks to athletes like Hubbard and Ward and Tolan and Derricotte and Fonville, they opened wide. Take a look at Michigan's "Hall of Honor" — its hall of fame for athletes and administrators. Black athletes are major representatives, and there will be countless more inducted as the years go by. Among many who have been enshrined are: Hubbard, Ward, Tolan, Franks, Watson, Derricotte, Fonville, Russell, Buntin, Ron Johnson and Lowell Perry (football), and Phil Hubbard and Rickey Green (basketball).

Ron Johnson

Ward, Tolan, Russell and Reggie McKenzie (football) are in the

Michigan Sports Hall of Fame. Johnson is a member of the National Football Foundation Hall of Fame, and Perry received a special silver anniversary award from the NCAA in 1977.

And how about football superstars like Anthony Carter (two-time U-M MVP), Desmond Howard (Heisman Trophy winner), and Billy Taylor, Gordon Bell, Paul Seal, Randy Logan, Russell Davis, Ron Simpkins, Butch Woolfolk, Jamie Morris, Tony Boles, Tripp Welborne and Buster Stanley — all team most valuable player winners.

Cazzie Russell — he put Michigan basketball on the national stage.

And look at basketball greats besides Russell and Buntin, such as: Henry Wilmore, Campy Russell, Wayman Britt, Rickey Green, Gary Grant, Glen Rice, Terry Mills, Loy Vaught, Roy Tarpley, Rumeal Robinson, Chris Webber, Jalen Rose, Juwan Howard, and more.

Among the great black track athletes I coached, Charlie Fonville, Tom Robinson, Kent Bernard, Lester Bird, Ken Burnley and Aaron Gordon were all national or international stars.

Today, it is disturbing to think of what successes Michigan's sports teams might have had in the first 50 years or so of the 20th century if there hadn't been so many closed minds.

◆◆◆

Chapter **15**

Some to Remember

◆————————————————————

Friends and Characters

One of the interesting aspects of being athletic director at Michigan is the difference between concept and reality. Nowhere is it more evident than in the rivalries. There are alumni who are bitter at the very mention of Ohio State or Michigan State, usually because of some loss on the field or some office wager that went sour. Coaches and athletic directors often see other schools and other athletic personnel in a

Jesse Owens returned to Ferry Field as referee of the Big Ten track and field championships in the late '70s.

different light.

One of the most popular people I've ever known was Ralph Young, former athletic director at Michigan State, who was the foundation on which that great athletic department was built. Another man who was extremely helpful to me and who became one of my close friends (I still keep in contact with his widow) was Clarence "Biggie" Munn, the athletic director who succeeded Young. Biggie was never very popular with Michigan alumni because he, as coach and director, led Michigan State to dominance over Michigan for many years.

One of the more recent athletic directors at Michigan State was Doug Weaver, a lawyer, former athletic director at Georgia Tech, and one of the most highly principled people who has served any institution. Weaver, Moose Krause of Notre Dame, and I engineered the withdrawal of our schools from the Western Collegiate Hockey Association to join the then-small Central Collegiate Hockey Association. We first tried to form divisions in the WCHA so as to keep travel time and costs down, but Michigan Tech scuttled that. The move to the CCHA followed the refusal. Doug and I were the committee to find a commissioner. We hired Bill Beagan who made the CCHA the premier hockey association in the nation. The prestige of the schools involved, plus a commissioner who knew exactly what he was doing, transformed midwest college hockey into a major sport in a few short years.

Ohio State has produced its share of characters and also outstanding athletic directors. The first OSU athletic director I knew was Dick Larkins. I will never forget him because he warned me not to hire Bo Schembechler. He said Bo and Woody Hayes were cut from the same cloth, "and you will end up with Bo just as I ended up with Woody," writing notes back and forth to each other, and not on the best of terms. Of course, that never happened and Dick didn't live to see the result of our relationship.

The next athletic director at Ohio State was a giant in the field. His name was Ed Weaver and I always knew where he stood on issues. Usually Ed and I were on the same side when things came to a vote. His successors, Hugh Hindman and Jimmy Jones, were also people who had integrity and vision. There were many others at different schools throughout the Big Ten. Elroy Hirsch at Wisconsin, Paul Giel at Minnesota, Bill Orwig at Indiana, Neal Stoner at Illinois, Bump Elliott at Iowa, Red Mackie and George King at Purdue, who served their institutions well. I miss them all.

George Allen

One of the most interesting of my friends was George Allen, the former Washington Redskins and Los Angeles Rams coach who, at 70 years of age, wound up coaching at Long Beach State. George and I had been in graduate school at Michigan in 1946 while I was assistant track coach. George and my wife Marilyn became quite good friends. He would come for dinner occasionally when we lived in a small apartment near the hospital.

George was assisting Cliff Keen in the Big Ten 150-pound football league and was a graduate assistant of some kind or other (no one really understood what job he did have) with Fritz Crisler. In his resume we made him an assistant to Fritz, who allowed George to observe practice and pick up towels I think, and even gave him a Michigan playbook. George had one ambition in life and that was to become a football coach at a major college. He had no idea he would end up in the pros. When it came time for him to graduate in 1947, my wife typed 200 letters to the universities in the NCAA that had football programs asking if they needed an assistant football coach. There were no copy machines or computers that could personalize a letter so each was hand-typed. At night George would come over and Marilyn would type eight or 10 letters for him, he would sign them and put in clippings and mail them out.

George Allen in a publicity shot when, at 70, he coached at Long Beach State. He needed a hard hat on that job.

In the spring of 1947 George received a call from Morningside College in Iowa where the football coach wanted to hire an assistant from Michigan, and Allen got the job without an interview. While

George was driving out in mid-summer to go to work at Morningside, the head coach died. By the time Allen arrived on the campus, he was the head coach and on his way. He attended every football clinic he could find, college and pro. He became friendly with George Halas, who eventually hired him as an assistant with the Chicago Bears. From there he went to the Rams and his ambition was realized.

Once a year George would either call or write to Marilyn reminding her that she typed all those letters for him and he would never forget it. Allen had a lot of critics, but I was not one of them. My wife passed away in December of 1990 and George called constantly when he found out she was ill. It meant an awful lot to her. Two weeks later Allen died from a heart attack. He was a friend I think of often.

Don Lund

It is pretty hard if you spend your life in athletics to always please everyone. Don Lund, my associate athletic director for 18 years, could do just that. I don't know of an enemy he ever had, nor do I know of

a time when he had a bad word to say about anyone.

As Michigan fans know, Lund was a great athlete in three sports — football, basketball and baseball, and one of our few nine-letter men. Don played major league baseball, succeeded Ray Fisher as baseball coach in 1959, and later took his team to the NCAA championship.

In 1963 he resigned as coach and went to the Detroit Tigers as farm director. He stayed until 1970, then returned to Ann Arbor as my associate director when Bump Elliott went to Iowa as athletic director. His greatest contributions were

Don Lund

He had no enemies.

not as an athlete or coach, but as an administrator. He was invaluable in fund-raising and alumni and university relations. It was Lund who mentioned that we should make an ice rink out of Yost Field House; no one thought of it before. To do that we had to move track elsewhere, so we built the Track and Tennis Building. Lund, thus, should get credit for both facilities.

I was never a sensation with small talk or greeting old grads. Lund knew it and made me look good on more occasions than I can count. The alumni relations we emphasized were primarily due to Don. He retired several years ago and won't be forgotten. The friends he made for Michigan have played a major part in its athletic progress and development over many years.

Bob Forman

Like Bob Ufer, Bob Forman was never employed by the University of Michigan athletic department, yet his contributions to athletics at Michigan were significant. His support of athletics was extremely helpful during my early days as athletic director.

He was executive director of the Alumni Association for 28 years, spanning the entire time I was athletic director. Michigan's Alumni Association is generally recognized as the best-organized group in the country. That is no accident — it is due exclusively to Bob Forman's efforts.

Bob Forman
Help when needed

His greatest contribution other than the organization of the association itself is the alumni travel program. While he didn't create alumni travel, he developed it beyond anyone's expectations. In addition, the association under Bob revised *Michigan Alumnus* magazine, establishing what is the finest magazine of its kind.

Forman's support of intercollegiate athletics was a vital factor in my early years when we were trying to fill the stadium. He integrated the athletic department and the alumni association far beyond anything that exists at other institutions. One only has to look at Ohio State — where the alumni association at one time led a movement to prevent the university's football team from participating in a Rose Bowl game. At many institutions to this day there is resentment toward the athletic department due to the publicity and attention athletics receives. Forman saw to it that it wasn't a problem at the University of Michigan.

Bob helped us promote ticket sales when we needed help and arranged alumni tours to away football games, Rose Bowl games, and events in other sports as well. *Michigan Alumnus* was a major supporter of our program.

Jesse Owens

The 1996 Olympic games reminded me of so many stories of a dear friend of mine, I must include him here. I first met Jesse Owens in 1934 in Chicago at the Central AAU Track and Field Championships. I was a sophomore in high school and had gone there to compete in a meet, only because Dave Albritton of Ohio was jumping. He was one of the leading high jumpers in the world and soon became the world record holder. I just wanted to say I jumped against Dave.

Albritton had gone to Cleveland East Tech High School with Jesse and then to Ohio State. After the competition was over, I went to talk with Albritton. He was very kind and we became acquaintances and later good friends. He wrote me often with the worst penmanship I ever saw. But, as we were talking, Owens came over. He had run an exhibition race or something in the meet. Albritton introduced us. Like everyone else, I followed Owens' career, but I did not meet him again until I became track coach at Michigan, 14 years later. Of course he did not remember me from 1934, but in the '50s and '60s our paths crossed many times at track meets, banquets, and various meetings.

It was not until 1957 I really got to know Jesse well. He was sent to Ann Arbor by the U.S. State Department to see if he could talk me into going to India with him to do some coaching and public relations work for the U.S. Information Services. I had been in Africa that fall and when I returned the U.S.I.S. asked me to go to India. I wrote the state department and said I just could not leave again that spring. It had committed Jesse to the India project and, because I had some friends in India in athletics and because the Indians had used my books for many years, it was requested I accompany Owens on his visit. We spent most of the evening talking about the possibility, but I just couldn't leave on another foreign trip that soon. Jesse went to India alone.

A remarkable thing about Owens was his modesty. When he returned from India he was in Detroit visiting friends, so he drove out to Ann Arbor to tell me about his Indian trip. I recall most his amazement about how he was treated. He couldn't get over it. "Don, you made a mistake not going with me. They treated me like a king. Can you imagine that after all these years?" He never did understand that he was the most-recognized athlete in the world. To this day, Owens is known far better than 90 percent of the athletes who have followed him.

When I was track coach I tried several times to have some sort of memorial or plaque constructed on Ferry Field denoting the place where Owens, in 1935, set three world records and tied a fourth, a feat that had never been done before and never will again. In the 1970s we finally did erect a memorial to Jesse and I'm only sorry it occurred after his death. His wife Ruth and his daughters

Jesse Owens had history's best track performances in Ann Arbor.

did come for the ceremony. It was a quarter-century late. The memorial was made possible by one of Jesse's friends in high school, Dr. Ralph Gibson, a U-M professor, and by the contributions of one of our great alumni supporters, Bruce Laing, from Dowagiac, Mich.

George Perles

How did a football coach from Michigan State get in this book? Mainly because off the field he was never an enemy of either Bo or me.

George Perles, like most well-known coaches, is different from his public image. His players and those who know him well have great affection for him. I have known him many years and I share that respect.

One illustration of his kindness occurred the Friday night prior to the 1987 Michigan-Michigan State game in East Lansing. Doug Weaver, the Michigan State athletic director, had mentioned to George one afternoon that it was my last trip to East Lansing as athletic director and the department was going to present me with an engraved clock. Perles, according to Doug, insisted he make the presentation. So, that Friday evening George left his team long enough to come to the press dinner, miles away, to present the clock to me with some kind words as well. Few coaches in my experience would take time to do that the night before a major contest. It was a nice thing for him to do and an act that meant a great deal to me. So much for bitter rivalries!

Walter Byers

A person who had great impact on Michigan during my half-century was Walter Byers. He served as executive director of the NCAA from 1951 until 1987. I was one of those at the NCAA convention in 1987 who helped "evict" Walter by giving a short speech when he retired. I said that, "no man had a greater impact on intercollegiate athletics than Byers." Through his leadership the NCAA not only became the greatest brokers of competitive athletics in the world, but did so in the best interests of the schools involved. The NCAA, under Byers,

Walter Byers never believed much in public relations.

instituted rules and fostered competition for both men and women far beyond what had been previously projected. He created order out of chaos.

The NCAA grew from five employees (Byers, Wayne Duke, and three secretaries in 1951) to an organization with a staff approaching 300 in the 1990s. That is indicative of what intercollegiate athletics has become under his tutelage, a major entertainment and economic factor. The NCAA now has a vast program for women and Byers was responsible for that. Many of us argued with him about integrating women. We thought women should have a separate organization. Many women felt the same. Walter won and probably was right.

One of his remarkable achievements was his founding of the NCAA basketball tournament that culminates in the Final Four. The gross income has grown from $500,000 to a figure approaching $70 million for the tournament in the '90s. The distribution of the funds to the NCAA basketball-playing schools is vital for the institutions.

Byers negotiated more than 50 different television contracts. I watched him first-hand as a member of the television committee for 12 years and twice when I was a member of the network negotiating committee. He was a tough negotiator and the NCAA schools were the beneficiaries. ABC, NBC, and CBS were all on the short end of negotiations with Walt, some more than once.

His greatest fault, and he had a few, was his total disregard for public relations. He never projected himself or the NCAA, so very few people knew him or of his brilliance. But more importantly, the public and media never understood the NCAA and the good it stood for. Byers spent very little time and no money publicizing what was going on within the organization. Few realize that everything the NCAA ever did was approved by the membership; and beyond office expenses all monies accrued to the NCAA were distributed to the membership. Yet the press painted Byers as an autocratic ruler. When NCAA rules and decrees came out of the NCAA office it was never the council or the NCAA membership, it was always Byers who was credited or discredited by the media. In reality, the member schools were the villains or heroes.

He always had a role behind the scenes as a member of most key committees, yet the final action and vote was not Walter's. While he seldom explained, he seldom complained either, and his stamp on the course of college sports will be there for decades.

James Blanchard

Because I was the athletic director at the university, I met and knew all the governors during my time. They were all sports fans. I campaigned for William Milliken during two elections and knew G. Mennen Williams reasonably well, as he often sat in the Michigan press box. He was a great Michigan fan. I must say my favorite governor, however, and the one I knew best, was James Blanchard, a Democrat. He and Senator Philip Hart were the only Democrats I ever voted for.

Jim called me one day and asked if I would serve on a citizens committee that was to survey the lottery and make recommendations to his office as to changes. We first met at the governor's house and there were about 20 people present. Some extremely impressive people sat around the table that day and for various other meetings during the year. Once that committee made its report, Blanchard appointed a six-man lottery oversight commission, of which I happened to be the chairman. We made recommendations and worked closely with the lottery commissioner, who was quite good. He was removed from office when the Republicans won the election in 1992, which seems to me a ridiculous way of running a government.

While I was serving as chairman of the lottery commission and by

Gov. James Blanchard — He almost got me into horse racing.

that time retired as athletic director, Blanchard asked me if I would consider becoming Michigan Racing Commissioner, as the present commissioner was retiring. I thought about it for some time and investigated it pretty thoroughly. I had been doing some work with the Harness Racing Association in marketing and promotion, so I knew a little about the problems and I had always been interested in thoroughbred racing. In the state of Michigan the only thoroughbred track is the Detroit Race Course, although there are many harness tracks.

It was on a Friday evening when I had a call from the governor's office asking if I had made up my mind. I said, "I don't want any announcement, but it looks to me like I will accept the job." The job paid, as I recall, $80,000 or $90,000 a year, and the offices were in Livonia, a commutable distance from where I lived. I thought it might be fun and I knew racing had some serious problems. I thought we might be able to get some changes made. The state of Illinois and other states have a racing commission, but Michigan has a commissioner and one-man rule is never satisfactory. I tried later to get a commission set up without success.

I went to my cottage on Harsen's Island and a man came up to me in the grocery store, someone I had never met. "Canham, if you want some good advice, I would not take that racing commissioner's job."

"Why do you say that?" I asked.

"Knowing you," he replied, "you will go in and try to change things and you will make some serious enemies and it doesn't seem to me like it would be healthy." It didn't seem to be a threat, but it could have been. He walked out and no one could tell me who he was. I never saw him again.

At that time I knew there was a narcotics problem at some of the tracks and I had heard there was some harness race fixing. I thought about it, and the individual who spoke to me was correct: I had planned to change things in a hurry and I probably would have been dealing with some tough characters who wouldn't be happy about it. I decided I really didn't need those problems. So on Monday I called the governor's office and said, "I'm sorry, but I can't take the job."

Jim was not very happy. Not long after that, a dozen or more race drivers were indicted for racing violations and the other problems continued. Blanchard lost the election and I probably would have been removed by the new administration anyway.

George Romney

Another governor I knew and one I always voted for was George Romney. My first association with Romney occurred when I was track coach and George was the governor of Michigan. He called a meeting of various people in athletics and we met in downtown Ann Arbor. Crisler had sent me. Romney's advice at that meeting has stayed with me for all these years.

The purpose of the meeting was to see if we could get high school and college facilities opened up for summer recreation for young people. Romney wanted U-M to lead the movement.

We sat around the table, probably 15 people, discussing how it could be done statewide. One after the other, people said, "If I had the money I could do this or that." Finally after five or six of those initial approaches, Romney took a pencil from behind his ear and threw it on the table and said, "Wait a minute. When are you people going to understand that not everything is solved with money? You solve the problems under your nose with the *tools under your hands*. Now let's proceed and see what we can do with what we have."

That changed the tone of the meeting and people began to innovate and talk about how it was going to be done. The thing that stuck in my mind was the simplicity of the statement and I've used it many times both in my business and in the athletic world. Everybody needs money, and more so today than ever, but there are often ways of doing things, as Romney said, with the "tools under your hands."

The second time I met Romney was in the Michigan football press box. He had been invited to the press box when they ran short of seats and someone came to me and asked if George and his wife Lenore could sit in my booth. I was delighted. That game started a long-time friendship with Romney. As any Michigan person knows, Romney was a great exercise advocate and I had recently been to

George and Lenore Romney
He should have been president.

Stockholm to study exercise for longevity, so we discussed my experiences and his own exercise program at some length.

Romney joined us in the booth other times and I saw him elsewhere from time to time. Twice he asked me to run for public office as a Republican, but I had no interest in doing that. "Name recognition is everything in politics," he said, and the Michigan athletic director usually has that. George knew that better than anyone. I liked and respected him. I think he would have been a great president of the United States.

Michigan solved many problems with the "tools under her hands" because of Romney.

Jimmy the Greek

It may seem strange to include Jimmy the Greek in a book on Michigan athletics, but I saw him from time to time at banquets and contests and I learned a valuable lesson from him. He was also one of the most entertaining people I knew. His advice was "priceless."

Once when I was being presented an award and he was the presenter, he brought to my attention that he "no longer took awards." When I asked why he said, "The guy getting an award never gets paid. It's usually a ploy to get a speaker free. So when they ask me to come to an awards dinner I only go as the Master of Ceremonies. He is the highest-paid guy on the dais." Jimmy then went on to remind me

Jimmy "The Greek" Snyder "Congratulations, Don — now let's have a free speech."

that on this night I was getting the award, and as a result, giving an "unpaid speech."

It was a lesson I never forgot — so when some service club or other planned to give me an award, I knew they just needed a speaker they didn't have to pay.

Coleman Young

I had two or three occasions to be with Coleman Young, the former mayor of Detroit, and I liked the man. I thought he had a great sense of humor and, while he may be a little earthy for some people, he always said what he thought. Michigan was host for the NCAA track meet in Cobo Hall, and later Joe Louis Arena, and I would see Young there occasionally. And when Michigan played in the dedication basketball game at Joe Louis Arena, I was at the game with him. He presented a trophy and as he was handing it to me, photographers were taking

Mayor Coleman Young of Detroit — He couldn't get rid of the trophy soon enough.

pictures. He said, "Canham, take this damn thing. It's getting heavy." I suppose the fans and the photographers thought he was congratulating me, or passing on some words of wisdom. I said, "Thank you," and took the trophy. It was heavy.

As I worked on this book I thought almost daily of someone else I should mention who contributed to Michigan's history and tradition. I finally had to stop. It was a never-ending task.

There are a few friends, however, who were of great help and support to me in the struggles we had sometimes to "change things." In good and bad times I could depend on them. Some, too, are just friends I admire.

Several were early Board in Control members like Ward Quall, Ralph Gibson, Howard Brabson, and my long-time friend and lawyer, Dick Katcher. Others are friends, fans, regents, and coaches like Cal Grove, Dr. Billy Graves, Leo Calhoun, Dr. John Magielski, Art McWood, Ed McNeil, Bud Van DeWege, Rev. Terry Smith, Chuck Trick, Gary Sandall, Greg Bevis, Bill Mazer, Jr., Tom Simon, Pete Pickus, Don Robinson, Jerry Hanlon, Alex Agassi, Tirrell Burton, Dr. Bob Brown, Jerry Dunn, Bob Nederlander, Paul Goebel, Roger Zatkoff, Deane Baker, Larry Deitch, Dave Rentsler, Clem Gill, Ed Borgioli, Jim McNamee, Muddy Waters, Andrea Fisher Newman, and the late Ernie Vick. Unlike Crisler I had more than three I called friends.

◆◆◆

Chapter 16

Days I Could Do Without

I Quit on Friday — Temporarily

William K. Pierpont

One of the first things I did when I became director of athletics was to call Bill Pierpont, the long-time vice president of finance at the university. Everyone had great respect for Bill and he was a friend of mine. I asked if he would send some accountants down to set up the athletic department books so they'd be compatible with other units on the campus.

When I had reviewed the financial statements after taking over on July 1, 1968, I'd found the books were still kept the way they were under Fielding Yost. The Michigan athletic department was a separate operating unit; all that was required of separate operating units was to post the year-end financial statement that had been examined by an outside auditing company. That was always done. But each year the auditors spent days converting our paperwork into a standard report for the regents. Responding to my request, Pierpont sent some people to set up our books and arranged for them to check each month to make sure our staff understood the change.

For many, many years the *banks* had been keeping our books. I don't know how many different accounts we had in how many different banks, but there was an account for travel, one for equipment, another for payroll. There was even a separate bank account for part-time work. Norma Bentley, Yost's and Crisler's secretary and bookkeeper, shuffled bank books at the end of the month to determine where we stood financially — hard to imagine in this age of computers. Once our new record-keeping was established, the year-end audits were easier and monthly visits from the university business office no longer needed.

Ten years after that system was put in place, disaster struck. I was in Chicago at the monthly Big Ten meetings on Oct. 19, 1978, when the Board of Regents met to review the outside audit report that had been completed in June. As usual, two or three people from Arthur Young and Co. had spent several weeks at our department, going over everything in great detail. Each morning I would answer any questions they had. I recall not being impressed with the lead auditor. His questions, I thought, were not germane, although we made every attempt to answer them. At no time did he mention to me a matter he reported to the regents that afternoon, a report that resulted in headlines in the *Ann Arbor News* and the *Michigan Daily* on Oct. 20.

Marilyn, my wife, alerted me to the disaster. When she called me in Chicago her first remarks were, "You're pretty big today in Washtenaw County." Then she read the headlines: one proclaimed "Canham Action Termed Improper," another "Canham Violates University Financial Rules." The stories said there was some "improper use of athletic department funds," which also was on the news wires that night and in the Chicago papers the next morning.

I had no idea what she was talking about. She read an article aloud. As she did I became furious because for the past 10 years I had made every effort to *prevent* any mishandling of funds in our department. I was certain there was none. The news report involved, "the unauthorized expenditure of nearly a million dollars" at Michigan Stadium for work done during the 1977-78 fall and spring. Most was for women's restrooms. The accusation was that I had provided A. H. Payeur and

Sons Foundation Co. of Ann Arbor with a million dollars of work on the stadium "during the past school year" without putting the job out on bids or notifying anyone; plus, no approval from the regents as required by the bylaws. Not so, but who knew?

The front page *Ann Arbor News* article reported President Robben Fleming's reaction: "He said there is no question this was not properly done and one cannot say of a project that goes on from fall to spring that it is an emergency." I had no idea what he was talking about. What emergency? The 10-year stadium renovation was never referred to as an emergency by me. Jim Brinkerhoff, who had become vice president of finance, and I had worked together for several years on the renovation of the stadium. Two university vice presidents were members of the Board in Control of Intercollegiate Athletics and should have known exactly what the situation was. I was astounded at so much erroneous information flying about without anyone saying, "Wait a minute, that's not how it is."

Later I learned that a financial officer, *not* Brinkerhoff (who was out of the country and couldn't attend the meeting), said I had told him, "the repairs were made in an emergency situation." I assume the financial officer said that to get off the hook one way or another, not knowing enough about the renovation project. I had said no such thing.

Fleming was quoted as saying, "This has been a long-standing problem stemming from the fact that the athletic department does not flow through the same channels as the rest of the university. That means you can find out about some projects after the fact ...We will certainly see that Don Canham — Athletic Director Don Canham — is aware that this is an improper way of going about this." He added that there had been discussions in the past about bringing the "athletic department under the control of the university." I knew nothing of that, either.

When Marilyn finished the article I was angry for several reasons. First, I didn't know that Brinkerhoff had been unable to attend the regents meeting. Thinking he'd been there, I was upset with him. More important, I was disappointed with Fleming's statements. I knew of no "long-standing problems stemming from the fact that the athletic department doesn't flow through the same channels as the university." It *did* flow through the same channels. The statement about "discussions in the past about bringing the athletic department under closer control of the university," made me even angrier.

When did all these discussions take place? I thought I'd had an excellent one-on-one relationship with Fleming, vice president Allan Smith, Pierpont and Brinkerhoff; at no time was there any discussion with me about bringing the athletic department "under the closer control of the university." In my first 10 years there were no problems at all, and we'd made changes to work even more closely with the deans, faculty, and administration. I was furious.

After hanging up I went to Big Ten commissioner Wayne Duke's room and talked with him and Elroy Hirsch, Wisconsin's athletic director. When I left them and started up to my own room I had made up my mind to resign as soon as I returned to Ann Arbor. I called Marilyn and told her there's no way I would continue with such a situation. There's no way I could win: the second headline is never remembered like the first one. I asked her if she would call Dick Kennedy, a vice president and a friend, and ask him to see Fleming and tell him I quit; to start looking for another athletic director. I was deadly serious. A day or so later I returned to Ann Arbor and found Marilyn had not called Kennedy. She knew I would calm down. She also knew how I liked a good fight, which we now had on our hands.

Brinkerhoff called me when he returned and said not to worry, he would straighten it out, that there was "nothing there." I felt better, but I wanted to make it a matter of record rather than just let it drift away. The story had gone from coast to coast. The facts of the situation were distorted in the Arthur Young financial audit for the year 1977-78 and the presentation at the regents meeting was a fabrication; yet it was in the minutes forever, I knew that.

After I'd heard the whole story and had more than just the newspaper accounts, I sat down to set the record straight in a letter. The facts were these: first, we had spent nowhere near a million dollars with a single contractor. An auditor should know that just by looking at the bills received and paid. Five other firms were paid more than one-half of the money for subcontracting work. The money was not paid to Payeur but went directly to the subcontractors. The renovation project

THE ANN ARBOR NEWS

Canham disputes critical auditor's report

on Michigan Stadium to restore the concrete and do other maintenance work had begun in 1968-69 and was projected at $4 million, and *was* put out on bids. For 1969-70 and 1970-71 we went with Michigan's plant department because its estimates seemed best. After two years, the department found the work to be more complicated than it had figured and suggested we again go out on bids. We did. Payeur Foundation's bid was the lowest we received, lower even than the plant department's. Everything about the project was studied and voted on by the Board in Control. Minutes of these meetings always went to the president's office and to the Board of Regents after every Board in Control meeting. Two vice presidents sat on the Board of Regents.

The critical issue concerned contracts. The audit report was wrong again by stating that maintenance work had to be put out on competitive bids each year if it exceeded more than $100,000. Ludicrous. The university rule was that, "new construction had to go out on competitive bids," but continuing maintenance did not and could not come under that rule. When one hires a contractor to renovate a building, new bids half-way through the work would be nonsense. The auditor should have known that. In any case, I wrote my letter and sent copies to everyone involved.

Brinkerhoff agreed that the athletic department had met all bidding requirements and came forward immediately to say that renovation work throughout the campus was too huge to report monthly to the regents meetings. No regent he talked with felt it should. Jim said the auditor's report was based on a misunderstanding (an understatement, in my opinion).

Two of the regents, Gerald R. Dunn and Deane Baker, came to the defense of the athletic department at that October meeting. But two vice presidents who had sat in on all of our Board in Control meetings didn't say anything. Why, I'll never know. Dunn said, "The auditor's report is full of errors ...We don't need to make a major case out of this." Obviously Dunn had read over the board minutes he received each time we met. Baker said, "Any move to bring the athletic department under the same administrative framework as the university could be a mistake." Baker has maintained that view through 1996; consistently he has been a supporter of the intercollegiate athletic department as it has been run since the 1920s.

Only one regent, Paul W. Brown, felt that, "Some day this sort of thing could get us in trouble. Someone should be advised when this type of expenditure is made." More than a few faculty people were very supportive, however. My letter on the 26th prompted a headline saying I disputed the critical auditor's report. Two days later, On October 28th, the *Ann Arbor News* ran an article saying, "Fleming erred in the Canham case."

To his credit, Fleming called a press conference that Friday and said he was mistaken to label the $1 million stadium expenditures by the athletic department improper. Typical of Fleming, he did not blame Arthur Young and Co. nor did he blame the vice presidents who didn't speak up at the regents meeting. He said, "The project had in fact been discussed with the vice presidents' office several years ago; with their knowledge and consent it had been decided that work had been properly classified as maintenance ...Therefore the capital expenditure requirements are not applicable ... I compounded the matter by labeling the procedure as improper without investigating the situation further. It should now be clear that the athletic department did proceed properly in this matter."

I know of very few presidents or others who would call such a press conference to correct their actions. But when Fleming did, it

THE ANN ARBOR NEWS

Fleming erred in Canham case

By Max Gates

didn't surprise me in the least. The original story was *not* contradicted in the Detroit papers or the *Chicago Tribune* or some others that had published articles saying I'd "acted improperly." Retractions seldom do get printed.

In my 20 years at the university as athletic director we built more buildings and facilities and fields than any other administration. By the time they were completed we'd spent 10 times more money than Yost. In every instance where the project was to exceed $100,000, we received presidential and regent approval. And, to his credit, Regent Brown of Petoskey, who had questioned the athletic department's expenditures and procedures at the regents meeting, said at the final Fleming press conference that he, "didn't see any need for the regents to consider tightening fiscal controls over the athletic department."

"Don has run a successful department in terms of solvency," Brown said. "There is no indication that any money was lost, wasted or misused."

The Michigan Daily

BAND DAY
See Editorial page

RAYS AND BLUE

Vol. LXXXIX, No. 45   Ann Arbor, Michigan—Saturday, October 28, 1978   Ten Cents   Twelve Pages

Canham clear on stadium renovations

By DENNIS SABO

That ended the matter as far as I was concerned. But it wasn't quite finished. A week or two later at the Go Blue luncheon held in the Track & Tennis Building Fleming sought me out. With people standing around he apologized to me in person. That's a pretty good indication of why he was Michigan's most popular president with the faculty, students, and with all those who knew him well.

Intramurals

Not long after I became director I was informed by a student group that Michigan was at the bottom of the Big Ten and maybe the nation in recreational facilities. The last recreation building built on campus for student activities was in 1928 when Fielding Yost built the intramural building. There had been some minor construction, including the swimming pool for women, on the central campus but nothing with much floor space for intramural basketball and volleyball and other activities. I had so many other priorities I couldn't see how we could do much about erecting intramural buildings even though I realized at the outset it was absolutely critical we do so. So I began to discuss the matter with Fleming my second year. We had to have a student fee; gate receipts couldn't do it. The former student fee under Yost and Fritz Crisler had been pledged to pay off the debt service on Crisler Arena, a situation I inherited as the building was completed the year I was named athletic director. We were without student fees for operations for the next 19 years. Fleming was extremely sympathetic and told me to start discussions with the Board in Control, which we did. And for a year or two we had the intramural project and designs as a priority. We had committee meetings it seemed weekly, trying to decide the real needs. We were working on it but the pace was slow. We had huge money problems.

That wasn't good enough for a few of the students and for a particular group that had an English student as a wild-eyed chairman. They felt because we didn't have play areas, they had to take over and use some of the areas the athletic department had. If there's one thing the athletic department was short of, it was available space at Ferry Field. When football, baseball, track, and softball are in season or practicing there is virtually no area for intramural recreation. So we started expanded recreation the easy way, with the development of outdoor play areas on the near north campus on Fuller road. That still did not satisfy the recreational group, but it helped. We also developed Wines Field for recreation and on the north end we planned a football-sized asphalt parking lot that was marked off for band practice. We later put basketball goals on the perimeter for recreation. So we were moving as fast as we could in view of our other problems to solve.

Once when we were ready to blacktop the band practice area on the north side of Wines Field, we had threats of violence by the student group. The English guy claimed if they put one yard of asphalt on north Wines Field, he would lie down in front of the 20-ton roller. It didn't help when the bulldozer operator told the newspaper, "If he does, I'll press him into the asphalt." With that we had a real confrontation. We waited a day or two and when the asphalt people came at 5 a.m. there was no one around and no one to lie down in front of the rollers.

The clamor continued. When we put a wooden fence around the baseball field, required by Big Ten rules that said all fields had to be fenced, there were efforts on two different nights to burn it down. Someone laid straw along the side, doused it with gasoline and ignited it. We had a groundskeeper living in a house where Schembechler Hall now stands and he quickly put the flames out both nights. We then put night watchmen on until the situation calmed down.

We finally solved the conflict when we put artificial turf in Michigan Stadium. We needed an artificial practice field but had no money. The recreation department, I knew, had funding from the university, so I presented a plan. If recreation would pay for the artificial turf on Ferry Field, about $250,000, we would buy lights and recreation could use it mornings and from 7 p.m. until midnight. That quickly was approved and for many years the intramural athletes played lacrosse, soccer, softball, and field hockey on the artificial football field at Ferry Field. The pressure was relieved.

When buildings on the central campus and on the north campus were completed, Michigan had more roofed square footage for recreation than any other school. A few years later we moved hockey to Yost Field House and converted the old rink into another large recreation building — giving Michigan play area few schools will duplicate soon.

Robben Fleming made it possible. From the outset he was behind the project when we suggested it to him. He prepared the regents and student body for the financing necessary and approved of the concept when the time came.

Howard Peckham, in his book, *The Making of the University of Michigan,* published by Bentley Historical Library in 1992, mentions

Michigan now has more recreation space under roof than any other institution. It started with Yost and the Hoover Street IM building. In my time we built the huge Central Campus Recreation Building and the one on the north campus. In addition, when we moved hockey to Yost Field House, we converted the former ice rink into a large recreation building.

that my legacy at Michigan might be the intramural and recreation buildings we built. I hope not. Paul Hunsicker, Earl Riskey, Rod Grambeau, and others were the first to show the needs, and I tried to do a few more things than build buildings. Student protests not only ended the Vietnam war, they had great influence on actually getting recreational facilities at Michigan.

Huffman

Politicians running for office sometimes gave us fits. They soon find out it's easy to get a name in the paper if one attacks a public institution. Because the university uses state funds it is always fair game. One of the most far-out charges against us resulting in widespread publicity came from Bill S. Huffman, a Democrat from Madison Heights. He provided a few days I could do without.

One evening I started to receive calls from newspaper, television, and radio people asking when I was going to start building the dome over Michigan Stadium. I had no idea where that story started, but in our wildest dreams we never contemplated doing that.

I quickly found out it came from Huffman, who had also accused me of several other things. His most serious charge had been that I was actually "hiding revenue" and that the university regents and administrative officers weren't privy to the amounts. Huffman claimed our actual revenue was $30 million or $40 million annually, and not the $8.15 million our 1980 audit report showed it to be.

One of our lobbyists in Lansing quickly supplied Huffman with the audit report that had been prepared by Arthur Anderson and Co. Huffman obviously could not understand a financial statement and he simply said, "It's not detailed enough."

The accusation quickly became a crisis because I knew the university had three key building projects it wanted done — and we had a fourth, a women's office building to be built on Ferry Field. I didn't know if the university buildings needed state approval, but the women's athletic building certainly didn't. It was not to be built with state funds. It was to be built, like all of our buildings, by the athletic department from reserves. When he found out about these building plans, Huffman immediately persuaded his colleagues on the senate appropriations committee to withhold approval of all four key university projects.

Huffman was tying university construction to his attack on the athletic department. He kept repeating he wanted detailed information on athletic department finances. He dared the university to try to build the $17 million worth of projects without legislative approval — *he* was chairman of the higher education subcommittee. I never heard anything directly from Huffman and never heard much about the entire matter after he called his press conference in Lansing and received plenty of publicity across the state. There must have been an election or fund-raiser coming up.

None of us could figure out what the Huffman agenda really was. He warned us to avoid any plans to add a dome to Michigan Stadium as it would be competition with the Pontiac Silverdome, which was sputtering financially. The Silverdome was represented at that time by lobbyist James Karoub, a close friend of Huffman. Both men evidently felt the exhibition professional football games I had held — and even the college games in our stadium — were competition for the Silverdome. Neither man wanted another domed stadium in the state, or at least that was the reason they gave for the outlandish accusation.

We learned with this attack and others that the quickest way for a politician to get attention and headlines is to either attack athletics or join it and be seen in a championship locker room. It's interesting that some college presidents have learned that lesson as well.

Bomb Threats

Some of the wildest times any of us in the athletic department spent were during the Vietnam War, when we were constantly worried about vandalism and defacing of property. Almost nightly we'd have people with spray cans spray that beautiful brick fence around Ferry Field with slogans like "Stop the War" or other anti-war statements against President Lyndon Johnson or the Pentagon, General William Westmoreland, or anyone in the establishment who was prominent in the papers. Those things we could handle, but what became a real concern were bomb threats. During one fall there was not a single football game where we didn't have at least one or two, and sometimes four or five, phone calls warning us that bombs had been placed in the stadium and we should cancel the football game.

Virtually everyone on our staff can recall those days because every morning of a game at 7 a.m. we would take every available employee and sweep Michigan Stadium. We had people who checked all the rafters. We had other groups check all the toilets. Others looked in every nook and cranny in the concession stands. We had crews that checked the players' lockers. Often we'd get calls saying the press box was the target, so we patrolled the press box constantly. And we put heavy security at the stadium starting every Thursday evening. At great expense during games we had the perimeter patrolled and other security personnel spread out through the stadium. Never did we allow any publicity. We didn't want to give anyone any ideas. We were dealing with enough nuts.

The tough part for me was that the police and others who got the calls left it up to me as to what to do if a call arrived during the game. The issue was if we should clear the stadium or not. The first time I was confronted with a game-time situation was during the first quarter of a game when a call came into the press box asking for me personally. We had a strict rule that such calls be highly screened because most of the time they were from gamblers asking for the score. Today that is not a problem because the games are almost always on television and the gambling houses know what the score is at all times. When the caller asked for me personally, I asked Art Parker, our press box liaison, who it was on the phone and to find out what the caller wanted.

Art called back up in my booth and said, "They say there's a bomb in the press box." That will wake one up pretty quickly. I immediately went to the security people and asked what they thought we should do. They were divided. Some wanted to sweep the press box immediately; others wanted to vacate the press box. That was no great comfort — it was up to me. Associate director Don Lund and sports information director Will Perry agreed we should sweep the press box and say nothing, as we had gone over it inch by inch that morning. We certainly didn't want a story in the Sunday morning papers giving some other fool an idea. We searched for the next hour and found nothing and said nothing. The matter never did appear in the papers, although I'm sure some of the newspapermen did know what had happened. None of them provided the publicity that people who make calls like that desire. We continued to receive calls often, some during games and some during the week. Callers usually claimed they were going to blow up this or blow up that unless we made a public address announcement denouncing the Vietnam War, or Lyndon Johnson, or ROTC, etc.

There were bomb threats at some major league baseball and football games at venues around the country that did empty out stadiums. We never considered it, but we took ultra-precautions with our searches and took each call seriously. The Vietnam War was not popular with anyone on the campus and all of us in the athletic department had seen some of our athletes killed in that theater. When the students who were active in organizations opposing the war came to us with requests, in most cases we tried to help. Usually it was a request to have a building for meetings or rallies. It's pretty evident that those of us who had draft-age children could understand the frustration of the youth. After all, many of us had similar emotions as we saw World War II coming in the early '40s. Spray cans and rallies we could tolerate. Bomb threats were another matter.

The Big Ten

A few times I found myself at odds with the Big Ten over policy that just wasn't in Michigan's best interest. Those were times I could have done without. The press usually had Wayne Duke and me portrayed as bitter enemies. We actually were friends.

In 1971 Bill Reed, a Michigan graduate, died in office and Wayne

Duke took his place as Big Ten commissioner.

Duke, a 1950 graduate of the University of Iowa in journalism, came to the conference with outstanding credentials. He was the first assistant in the NCAA for 11 years and the conference commissioner for the Big Eight for eight years. He served the Big Ten with distinction until he retired in 1989.

We had several disagreements that became public. Most of our problems occurred because athletics were changing rapidly. Wayne was a great traditionalist, something the Big Ten needs badly today. He understood the conference and its traditional role in intercollegiate athletics like no other administrator. For that reason he was slow to change marketing, television, and promotion. That's where we often had difficulties. His approach and mine were different.

The surprising thing is that two of our major differences occurred because tradition was not followed. I found myself fighting to maintain the status quo, and that was a switch. The most significant trouble occurred in the fall of 1973.

We Lose the Rose Bowl ... by vote, that is

That year Michigan and Ohio State had played to a 10-10 tie in the final football game at Ann Arbor and we had not lost a game that season. So with a 10-0-1 record, the same as Ohio State's, we figured we would get the Rose Bowl vote for two reasons. First, the Big Ten always believed in the philosophy that all Big Ten schools should get the opportunity to play in Pasadena, and at one time had a no-repeat rule on the books — meaning teams regardless of standings could not go two consecutive years. Ohio State had been to the Jan. 1, 1973, Rose Bowl so everyone — alumni, media, players, and coaches — assumed Michigan would be at the Rose Bowl January 1, 1974. The athletic directors were to vote on Sunday following the OSU-UM game.

But, shockingly, the athletic directors voted for Ohio State to go to the Rose Bowl to again face Southern California. The vote was 6-4 in a secret ballot.

Why did the vote go to Ohio State? Frankly, I think it was a very simple reason. The Big Ten directors felt they had to start winning some Rose Bowl games for fear the pact with the Pacific-10 Conference would not be renewed. There was media pressure on the West

Coast to go for the best teams regardless of conference. The athletic directors thought Ohio State had a better chance because Michigan would be without our starting quarterback, Dennis Franklin, who suffered a broken collarbone in that last game.

Coach Bo Schembechler and I were both furious at the vote, but we disagreed over whether Duke orchestrated it in Ohio State's favor by making phone calls to recommend the Buckeyes because of Franklin's injury. Some people, meanwhile, forgot that Larry Cipa, our backup quarterback, had been our quarterback in the Rose Bowl as a sophomore and was totally adequate.

The Franklin injury was hardly a reason to vote against us as no one knew how long he would be out when the vote was taken. Schembechler and others felt the athletic directors had it in for Michigan because he had won so much and lost so few games since coming to the university. There was some truth to that.

Wayne denied Bo's accusations and no director since has ever acknowledged receiving a phone call that Saturday evening from Duke. I have never known him to fabricate anything and he steadfastly denies calling anyone. More than 25 years later we have no evidence that he ever made those phone calls. Originally I also felt he might have done so. I was so mad I would have believed anything.

Schembechler's suspicion of Duke arose because after the 10-10 tie Duke went to Metropolitan Airport and called the press box from there and asked to talk to Perry. His first question to Perry was, "How is Franklin?"

Perry had reports from Dr. Gerald O'Connor, one of the team physicians, that it appeared Franklin had a broken collarbone but it was not certain. So Duke did know, before the vote was taken Sunday morning, about the injury. Bo felt that phone call was to get information for the bowl voters, but Duke said it was only for his concern about Franklin.

When I was told the vote went 6-4 in favor of Ohio State, it was easy to calculate three of Michigan's votes. One, of course, was from Bo's predecessor, Bump Elliott, who was the athletic director at Iowa. Another was from Bill Orwig, who was A. D. at Indiana. And, of course, the Michigan vote. As for the fourth vote, I felt it probably came from Cecil Coleman, athletic director at Illinois, because Orwig and I had been instrumental in getting Cecil his position at Illinois and he was a stickler for rules. He certainly didn't have any animosity toward Michigan. I didn't expect any favors, but I felt Cecil would vote his conscience in our favor. But as I later found out, that fourth vote for us came from Paul Giel, the athletic director and great all-around athlete from the University of Minnesota. It should not have surprised me. Giel called me to say how sorry he was that Michigan didn't get the vote. He didn't tell me how he voted, but I knew at that time if he had voted against us he wouldn't be making a phone call to me.

The biggest surprise, of course, was Michigan State voting against us. That vote was cast by Bert Smith, the athletic director, who told me sometime later he wanted to vote for Michigan (he was a Michigan graduate) but he was instructed by MSU vice president Jack Breslin how to vote because the Spartans didn't want to see Michigan go to the Rose Bowl. "So vote for Ohio," Breslin instructed. The Wolverines had become the dominant team in the state under Schembechler and Michigan State wasn't enamored with being No. 2. It was a situation that continued during my time and after.

The key votes were cast by three shown in this picture. I was confident Elroy Hirsch (2nd from left), Bert Smith (center), and Cecil Coleman (far right), would vote for Michigan. None did. Wayne Duke, far left, didn't have a vote.

Smith's vote probably eventually cost him his job. The newspaper people in the state of Michigan were furious when they found out he had voted against Michigan. It deprived all of those sports writers, sports editors, and even some of the publishers, of a trip to California.

Michigan State took all kinds of hell from the legislature, too. Many legislators were Michigan graduates and couldn't understand how Michigan State would cast a vote against its sister institution. "It just wasn't good for the state," they said. Many had made plans to see Michigan play in Pasadena.

Schembechler had been at U-M for five years and the disagreement with me over Duke's involvement in the vote was our first. Hardly a day went by, it seemed, when Bo wasn't railing to the press about the injustice of the vote, Duke's alleged involvement, and the "gutless" faculty representatives who would do nothing to change the decision. That made *me* popular at the Big Ten meetings I had to attend every week or so while this was going on.

I was as upset and disappointed as Bo was, but I learned a long time ago not to make a two-day story out of a one-day story. I said as little as possible other than there wasn't much that could be done. I then started to get letters and calls from the media as to why I wasn't backing up Schembechler on his efforts to get the vote changed — an impossibility, if anybody knows how intercollegiate athletics is run in the Big Ten. Votes are not changed by pressure.

Compounding the situation was that regent Paul Brown went public saying that Michigan should withdraw from the conference over the incident. He said other regents were considering such a move and it seemed clear Brown's anger was getting the better of his judgment. Michigan had been that route before with sad results.

Letters began flooding my office about why the Wolverines should bolt the Big Ten, or stay put. It seems no one remembered the disaster that had occurred when Yost had forced Michigan out of the conference from January 1908 to November 1917. Who do you play was not a concern of those who wanted to leave.

Finally, a special meeting was called by the conference. Duke, meanwhile, was incensed about the accusations he manipulated votes. Faculty reps were angry because they were being called "gutless." And athletic directors were mad that their votes had become public. And why didn't I "shut Schembechler up?"

I took it from all sides. The conference was prepared to hand Schembechler a severe disciplinary sanction "for being unsportsmanlike" and wanted him to apologize. I knew there was no chance of an apology. I agreed to get Bo to be quiet or they would have kept him off the sidelines all the next season. Schembechler did agree to calm down, but would not apologize. I really never asked him to. The vote was wrong, but he finally ceased talking about it.

Bo was on his good behavior on that incident until 1994 when Bo and I had a TV interview with Don Shane, sportscaster of Detroit's ABC affiliate, WXYZ, Channel 7. The show was about Michigan's series with Notre Dame, but somehow the 1973 Rose Bowl vote came up. Once again Bo gave everyone hell — but there was a whole new cast of characters presiding over the Big Ten and nobody took notice or worried about the 20-year-old vote. They had not been involved.

Basketball

The second difficulty I had with the Big Ten and primarily with Duke concerned basketball. A surprise announcement by him brought both of us some unwanted publicity. I had long been opposed to anything that diminishes the importance of a Big Ten championship in any sport. Duke always felt the same. Wayne, however, wanted the Big Ten to follow the example of the Southeast Conference, and others, to hold a conference basketball tournament after the season, the results to determine the representative to the NCAA championships.

Evidently there had been some discussion of the matter privately with some coaches and directors and Wayne disclosed his proposal in an announcement one weekend in 1978. He suggested the tournament begin in 1979 as a "vehicle" for selecting the Big Ten's representative to the NCAA tournament. He predicted it would gross $750,000 or $800,000, in those days real money. I was astounded when I read the release in the newspaper. It must be remembered that in 1978 there were not 64 institutions invited to the NCAA Basketball Tournament; the tournament champion in each conference was selected to compete for a spot in the final four. In addition a few at-large teams were invited.

The strength of the NCAA and of college sports in this country is based on conference play. I felt that to force a conference champion, after season-long play, into a tournament to qualify for the NCAA championship was an affront to the true champion. I was particularly sensitive to this because of track. I had watched the NCAA turn away from making the conference champion eligible — first for outdoor track, then indoor — in favor of times and distances. I thought then it was a terrible mistake. My view: a champion is a champion and he should be in the championship meets.

When I started the NCAA Indoor Track Championship in Detroit, we invited the champion of each conference in each event. We also had spots open for non-champions with outstanding performances. To this day there is no way indoor performance marks can be an accurate yardstick for selection. Some are made in tobacco barns and others are made running downhill, some on long tracks, like Illinois, or small board tracks in the east.

In basketball the season-long champion cannot be denied. For that reason I vehemently opposed the tournament. It also concerned me that Duke made the announcement without prior discussion and vote by the athletic directors. It was unlike him. I assumed somebody had been talking about it. Maybe it was a trial balloon. I wasn't sure.

I immediately called Indiana basketball coach Bob Knight because he'd been quoted as opposing a tournament, as had I. I told him he'd better round up his coaches and inform the athletic directors and hope we could turn it down at our next meeting. Knight said he wasn't sure he could get a majority. He pointed out that a post-season tournament is for losers and half the teams in the second division would probably vote for a tournament giving them a second chance. Few athletic directors are going to vote against their basketball coaches, but huge gate receipts would also be a factor in the vote.

So, I had a real concern there might be a 6-4 majority in favor of a basketball tournament. I had talked with our Board in Control and it was absolutely opposed to extending the season with a tournament. I was baffled because I'd heard so many presidents in those

Bob Knight

days (and to the present) talking about *overemphasis* and lost class time and how we must control intercollegiate athletics expansion. With that philosophy, how could the presidents approve of a post-season tournament? But my confidence in many of the presidents on athletic matters was not high, frankly.

The arguments against the tournament were threefold: 1) the conference champion should be the designee, due to performance over several months, 2) everyone was on record as being opposed to extending the season in other sports, why not in basketball? and 3) a tournament after a grueling round-robin schedule in the Big Ten was not the best way to prepare our champion to compete against the best in the nation.

Knight agreed with me as did athletic director Doug Weaver at Michigan State. As we tried to count the votes, we weren't sure where we were. Schools like Indiana, Michigan, Purdue, and Michigan State were vehemently opposed. We banded together and said that if you hold your tournament we won't be there. Our Board in Control said it would be in favor of that approach. The move thus ended; it couldn't be of any value to anyone if only six schools showed up. It was realized the vote in favor had to be unanimous.

The future proves the wisdom, because now five and even six Big Ten schools are usually invited to the NCAA Tournament without a conference tournament, as the field has expanded to 64 teams. One sidelight is that the Pac-10 briefly attempted a tournament and abandoned it after two or three years for the very reasons we opposed it in the first place. Now, however, in 1996 it is talking of starting it again as a source of revenue. The Big Ten is also discussing the possibility for the same reason. James Delaney, the Big Ten commissioner, is no genius.

Chapter 17

Some Laughs Along the Way

◆————————————————————

Funny How Things Happen...

Al Renfrew didn't cancel "Big Mouth's" tickets as requested.

Major issues, games, decisions, and changes demanded the most attention during my years at Michigan — but not everything was serious. Humorous incidents punctuated the years and some of them still stand out.

Take the time I got a telegram from a man I'll call Elmer Hanson. It was January 1982 and Bo Schembechler's football team had just lost another Rose Bowl game, a situation that seemed to crop up frequently in those days.

The telegram read: "Cancel my season tickets until you get rid of Schembechler....signed Elmer Hanson."

I called ticket manager Al Renfrew to find out what kind of

season tickets Hanson had. Al looked it up and called me back. "Boy, this guy is on the 50-yard line with four seats," he said. "How did he get there? We have a waiting list in that section."

So I wrote to the man and told him, "We're sorry to lose you as a fan, but we can certainly use your tickets because they're among the best we have." A day or two later I received a telegram from his wife, whom I'll call Louise. It read, "Big Mouth was not authorized to cancel *my* season tickets. I had those tickets before we were married and I wish to retain them. Please ignore the telegram from Big Mouth. I, not Elmer, will use the tickets in the future."

With that message I decided I wouldn't do anything. Louise still had her tickets. I told Al of the situation so there wouldn't be any slipup, and then forgot about it. A day or so later a phone call came in from an alumnus in Detroit. "Did you get a telegram from Elmer Hanson?" he asked. When I replied I had, he said, "Well, he's in deep trouble with his wife and I think if you don't pull his tickets I can get him to join the Victors Club."

At the time, the Victors Club cost $1,000 a year to join, or $10,000 for a life membership. So I said, "OK," and didn't tell the caller I'd already decided not to cancel the tickets.

About a week later I received a letter from Hanson. It didn't mention the telegram, but enclosed was a $1,000 check for a Victors Club membership. I then wrote to Mrs. Hanson saying all is forgiven and she now was a member of the Victors Club. The last time I looked, Elmer Hanson was still paying his dues.

There's a story Renfrew told of a couple who split up and the husband said he wanted to change his ticket so he'd be as far away from his wife as possible. Al had the same request from the man's wife — and so both were moved. When the next season began, the couple's tickets were 180 degrees from where they had been — and they wound up sitting next to each other *on the opposite side of the field*. It was the only spot we had to put singles and the computer made the moves.

Over the years the well-being of Michigan football players has been in the hands of excellent team physicians. Dr. Jerry O'Connor and Dr. Bob Anderson held the post for more than 30 years. With minimal compensation and maximum expertise they provided U-M athletic teams with medical care second to none.

Some thought O'Connor and I resembled each other. Once after my retirement, at a U-M game being played in Iowa City, Jimmy Barrett, a sideline radio reporter from WJR, grabbed O'Connor who was on the sidelines, called up to the radio booth and told the announcing crew he had an interview coming up with Don Canham. Jerry Hanlon, the former assistant football coach, happened to be on the other end of the phone. "If that's the case, it's the first time in history that Canham ever set foot on a football sideline," he said. "I don't think you have Canham."

Barrett assured Hanlon that he certainly did, and proceeded to ask O'Connor questions. Tongue in cheek, the doctor didn't correct the

Jerry Hanlon and Dr. Jerry O'Connor
O'Connor once put words in my mouth; Hanlon was skeptical.

reporter and supplied answers I never would have given — and O'Connor knew it. It was mystifying: friends kept saying they had heard me on the radio at half time. O'Connor had made a wild statement or two, I heard.

Not many weeks afterward I was walking around the stadium at a home game when a young man came running up to me. "Hi, how are you?" he said, greeting me like a long lost friend. I had no idea who he was, but I entertained the possibility we might have met somewhere until he said, "You know, my internship under you was the most important time in my career!" I don't know who should feel more insulted, Dr. O'Connor or I, but at least I didn't advise the young doctor how to operate.

Later that season Barrett was interviewing tailback Tyrone Wheatley. After the broadcast he called up to the booth and asked how the Wheatley interview went. Hanlon, with his pixie humor, said, "It went fine, but you didn't have Wheatley." This time he did have the right guy.

It usually was the coaches who kept me in good humor and one of the best of those was Johnny Orr, the former basketball coach who moved on to coach at Iowa State for many years. One March during recruiting season John met me in the hallway, on his way to recruit a great center in Chicago. John knew I was from Oak Park, just outside Chicago, and asked if I could help in any way. I can't recall if I had any input or not, but during our conversation Johnny said, "You know, I think the mother is going to determine where that boy goes to school. So when I go to Chicago, I entertain the mother, and when Digger Phelps [the Notre Dame coach] goes, he spends time with the kid."

Maybe weeks or even months later I remembered to ask John about that big center and if we were successful in recruiting him. Orr said, "Aw, hell, Don, the kid went to Notre Dame." Then he wheeled around and with a big grin said, "But the old lady is coming to Michigan." I never did follow up to see if the kid ever played for Notre Dame. The story has been used since, but John was the originator in 1969.

No coach is more recognizable than Bob Knight, the famed basketball coach at Indiana University. Like all fine coaches, Knight is also an actor — Knight in private is not the volatile Knight in public. I like him immensely and have a few stories I could tell about him, but I won't.

On occasion when Indiana played in Ann Arbor, he and Bo Schembechler would meet me at my factory so no one would bother us. On one occasion when Knight came in, my secretary ignored him.

She is a knowledgeable sports fan, didn't like Knight, and "had her reasons," as she usually does. While we were sitting in my office, I mentioned to Bob that Peg, my secretary, hated him.

"What?" said Bob, and with that he went back into her office, took her by the hand, brought her in, and sat her down between him and Schembechler. For two hours she sat there while he charmed her to death — and to this day she's one of Knight's greatest defenders. He can do no wrong in her eyes. She was tough to convince — I know because that secretary is now my wife.

Peg Schoemer, the secretary who hated Bob Knight — until she met him. Now she has other problems. She is my wife.

I've seen him turn on that charm a few times. One time when he didn't was at a basketball game in Ann Arbor the year after Johnny Orr had resigned and gone to Iowa State. I was standing in the arena tunnel with Knight before the game started when a little old lady leaned over the railing and called, "Bobby Knight, Bobby Knight, I know Johnny Orr." She was all decked out in maize and blue, complete with "M" and pompons. He walked over to the rail, looked her in the eye and said, "Screw Johnny Orr," then turned around and walked back to me.

"Why the hell did you say that?" I asked.

"Because it's something she'll remember all her life and just think what she'll tell her friends," he said. She's no doubt done both.

One of Biggie Munn's Michigan State football assistants told me a story about Biggie's lesson on how to deal with critical letters of complaint. The team was having a particularly ordinary season and letters began to pour in. Biggie called a staff meeting and said he didn't want the coaches to be worrying about some nut writing a critical letter about the coaching. He reached into his file, pulled out a letter from a fan, and began to read it. It was a very derogatory note concerning the way the MSU football program was being run. "You see what I do with letters like this?" he said, and crumpled it and threw it into a wastebasket. The meeting continued. A few minutes later he wheeled around in his chair, fished the letter out of the wastebasket and started to smooth it out again, muttering, "*What* did that bastard say?" So much for a lesson in ignoring criticism.

People have come to expect 100,000-plus crowds for every Michigan home football game, and the NCAA record attendance is 106,867 for a game against Ohio State in 1993. But, *unofficially*, more than 110,000 spectators packed Michigan Stadium for a game against Purdue during the heyday of Schembechler's teams. How's that? It's another funny story, although it wasn't particularly so at the time and there's no way we can take credit for that "record" turnout.

One sunny Saturday as I looked down from the press box I could see every aisle was packed with people. Many of them were Boy Scouts. No one could move in or out of the stadium, a situation brought about by a miscalculation concerning *which* game was going to be free-admission Boy Scout Day.

Vern Rose, who was in his mid-80s, had done a lot of printing for Michigan. He was also very active in the Cub Scout and Boy Scout organizations. Prior to sellout years we had 10,000 to 20,000 empty seats in the stadium and we'd pick a day and give Vern 6,000 free tickets he could pass out to various scouting groups. It was one of the highlights of his life and as a result he was extremely popular with the scouts. He could hardly wait for Boy Scout Day to arrive each year.

When Renfrew came to see me that year about which game we'd choose for the scout tickets, we both picked Northwestern. Historically it had the smallest draw. Two years earlier, however, Purdue had been the opponent on Boy Scout Day. Perhaps with that in mind, Vern printed the complimentary tickets for the Purdue, not the Northwestern, game.

By this time Schembechler's teams were in the habit of having outstanding seasons and the crowds were growing, with some sellouts. Purdue had a new coach and, if I recall correctly, it was Jim Young, a former member of Bo's staff. The Boilermakers were becoming a formidable rival. On game day it was bright and sunny and as I pulled up to the stadium I saw long lines of people trying to buy tickets. We had a tremendous gate sale, I remember, maybe the best ever.

Boy Scouts and Cub Scouts were pouring into the stadium. I didn't think much about it until I got to the press box and looked down. So I walked down into the stadium and found that people were furious. The scouts had arrived early with their sandwiches and Coke and apples, and they were seated in the seats we'd sold to paying customers.

Some of the Boy Scouts wouldn't move and as I walked in one guy, who must have had a few belts, yelled out at me, "Canham, get these little bastards out of our seats!" Some others had a few choice words for me and my promotions. Among other things, they accused me of selling their seats twice. Immediately I realized what had happened and went off to find Bob Flora, who was in charge of building and grounds and my game-day right-hand man. I found him at Gate 2 and said, "Bob, get some people and take these Boy Scouts and spread them out through the stadium or seat them in the aisles. Just be creative."

It eventually worked out beautifully. Most people moved over to make room and some of the Cub Scouts sat on people's laps. They can all look back now and say they attended the football game with the largest crowd in the history of pro or college football. Of course, if the fire marshal had walked in he would have closed us down. We were so oversold it was comical. The next morning at the ticket office Renfrew was beside himself. There had been a couple of stories in the papers about the mix-up and we were all trying to protect Rose. Al took the blame. When I walked in he thought I was about to take his head off, something for which I had been known to do on occasion. But when I started to laugh he soon realized the humor in the situation. The damage was done and what could we do about it? The sad part was we couldn't claim the all-time attendance record.

Doug Hobbs, the faculty representative at UCLA and a very funny man, had an experience at the Huntington Sheraton Hotel in Pasadena that deserves retelling. Hobbs and all the faculty reps in the Pac-10 always stayed there during Rose Bowl week each New Years. One year when Michigan was there, someone set off a fire extinguisher system at 3 a.m. that clouded the fourth floor with dense fog. Alarm bells went off. Doug, who was on that floor, flew to the rescue, running up and down the hall in his nightgown pounding on doors. Then he remembered the team was on the fifth floor so, still in his nightgown, he ran up. Although no extinguisher smoke was in evidence, fires do spread, he felt, and he started beating on the doors to alert the team. One by one the players opened their door, took one look, and shut the door in his face. The next morning they told about the nut in a nightgown who woke them up in the middle of the night. (The fourth floor people, including members of the press, had fled to the streets but soon returned to their rooms when everyone realized it was a false alarm.)

That evening at a joint conference dinner, Doug was scheduled to speak. With tongue in cheek he started to tell his story about the events of the night before — the smoke, the fire alarm, and the "total lack of concern the players had for Paul Revere." He concluded by saying, "The next time that happens I'm going to let the S.O.B.s burn." Hobbs is the one I still suspect of engineering my invitation from UCLA to become athletic director after the death of famed athletic director J.D. Morgan.

In 1956 when I was returning from Africa, I stopped in Rome to visit George Oberweger, the Italian national coach. During our conversation he suggested I tie up some rooms in Rome for the 1960 Olympic Games and run a tour because the critical problem for the '60 games as he saw it would be lack of accommodations for the visitors. I did just that when I returned to the United States, through Kurt Thrun, a travel agent in Plymouth. I then recruited Jeff Mortenson, track coach at Southern California; Dave Rankin, track coach at Purdue; Leo Johnson, track coach at Illinois; and Chick Werner, track coach at Penn State, to help me run a tour. We called it the "Five-Star Track Coaches' Tour." I originally tried to get Larry Snyder, the Ohio track coach, but he was named the Olympic coach, so he couldn't be with us. In very short order we had 160 people who wanted to take our tour to the

Olympic Games.

After a tour of Paris, the group ended up in Rome and we were having a dinner party at a very nice out-of the-way restaurant. All 160 people showed up because Bud Winter of San Jose State, Snyder, and several other Olympic coaches were there. As we were about to leave, a good portion of the tour group said, in effect, "Let's stay and continue the party, we haven't anything to do tomorrow." The

Dave Rankin, Purdue track coach, finally checked his watch pocket, two weeks late.

proprietor said we could, but we needed to put up $300, which in Italian money amounted to thousands and thousands of lira. The people who wanted to continue the party chipped in the money and we had a stack of Italian lira a foot high. We went to the cashier, changed it into two very large lira bills and Rankin became the banker. The party went on until 3 a.m. and when it came time to settle the check, Rankin had lost the two bills. We looked everywhere. Johnson, Werner, Dave, and I put in our own money and paid the $300 check.

Following the Olympic games Rankin, Werner and I went to Switzerland for a week. We did a little fishing and one afternoon while we were sitting in a bar overlooking Lake Thun, Rankin leaned back, put his thumb in his watch pocket and almost fell off the stool. He'd found our thousands of lira. Needless to say, Rankin was never the banker on tours we subsequently ran to the Olympics in Mexico City and Tokyo.

Some of my most humorous moments were spent with a man named Ted Bredehoft, athletic director at the University of Wichita (then Wichita State.) I constantly included him in the Michigan seminars I ran around the country on marketing management and promotion. He was always the hit of the program. Ted's first claim to fame was that he started a crew team at Wichita, which is in the middle of Kansas. It was a neat trick, seeing as how there wasn't a team to compete against for 1,000 miles. It was the only crew team in that part of the country and I don't know what river or pond it rowed on. It was a bit incongruous — but then, Admiral Chester Nimitz, commander of the U.S. Navy in the Pacific theater during World War II, was from Kansas. Bredehoft put together the team at the behest of some Ivy League people interested in crew. They were willing to finance the team, giving them an excuse to attend the NCAA championships, usually in the East.

But Ted's greatest claim to fame was his approach to selling football tickets. Like Michigan, he set out to make the spectacle of football the focal point, although his approach was somewhat different from ours. In our marketing and promotion we hammered away at the difference between professional and college football. "Three-plays-a-minute" was a magic phrase for us. Then there were the tailgate picnics which brought children into the campus atmosphere. And every time we did anything different, such as when we installed artificial turf, we ballyhooed it. But Bredehoft had another agenda.

Once I read in the newspaper that Wichita had agreed to refund the ticket price to any season ticket holder for any game the Shockers lost. I phoned him. "Ted, are you out of your mind?" I said. "You've got a lousy football team coming up and you've got a murderous schedule. How in the world could you refund the money and even come close to meeting your budget?"

He just laughed. "I haven't announced how they're going to get the refund. I won't announce that until I've sold all the season tickets I can."

"What magic formula are you going to use?" I asked.

"Well," he said, "we have a farm 50 miles out of town and the refund desk is going to be set up at this farm from 3 to 4 a.m. on the Sunday morning following the game."

"Ted, they're going to kill you," I told him.

His answer was, "I don't think so. Most people are going to know how I operate and think it's rather humorous. But secondly, after a football game nobody feels like getting in his car and driving out to get six dollars on a ticket when the team lost a game." He was correct — and he did survive.

While we were running a seminar in Anaheim, Calif., I asked him how his ticket refund gimmick worked out. "The first couple of weeks nobody showed up." he said, "and after that I never bothered to open up the farm." I wondered if he'd had any complaints and he said there were one or two. "But when we checked them out we found they were from people who didn't even buy tickets." Few copied his marketing of football, though.

On another occasion, Bredehoft had seen a TV show where some camels were used in a promotion to open a supermarket or a theater or something out in Los Angeles. He called the camel owner and asked if he would bring the camels to Kansas and put them in a race at halftime of a Wichita football game.

The owner said, "Sure, for $6,000." So Bredehoft flew in the camels and put them up at a friend's farm, out in an orchard, prior to the big race. You can imagine the kind of wild publicity he received with a camel race scheduled for

Ted Bredehoft
He sold football tickets
in many strange ways.

halftime, and ticket sales were brisk. The race was to be for a quarter-mile around the running track outside the field and that's the way they hyped it. But then the camel driver arrived. "Don't you know a camel can't run and turn?" he said. "A camel runs and stops and then makes a turn. We can't run around a track."

It was not a great day and the field was a little muddy. But that didn't daunt Bredehoft. He said, "OK, we'll run up and down the field four times instead of having a quarter-mile race around the track." And that's what they did. The camels ran up to one goal post, stopped, turned around and ran back. It was not a great spectacle, but it sold an awful lot of Wichita football tickets and ruined a football field, too.

The next time I saw Bredehoft I asked how the race came out. He said it ended up OK, "But the damn camels ate all the bushes at my friend's farm and now I have to replace the shrubbery."

One could go on and on with Bredehoft stories alone. But they illustrate the mindset we had in those days when college sports were promoted only by a few; and, when promotion caught on, it sometimes developed some outlandish and spectacular marketing programs. Just about anything that could sell tickets was tried, and it certainly was more fun, too. I have not heard from Bredehoft lately. He subsequently left Wichita State, but I did hear he was selling oil wells. He's no doubt a multi-millionaire now.

Bob Flora, my long-time manager of facilities, had been a football

Lilyan Duford

"Don, that crazy Flora is going to take the flag pole out of the stadium."

player at Michigan when I was in school. His brother "Flop" had been a Michigan All-American. Bob became an assistant to Forest Evashevski at Iowa, and later assistant athletic director when both he and Evy retired from the football scene. I saw him from time to time over the years and one fall when we were there to play Iowa I met him for breakfast. Flora was not happy. It seemed that after Evashevski had departed, Flora had been fired by the powers that be. I happened to be looking for someone with his background, although he didn't know it at the time. After talking with him, I made up my mind I was going to hire him. It was a decision I never regretted.

When he reported for work about a month later he tried an experiment that has stayed in my memory ever since. It seems that when he came into the office several people told him if he wanted something done he should come to them and *they* would see Canham about it. Flora was determined to find out which of them was the real pipeline to the director's office. So he told four different people that he was going to remove the flag pole in Michigan Stadium because it really wasn't necessary anymore.

The next morning, Lilyan Duford, who had been my secretary when I was a track coach and was now the business manager, came into my office. "Do you know what that crazy Flora is going to do? He's going to remove the flag pole in Michigan Stadium!"

"What?!" I said. "Get that guy in here."

When Bob came in he had a big grin on his face and said, "Now I know the pipelines around here."

From then on, when Bob wanted to plant an idea with me and I was busy or preoccupied, he would go sit in Lilyan's office and pass it on to her, knowing that at some point she would walk across the hall and tell me his latest brainstorm. Most of the time, however, Flora didn't need my approval on things he thought needed to be done. He was a great one on maintenance and knew we both thought along the same lines.

Track and field seemed to produce more than its share of light moments. Michigan's two-mile relay team was invited to the once-famous Coliseum Relay in Los Angeles where 60,000 spectators often showed up. Our plane landed at the same time as that of Clyde Littlefield, the famous coach of Texas, with one of his relay teams. Our host was a young man who met both teams with transportation. Littlefield wanted his team to stretch and jog a bit before we went to the hotels. "Young man, where can we

Clyde Littlefield
Not one to celebrate

loosen up a little around here?" he asked. The kid looked surprised. "Hell, Coach," he said, "there are all kinds of joints up and down this boulevard." The loudest chuckle came from Littlefield who probably never had a drink in his life.

One of the more memorable people I ever knew, again in track and field, was Frank Hill, who coached at Northwestern. From his youth he was crippled and had to use a cane. He usually sat on the edge of the track in a chair and told great stories about Knute Rockne and others he had coached with. Frank had one of the sharpest senses of humor I ever encountered. Rankin and I started to coach when we were in our twenties. We were befriended by Hill, probably more than by other coaches in the senior group, so consequently we spent a great deal of time with him. They called him "Hurry Back Hill" and I asked him one time how he'd acquired the name. He said that his first cross-country team at Northwestern was not very good and when they were about to have their first race of the season, the captain came over to him with the rest of the team trailing behind and said, "Coach, do you have any last minute instructions for us?" He looked them in the eye and said, "Yes. Hurry back." The nickname stuck for good.

Frank Hill
They called him, "Hurry Back."

One humorous story happened on the Ohio State campus at the Big Ten Championships in 1960. Illinois and Michigan were locked in a battle for the title. It came down to the last race before the relay. We both had outstanding two-milers and it appeared the team that scored the most points in the two-mile would win the championship. The pressure was a little hefty for me and I left French Fieldhouse and went into St. John's Arena, which connects to the running track. I started to walk around the concourse at the top of the building. There wasn't a soul around and then I heard clicking heels. I turned the corner and bumped into Leo Johnson, the Illinois track coach. We'd caught each other pacing around a quarter-mile away from the running track. We started laughing like a couple of fools. Neither of us would ever admit where we were during that two-mile run. We walked back to the track and Michigan had prevailed. Years later when I became the athletic director I received a note from Leo: "If you ever get in trouble and need help, and I know you will at some time, you might hear clicking heels and I'll be there. Best of luck, Leo." It's a note I've treasured and always will. I gave the eulogy at Leo's funeral when he passed away at age 98 — one of my all-time favorite people.

Gerry Faust, the former football coach at Notre Dame who later coached at Akron, was a beauty. Once when Perry and I were consulting at Akron, Gerry took us on a wild car ride to the Glass Bowl to show us the new locker rooms. We found ourselves going down a one-way street and when I said, "Gerry, you're going the wrong way on this street," he merely said, "It's a short-cut." Will and I just looked at each other and grabbed the seat belts.

Shortly after Faust was hired as coach at Notre Dame I had an occasion to speak with the athletic director, Gene Corrigan. I asked Gene how he was getting along with his new coach and he said, "Fine, but I need to give him instructions once in a while." Corrigan, who's a good friend with a great sense of humor, told me his instructions were, "Gerry, the first time we play Michigan I want you and your team prepared, and my words of wisdom to you are — when the Wolverines take the field, *don't laugh at their helmets!"*

There were many times when humor was provided by opponents. One time was when Michigan played Wisconsin for the NCAA Hockey Championship at old Olympia Stadium in Detroit. The game was going into overtime and Elroy Hirsch, the Wisconsin athletic director, and I went to the Olympia Room for a drink. When overtime started I went back into the arena and Elroy went to the men's room that was situated in the back of the Olympia Room. The custodian, who had been instructed to stay in the room, thought it was empty and decided to lock up and go into the arena to watch the overtime. Elroy was inside. As he tells the story, he tried the door and it wouldn't

Elroy Hirsch

budge, the crowd was going wild, and no one could hear him beating on the door. Wisconsin won the game, the door was unlocked, and the Olympia Room was flooded with people. Poor Elroy had to learn of the Wisconsin victory second hand.

Hirsch became the only athletic director in history whose school won an NCAA championship while its athletic director was locked in the men's room, and until now — I'm the only one who knew it.

Don Lund at one Rose Bowl game was in charge of allotting courtesy cars to our family party of coaches, directors, faculty and others. There were probably 50 or more cars to be assigned. Ford, Chrysler and GM always provided the cars to visiting Rose Bowl participants. They would park them in certain spots and put the keys in a large brown envelope for Lund to pass out. On this occasion, Cadillac put two sets of keys in the large envelope rather than the usual one. Don passed out all the keys, not knowing there were duplicates. In a short time he had a report one of the Cadillacs was stolen. Lund called the police but before they got there the "thief" had returned the car. As police arrived another car was reported stolen and then another. Reality soon set in when we found the duplicate key situation.

Lund had another experience with car keys. He was moved into a full lot by an attendant near Cobo Hall in Detroit. "I'll find a spot for you," the attendant said — and Don tossed him the keys and left. When he returned for the car later a different attendant was on duty and the key board in the shed had no keys for Lund. It seems the official attendant, when the lot filled up, locked the shed and left. The guy Lund tossed his keys to was someone just walking by.

He did find a "spot" for Don's car, probably in Mexico.

Don't talk to Don Lund about keys.

◆◆◆

Chapter 18

Changes

◆————————————

Title IX and the CFA

T itle IX drove me nuts from 1972 until I retired in 1988. I was very much in favor of women's athletic competition and had seen a good deal of talent and interest in Europe when I coached women's track there during several summers in the 1950s and '60s. What those of us in administration hoped for when Title IX came along and what we received were vastly different. The amendment Congress attached to the bill and the interpretation given by government agencies were miles apart. For more than 25 years schools have been regularly confused by bungling bureaucrats and, of late, by some judges who were simply uninformed. Some less-than-courageous college presidents didn't help matters, either.

Due to recent publicity, many think women's sports started with Title IX. That's not so at Michigan or other schools. Title IX did expand opportunities for women without question, and

Babe Didrikson and others competed long before Title IX.

from that standpoint it has been valuable. Some of us remember how the athletic fame of all-around athlete Babe Didrikson, skater Sonja Henie, and swimmer Esther Williams gave women's sports a tremendous shot in the arm. We recall, too, that the interest wasn't sustained until television put women athletes in living rooms across the country. Title IX has fostered women's sports on all levels, but the price of this expansion has not always been fair or pleasant.

MINOR SPORTS WOULD SUFFER

Canham slams Title IX rules

Don Canham

HOUSTON — (AP) — University of Michigan athletic director Don Canham said Tuesday proposed federal guidelines for equal funding for all men's and women's intercollegiate athletics could mean the end of competition in some sports for both men and women athletes.

"Track and field would be one of the first to go, because you're dealing with numbers," said Canham, here to address an alumni meeting. "You're dealing with a non-revenue producing sport. What they're talking about now would end a lot of things for both men and women athletes."

Canham is one of the more vocal critics of proposed guidelines outlined under Title IX of the Education Act of 1972, which says men's and women's intercollegiate athletic programs must be matched dollar for dollar.

CANHAM suggested that revenue-producing sports like football be removed from the guidelines and let all non-revenue sports be treated equally.

"What they have done is tell us to put all men's athletics into a pot and come up with a per capita expenditure for the men's program," Canham said.

"Then they say you have to spend that much for the women. It just won't work.

"We spent $1.5 million on football last year but we netted $5 million."

CANHAM SAID the plan means that if a university has 300 men athletes and only 100 women athletes, the next 200 women to join a team would automatically get a scholarship.

"As affluent as we are in Ann Arbor, we couldn't spend another $1.5 million on women's athletics," Canham said. "If it would cause us trouble, what about some of the other institutions."

The Michigan athletic director said non-revenue sports should be treated equally adding "you can't just build in 300 scholarships for women's athletics."

"Why don't they say every male nurse gets a scholarship until there are as many male nurses as female," Canham said.

An article in a Houston, Texas newspaper from a speech I gave in 1974, over 20 years ago. The problems raised then are still with us in 1996.

In a 1974 speech in Houston I went on record opposing the Title IX guidelines as set out by the Health, Education and Welfare Department (HEW) at the outset in 1972. They were not what Congress intended them to be when the equal opportunity athletic bill was passed. It is 25 years later and I have not changed my mind. Schools are in courts constantly these days over the very issues I raised then, plus the added "gender equity" requirement.

HEW originally was responsible for interpreting Title IX for educational institutions. It was a disaster. Those of us who supported the original legislation were soon amazed as the department attempted to impose its idea of compliance. When HEW agents visited Michigan, for instance — and there were seven of them at one time with their little notebooks — they made it clear at the outset that equal opportunity meant equal expenditure of dollars, equal coaching salaries, equal numbers of athletes on a squad, and identical locker rooms and training rooms. No consideration was given to the difference between getting a new program off the ground and maintaining an established 100-year-old program. We had 120 or 130 athletes turn out for football alone, 50 or 60 for track, and to come up with equal numbers for women couldn't be done by waving a magic wand or a regulation.

The original group that came to Ann Arbor counted the number of shower heads for men and women and the thickness of the carpet in the men's locker room vs. the carpet in the women's areas. The number of trainers who were male and the number who were female seemed a major concern. None had any experience in athletics and not much common sense, either.

Other institutions had experiences similar to Michigan's and by 1974 the NCAA council protested to HEW that they should put out some reasonable standards to avoid legal action that was sure to come. HEW eventually issued new guidelines that solved nothing. It claimed equal opportunity was "financial proportionality," and the specter of quotas appeared for the first time. In the spring of 1980 the administration of Title IX passed from HEW to the U.S. Department of Education. There was no change in approach, but equal numbers or "gender equity" were added to the guidelines.

The Title IX that passed Congress actually did not specifically apply to athletics in high schools and colleges. The law is a broad educational bill. Bureaucrats zeroed in on athletics. The rules of enforcement by HEW and the Department of Education have changed from administration to administration. For years no one has known exactly what is expected from Title IX enforcement. The courts originally stated that Title IX did not apply to sports. It wasn't until 1987 that Congress overrode a 1984 Supreme Court decision that the law didn't apply because sports received no direct federal financing. The ruling has made no difference to the Education Department.

A federal judge in 1995 decided Brown University was in violation because of the proportionality guideline. The judge decided it no longer matters whether a college gives men or women equal opportunity to play varsity sports: "Equal opportunity is not what the compliance test measures," she said. So things are no different than they were in 1974. Athletes out for sports must consist of 50 percent men, 50 percent women, or it's a violation. That's logic?

After 25 years of Title IX it is true women's athletics at Michigan and other institutions is better off. However, the price has been high for men's athletics. If a sport hasn't been dropped, it has restrictions on squad size to comply with directives calling for proportionate quotas. Everyone would prefer progress without threats and ridiculous lawsuits against institutions for so-called violations. The legal fees alone would finance a lot of team travel for men and for women.

The saddest result of the government bungling is that young male "walk-ons" (those not on scholarships) are a thing of the past. Even more important is many schools are dropping men's sports to make their numbers acceptable to investigators. Arkansas, for instance, dropped swimming; Arizona State, men's gymnastics; Brown University, men's water polo and golf; Drake, wrestling; Fresno State, men's swimming; Illinois, men's swimming and diving, and fencing. Iowa State dropped men's gymnastics and tennis; Notre Dame, wrestling; Princeton, wrestling; and UCLA, men's swimming and gymnastics.

How it will play out is only a guess. Louisiana State and Brown University and some others have ended up in court, and that is where the matter will be settled. Until then, the men's programs will decline in size — to make "equal numbers."

The Freshman Rule

A radical change in intercollegiate sports has been the elimination of the freshman rule, something that came about because small schools were in favor for cost-cutting reasons and had more votes at the NCAA convention. Freshmen became instantly eligible to compete. Michigan and most major universities saw problems ahead and voted against the rule change in 1972. Athletes at some institutions were quickly regarded as disposable objects: some coaches recruited athletes they knew couldn't last more than a year — or a semester. They began to take those who never should have gone to college, or who should have gone to a junior college to get their academic feet on the ground.

It's also incredible that freshmen athletes can be admitted to school prior to the start of classes and compete in football and cross country meets before they even know where the library is. Every time some of us in Division I schools tried to bring back the old rule requiring freshmen to put in a year before becoming eligible, we failed. If presidents really want to reform athletics as claimed, they again should make freshmen ineligible. Sadly, they won't do it because of the cost. Those 25 freshmen football players on athletic scholarships would be sitting on the bench and who would be taking their place on the field? Who did it before frosh were eligible?

Professional Sports

Some of the changes over the last several decades have caused hardship for athletic departments across the country, the most important being the rise of professional sports. In Detroit, for example, we now have: a National Hockey League team; a minor league hockey team promoted like an NHL team; an indoor soccer team; a National Basketball Association team, that in my day was playing in Indiana; an American League baseball team; and a National Football League team.

For a multitude of reasons the pros have dominated the news media. It's hard to find college sports coverage in the big metropolitan newspapers on any level close to what it once was. College baseball at one time drew large crowds at Michigan and other schools and was well-covered by metropolitan newspapers. Today a school is lucky if it can get its game scores in the paper. Radio and TV news shows use their three minutes of sports primarily to cover the pros.

The College Football Association

Some changes in athletic administration took place during my time, some that altered athletics forever. Michigan's point of view wasn't always with the majority, and several changes had lasting impact on collegiate athletic program. Usually the Big Ten was involved and included Wayne Duke, the Big Ten commissioner. Wayne and I often saw things differently.

My opinion did *not* prevail in a crucial issue in the '70s and '80s. It concerned the College Football Association, the CFA. It was formed after several of the major institutions at the 1970 NCAA convention, including Michigan, were unsuccessful in reorganizing the NCAA itself. Those of us in major college football had become frustrated by our inability to determine our own destiny. Specifically, we opposed the policy that allowed virtually every small school in the NCAA to vote on matters important to our programs and that were of little concern to theirs.

It was so bad that non-football-playing schools were voting on football matters. The CFA, in my opinion, was formed primarily to change that and other problems within the NCAA. I certainly was in favor of that change. I felt the CFA was not started to destroy the NCAA, as claimed.

Chuck Neinas, who had been with the NCAA and then commissioner of the Big Eight, eventually became CFA director. He is a very bright man, a friend, and possesses a background in athletics second to none. I also knew most of the people who formed the CFA. Shortly after Neinas became director, I was invited, along with another Big Ten representative, Bob Knight from Indiana, to attend a three-day meeting with CFA principals on an island off the Georgia coast.

Bob Knight, Indiana University basketball coach, and I at the time felt the CFA was something the Big Ten should consider.

The time was not spent trying to destroy the NCAA, but rather on discussions about how to raise academic standards; put sanity into recruiting; eliminate abuses, particularly those that exploited the student-athlete; and, of course, about how to create financial equity for intercollegiate football programs and give major schools more control of their own destiny. So I knew a little about CFA matters early on.

CFA membership consisted of 66 Division IA football-playing institutions. Only the Big Ten and the Pac-10 of the major conferences failed to join at its founding. I thought we should have.

It was my firm belief the CFA was founded to improve intercollegiate football. I campaigned for years to get the Big Ten to join, without much luck, I'm sorry to say. Had the Big Ten, and possibly the Pac-10, joined, it might have prevented mistakes the CFA, like any new organization, made. Football television, for instance, might still be controlled by the NCAA as many feel it should be.

We needed an autonomous Division I. That was high on the CFA agenda. The best example of the need was when the NCAA legislation made freshmen eligible. It was passed by a very small margin. Virtually every major institution voted in opposition; again, the day was carried by the small schools. If we'd had divisional vote at that time I doubt if the major institutions would be playing freshmen as they are today, to the relief of many coaches.

Wayne Duke and I differed on the College Football Association. His position prevailed. Of course I was right — I think!

Duke and I had distinct differences of opinion regarding the CFA issue. As one of the first employees the NCAA had, he was extremely loyal to the NCAA and to its executive director, Walter Byers. Both Wayne and Walter felt the CFA was originally conceived to take the place of the NCAA among the major institutions. Duke, at least, felt that without the Big Ten and the Pac-10, the plan would be impossible. That was true. I just believed that when 66 major institutions band together to discuss intercollegiate football and its future, *someone* from Michigan should be sitting in the room, and the

Big Ten should have a vote on what was going to change.

Further, I felt with the leadership available in the Big Ten (men like U-M president Robben Fleming), and in the Pac-10 (men like UCLA's president Chuck Young), both conferences could influence the direction of the CFA.

The Board in Control of Intercollegiate Athletics at Michigan discussed the matter at length. Our board at that time felt it might be worth exploring but they were not as enthusiastic as I was. At Big Ten meetings the directors of athletics were probably more in favor than against, although we never took a vote in the preliminary discussions. At one point the Council of Ten — the presidents of the Big Ten — asked for a director to address their group. The directors chose me. My guess is the invitation was the result of chairman Fleming wanting to make sure both sides were heard. During that meeting several of the presidents shared my view and spoke in favor of joining the CFA, but the group voted not to join that afternoon.

For all the good it accomplished, the CFA made two major mistakes. I'm absolutely certain the Pac-10 and the Big Ten could have prevented them. Both mistakes revolved around television.

I recall the time when I began to have doubts about the CFA. It had announced that NBC was going to produce a fall CFA television series of games worth millions of dollars. The games would be in competition with the NCAA program. It was the first time I thought Byers and Duke were correct in their appraisal of the CFA. It made a mistake in that move.

Walter Byers points out in his book, *Unsportsmanlike Conduct,* published by the University of Michigan Press in 1995, that the CFA felt the NCAA television plan, of which I happened to be a committee member for many years, was strangling them financially and the Big Ten and Pac-10 were favored with more than their fair exposure. Ignored by the CFA was that 30 percent of all TV sets are in the Big Ten area; and the East is more likely to tune in the Big Ten than to conferences in the plains states or the Southwest. The networks wanted more Big Ten games. Neinas had sold the CFA on the premise that cable and pay-TV would bring tremendous wealth if only the major football-playing schools could control their own destiny and get more games on the air than the NCAA plan allowed.

In fairness, almost everyone thought pay-TV was going to be a gigantic income source for college football. The CFA threw out wild figures on the value of pay-TV cable football. Would the Ohio State-Michigan game be worth $10 million or even $20 million? What about Army-Navy on pay-TV? And almost any game Notre Dame played would be worth a fortune. Time has shown the market to be minimal for college football on pay-TV, because barn-burning games are scarce among the hundreds of televised games each season. That was the second CFA television miscalculation. That market never developed.

Fred Davison, then the Georgia president, and Neinas were the leaders in the CFA plan that was to go head to head with the NCAA football telecasting contract. But in August of 1981, when the CFA put the plan to a preliminary vote of their institutions, there were only 33 schools in favor, 20 against, and eight abstaining. A majority wouldn't be enough. It had to be unanimous, or close to it. No network would pay millions of dollars for a handful of teams competing against the NCAA package. We all knew that. The NBC offer did not materialize.

The CFA soon voted to sue the NCAA to break up control of college football television. The case was filed in Oklahoma City with the University of Georgia and the University of Oklahoma as plaintiffs. The court ruled the NCAA television controls, "did not contribute to competitive balance and were in violation of anti-trust laws." The appeals court concurred. Now the NCAA was being judged on pure business anti-trust laws. So, after losing the case in Oklahoma City and then again in the Tenth Court of Appeals in Denver, the NCAA appealed to the Supreme Court. There, only William Rehnquist and Byron White, former University of Colorado All-American football player, voted for the NCAA. The other seven justices found the NCAA in violation of the anti-trust laws. Schools now had no restrictions on televising their football games.

The sad part of this matter is time has shown that free and unlimited television hasn't been the best move for college football. It has led to most major schools, including Michigan, telecasting their entire season. While the money may be close to what we received under the NCAA restricted television package, our exposure under the NCAA plan was limited to only two or three games. The games were scarce and thus valuable, and were becoming more valuable.

The NCAA plan was designed to protect large and small schools alike. The most damaging effects of the Oklahoma-Georgia lawsuit have been felt by small schools, as the NCAA television committee predicted it would. Small-school conferences throughout the country have seen their attendance dwindle. And their opportunities for occasionally telecasting a game have dried up as the major schools gobble up all the time slots and bring several televised games of the majors into their areas each week. Television has eroded the small schools' attendance just as it destroyed small town theaters. On the other side of the coin, major institutions generate more fan interest for themselves as they appear in living rooms week after week. Women and children have been exposed to the game as never before, and attendance has not been appreciably damaged at most major schools. Many have even seen attendance increase because new fans are being created.

In retrospect, one wonders what might have happened had the Big Ten and the Pac-10 joined the CFA in the first place. It's my feeling they would have been able to guide the organization in a different direction with regard to television, away from the CFA's miscalculations involving pay-TV and the effects of unlimited football telecasts. Whoever put a pencil to the figures didn't understand that a Mercedes Benz costs $70,000 or $100,000 because so few are produced. Scarcity is what sells in any market.

The 10 years or more of the CFA's financing was based mainly on its role in free and unlimited televising of football and its TV rights. But TV also led to the demise of the organization. During the 1994 season Notre Dame pulled out of the CFA plan and went on its own. Other conferences followed. In May of 1996 the CFA voted to disband by 1997 as, once again, it can no longer present enough televised games to sell to the networks under the CFA umbrella.

It must be said, however, that during its life, the CFA with Neinas as director, had a major positive effect on intercollegiate athletics. Most of the reforms the CFA advocated at the outset were eventually passed in NCAA legislation. Its members were among the giants in NCAA governance during my time, and the CFA didn't destroy the NCAA.

◆◆◆

Chapter **19**

Final Days

◆────────────────────────────

There Were Better Times

J anuary 1988 I attended my last NCAA convention. I was about to retire that June and there had been some publicity about Michigan's search for a new athletic director. I was in a committee meeting with several presidents when one of them — I believe it was Otis

Peg and I in Sorrento, Italy, in 1996, obviously doing research on the book.

Singleterry of the University of Kentucky — turned to me and said, "Don, you're going to find there are three stages of retirement. The first is, 'We're losing a legend; we'll never be able to replace him;' the second is, 'We've hired a genius, the best in the land;' And the third is, 'That old guy didn't know what the hell he was doing; how are we ever going to get out of the mess he left us?'"

I realize now I went through those stages, but it wasn't *after*

I retired. If I could wipe out one period as athletic director it would be the final year; it was one disappointment after another. I ended up at odds with one of my favorite people, President Harold Shapiro; lost faith in a board of regents and the search committee's handling of football coach Bo Schembechler; and was disappointed in a young person I had hired years before. I concluded that a lame duck athletic director doesn't have much of a chance.

From past experience I knew that a change in administration always produces some uncertainty within a department or institution. I watched it happen when presidents Harlan Hatcher and Robben Fleming left, and again when Shapiro went to Princeton. I remember in particular the concerns we all had when Fritz Crisler retired. It's human nature to worry about who your boss is going to be. My leaving was no exception. Even though I understood the dynamics of administrative change, I never imagined I'd be as uncomfortable or as eager to get out as I was in 1988.

One problem started in late January 1988 when a group of alumni from Detroit, led by a prominent lawyer, came to me saying they wanted to go to court over age discrimination so I could stay on longer. They cited the case of Bob Devaney, Nebraska's great athletic director and football coach, who remained on the job until his late seventies because an age discrimination ruling prevented him from being forced out at 70. I told them I had no desire to stay on; in fact, if I could walk out the door right then I would. They didn't seem to be convinced. My concern was that the newspapers might make something of the move and I didn't want that. I'd enjoyed the job so much I always felt I was in a toy store. Coaches and athletic directors are lucky; the job satisfactions usually far outweigh the problems. I felt that way for my entire life in athletics.

My disenchantment actually began two years before my scheduled retirement, in the spring, 1986, when Shapiro called me to his office and said, "Don, we want you to retire next year and I want to make plans for a big retirement party for you." That was exactly the way he started the conversation. Up until that time I'd been preoccupied with getting things wound up and assumed I'd have until my 70th birthday in 1988. The most pressing matter was the completion of the new swimming natatorium. In addition, I had made specific plans about when

I'd return to School-Tech, the corporation I had put into trust in 1968. I said to Shapiro, "Harold, I don't want to retire a year early. I have too many obligations and too many things I'd like to complete here, the pool being one."

He replied, "Well, we have some other problems and we really want you to retire in July of 1987." With that he stood up and said, "I want you to think about it." The whole thing was a stunner for me.

I said goodbye and left. I wasn't going to think about it, I was going to fight it because I knew what the regents' bylaws stated. But the last thing I wanted was a public squabble. I returned to my office and phoned my good friend Tom Roach, an attorney and one of the best regents Michigan ever had, and asked if there was a time he could come down and see me. "I can see you in the morning," he said. "We're having a regents meeting and I could meet you at 9 o'clock."

As usual, he was early. After telling him about Shapiro asking me to retire a year early, I added, "I'm simply not going to do it. The regents' bylaws allow me the privilege of staying until I'm 70. I want you to talk to him because I don't want any trouble on this thing; but I am absolutely adamant." I handed Tom a copy of the regents' bylaws which I'm sure he knew by heart. In section 5-19, paragraph 1, it stated: "The term of service of the President, the Executive Officers, and the members of the Faculties, shall terminate no later than the end of the fiscal year in which their seventieth birthday occurs." The bylaws also said that there was a terminal furlough year that paid full salary between the 69th and 70th year, but it did not have to be taken. And, "Individuals appointed on or after January 1, 1984, are not eligible for the terminal furlough year." In any case, on July 25th I received a letter from Shapiro, stating I would

With President Harold Shapiro

THE UNIVERSITY OF MICHIGAN
ANN ARBOR, MICHIGAN 48109-1340
(313) 764-6270

HAROLD T. SHAPIRO   July 25, 1986
President

Mr. Donald B. Canham
Director
Intercollegiate Athletics
1000 South State
Campus Mail

Dear Don:

The purpose of this note is to summarize the nature of the understanding we have reached regarding your retirement as Director of Intercollegiate Athletics and the time-table for searching for a new Director. For brevity's sake, I will outline our understanding in a series of points:

(1) Because of your long and outstanding service to The University of Michigan and your desire to complete certain ongoing initiatives, we have agreed that you will forego your furlough year and serve as Director of Intercollegiate Athletics through the 1987-88 academic year. During the 1987-88 academic year you will have reached the mandatory retirement age of 70 and will, therefore, complete your service to the University at that time.

(2) In early March, 1987, we will jointly announce your prospective retirement, together with a description of the procedures the University will use to secure the best possible replacement....

The letter agreeing to my not leaving early

serve as director until July 1, 1988. That was the last I heard of the matter and I never mentioned it further to Roach. My relationship with Shapiro was never the same.

At the time I had no idea why Shapiro would ask me to retire a year early. We had worked well together. I was always supportive and loyal and he, in turn, had publicly supported everything I did. He had given me raise after raise until I was the highest-paid athletic director in the Big Ten, maybe in the country. From my perspective now, I can see two or three possible reasons. I never tried to find out, however, as there wasn't much point in pursuing it.

The first might be that he knew he was leaving Michigan and wanted to appoint the new athletic director himself. In 1984 or 1985, in a casual conversation, Harold mentioned to me that he would never appoint football coach Bo Schembechler as athletic director. And maybe that was his concern: that Bo had gained such popularity and respect that the regents and search committee would appoint Schembechler against his wishes. In addition, he knew I favored Bo — but only if he gave up coaching. That had been in the papers.

Another reason might have been anger over a vote at the NCAA convention. The Board in Control and Schembechler and I had all voted against the motion to drastically reduce the numbers of football tenders and assistant coaches. I was to speak against the bill to a group of presidents and Bo was to talk to the convention itself. That was before we learned that Shapiro favored the motion. I explained to Shapiro some time later the background of Schembechler's and my involvement, that we'd been put on the convention agenda weeks before he had expressed his feelings. He never seemed angry about it and, in fact, didn't mention the convention at all when I saw him. But maybe it bothered him more than he said. After all, his opinion on the matter

Appointing a committee to consider changes in intercollegiate athletics

MEMORANDUM

TO: Harold R. Johnson, Chair
          N. Harris McClamroch
          Virginia B. Nordby

FROM: Harold T. Shapiro

DATE: June 23, 1987

SUBJECT: Review of Department of Intercollegiate Athletics

I very much appreciate your willingness to serve as the small, special committee to advise me regarding the governance and organizational structure of the Department of Intercollegiate Athletics. I hope that you can begin this consideration immediately and that you will be able to present your recommendations to me by the end of the summer.

I consider this an extremely important undertaking and one that needs to be concluded well before we enter the final stages of the search for a new Athletic Director. I anticipate that we will be at that point by late fall and, therefore, wish to use the first part of the fall to consider and plan whatever changes we may choose to make as a result of your review and recommendations.

Harold Johnson has agreed to serve as the Chair of your group, and I recognize that Virginia Nordby has long-standing plans to be away for most of the month of July.

I am grateful for your efforts in this matter.

sd

bc: Robben W. Fleming
     Richard L. Kennedy
     Donald B. Canham

was on record with the presidents, and it was an opinion opposite to that expressed at the NCAA convention by his A.D. and his coach. A saving circumstance was that some of the presidents changed their votes to "no" on the motion and the Big Ten vote went from "yes," preconvention, to "no" at the meetings.

The third possibility is that he intended to reorganize the athletic department before a new A.D. came on board and prior to his leaving for Princeton. Some indication of this was in a copy of a memorandum I received from him July 8, 1987, a year after his request that I retire early.

The chairman, Harold Johnson, was a professor who had served on the Board in Control of Intercollegiate Athletics. His agenda, I felt, would favor the faculty having more control over the athletic department with only limited input from the A.D. Johnson was bothered — and he said so to me — that the athletic director was chairman of the Board in Control. He and I never agreed on much concerning

THE UNIVERSITY OF MICHIGAN
ANN ARBOR, MICHIGAN 48109-1340
(313) 764-6270

HAROLD T. SHAPIRO
President

MEMORANDUM

TO: Robben W. Fleming (Chair)
        Richard L. Kennedy (Vice-Chair)
        Gwendolyn S. Cruzat
        Paul W. Gikas
        Thomas Goss
        Sarah S. McCue
        Wilbert J. McKeachie
        David M. Nelson
        Robert M. Sellers
        Lillian M. Simms
        John P. Weidenbach

FROM: Harold T. Shapiro

DATE: July 7, 1987

SUBJECT: Athletic Director Search

    I am writing to confirm your appointment as a member of the Search Committee for a new Athletic Director and to thank each of you, especially President Emeritus Robben Fleming, for your willingness to serve the University in this capacity.

    The position of Athletic Director at The University of Michigan is one of the most prominent and desirable such positions in the country. Thus, I am confident the search will attract a pool of quite distinguished candidates, and I am hopeful things can proceed expeditiously enough for us to be able to make an appointment before the end of the fall semester. There is, of course, widespread interest in this particular search, and there will be some especially sensitive aspects to it, which is why I have considered it so important to select a committee of highly-respected, broad-minded, trustworthy individuals.

athletics. That's quite a different situation from 1990 when President James Duderstadt practically eliminated faculty control of intercollegiate athletics. It's possible Shapiro thought we needed to reorganize the board and that it would be easier if I weren't sitting as chair.

I never really talked with Shapiro after that time — unusual, because during his tenure we had talked often. He soon left for Princeton but before going he appointed retired president Fleming as chairman of the search committee for a new athletic director.

Several of those named to the search committee–Kennedy, Cruzat, Gikas, Simms, McKeachie – had served on the Board in Control. I felt they understood the complexities of the position. They may have but the Regents might not have.

The changes that took place in my 20 years weren't the same changes the next athletic director would have to cope with. The search committee was diversified and experienced enough to realize that. In a meeting in October 1987 I gave Fleming, at his request, a list of my recommended candidates: Schembechler, Red Berenson, and Tom Jernstead of the NCAA. Goss and Nelson knew that.

I had recommended Bo but only if he gave up the coaching position, as I thought he probably would. On several occasions he had mentioned to me that he was not as good a coach as he was a few years before. Two heart operations and 40 years of coaching had taken their toll. It happens to most; enthusiasm is hard to maintain over a long period. A.A. Stagg, Woody Hayes, and Joe Paterno were memorable exceptions. Bear Bryant near the end delegated almost everything.

In early March the regents gave Schembechler their one condition: if he quit coaching he would be named athletic director. Bo was not ready to quit coaching. That put the regents in a dilemma because, as they saw it, there were no other appropriate candidates. Regents Deane Baker and Veronica Smith were the only ones who held out for Schembechler throughout the discussions.

After Bo refused to quit coaching, the name of John Swofford, athletic director at North Carolina, kept coming up as a candidate in the press. That was disturbing to knowledgeable Michigan people. I had no idea how he got on the list in the first place, but he certainly wasn't the right man. John, I think, knew it: a southerner with no Michigan connections coming to liberal University of Michigan is not

going to rally the M-club or alumni behind him, particularly over a
Michigan man. Someone kept leaking stories about other candidates
to the *Ann Arbor News*, and Swofford had a champion pushing him in
the papers. However, Ron Kramer, the U-M football All-American,
had heard that Swofford might be the number one candidate and, I
later learned, wrote Swofford a letter telling him that Michigan was
not the place for him. After Kramer's letter there wasn't a chance
Swofford would take the job even if it were offered. Rumor had it that
it was offered; if so, the regents just didn't understand Michigan
athletics. I had served on the TV committee for the NCAA with
Swofford and he is a very nice man, but he was not the candidate for
Michigan by a country mile.

A surprise soon occurred. On March 17, 1988 I received a phone
call from Bruce Madej, our sports information director, who was in
Salt Lake City, Utah, with our basketball team at the NCAA tournament. His first words were, "Canham, you won't believe this! But I
had a call from Keith Molin saying the regents voted to name Jack

Weidenbach the director
of athletics. What the hell
is going on?" Molin was,
I believe, a spokesman for
the university or the re-
gents. Jack was the head of
the university plant department — a sports fan who
often helped Renfrew in the
will-call ticket booth at
away games.

Weidenbach had been
down to see me just that
morning, I told Madej. He
had been offered the job as
athletic director and he
asked me what I thought. I
had said, "Jack, there is no
way you're qualified for the
job as athletic director at

Bruce Madej and Anthony Carter.
Bruce received a strange call from
Keith Molin.

this school or any other school at this level. This is not some backwater high school situation. Someone must be kidding." A note on my calendar confirms what I said.

Jack, a longtime friend of mine, looked at me and said, "Don, you know, I agree with you. I wouldn't know where to start here." So I assumed it was only exploratory conversation. Jack and I talked about other things and he left. I don't know what the ensuing scenario was, but my guess is that Weidenbach went back to the regents and said, "You know, I don't think I should take that job." But Molin had not been clued in and he called Madej. Why he called Madej in Salt Lake City is an interesting mystery, as the following letter points out. The call was a day or so before I received this memo from Madej:

FOR INTRA-UNIVERSITY CORRESPONDENCE

THE UNIVERSITY OF MICHIGAN

March 22, 1988

MEMORANDUM

TO: Don Canham

FROM: Bruce Madej

RE: AD Announcement

Last Thursday, Keith Molin contacted me in the Doubletree Hotel to inform me that the University of Michigan would announce the statment saying Jack Weidenbach has been asked to take the position of Michigan Athletic Director.

He was to have ten days to think about the decision and come back with an answer.

At that time I felt, the decision to make such an announcement was not in the best interest of the University of Michigan and the Athletic Department.

During the conversation with Molin, he added that the Regents were 6-2 in favor of the appointment. He also told me that Interim President Robben Flemming had talked with both you and Bo Schembechler.

He had said that Fleming noted Bo would support the announcement but he didn't think you supported the decision but had agreed not to comment.

Since I was in Salt Lake City, and I did not want the announcement made, I talked to you and Bo Schembechler about the statement and both of you agreed the statement should not be made until an Athletic Director was named.

I returned the call to Molin and strongly encouraged him to ask Fleming to wait until Weidenbach had made a decision.

The following day, the Ann Arbor News had the statement, in a way. It did not officialy come from the University nor the Athletic Department. According to Molin, he felt a Regent had leaked it to the press. Of course, there was no comment from the Athletic Department.

Again, I tried to keep the statement from the media, and I did talk to you and Schembechler about the way it should be handled. I did not feel I could represent the Athletic Department unless I had discussed this matter with you, and knowing Schembechler's feelings made it imprative for me to contact Molin and ask him to hold the announcement.

"Weidenbach is to have 10 days to think about the matter," Molin had said. If that was the case, why were they even thinking about making an announcement? Bruce told Molin that he did not want to make any announcement until he talked with Schembechler and me. He felt Bo was the logical candidate and would get the job and a switch to Weidenbach was strange. Any statement, he felt, should be approved by my office. I was still the athletic director, but wasn't sure at that point.

Bruce, after thinking it over, called Molin back and strongly encouraged him to ask the regents to wait at least until Weidenbach had made a decision before making any tentative announcement. But

---

THE UNIVERSITY OF MICHIGAN
Department of Athletics
1000 South State Street, Ann Arbor, Michigan 48109-2201
Phone (313) 747-2583

Don Canham
DIRECTOR OF ATHLETICS

March 21, 1988

Mr. R. W. Fleming
Interim President
Fleming Building

Dear Bob:

    I was extremely disappointed to receive a phone call from Bruce Madej in Salt Lake City on Thursday, March 17th, about an hour after I talked to you on the telephone regarding the athletic director situation. Madej said he just received a phone call from Keith Molin saying that the Regents were going to issue a press release on Friday stating that Jack Weidenbach had been named Director of Athletics, and that Canham opposed it. That's incredible for more than a few reasons.

    First, the Regents had not met yet and Molin is calling around the country to my sports information director as to what the Regents will do when they meet. In addition, he attributed sentiments to me that I never had and I resent it very much.

    As you know, in our conversation that I assumed was private, I did not object to Jack Weidenbach. He is one of my close friends. I objected to the fact that an individual, without an athletic background, was being considered for the directorship at The University of Michigan, and that a great many outstanding administrators in athletics have never been approached by the University. That is all I stated in my conversation with you and I have not discussed the matter with a single other individual.

    If people in Salt Lake City knew about this from Keith Molin's phone calls, it's no wonder that the story was in the newspaper before the Regents met concerning the matter.

                    Sincerely yours,

                    Don Canham
                    Director of Athletics

DC:cl

the story again got into the papers. The leaks were obviously intentional. They didn't come from either Madej or me.

Fleming was still the chairman of the search committee and I wrote to him after talking with Madej, a day before I received his report in writing.

Fleming answered on April 1. Five paragraphs follow from his

THE UNIVERSITY OF MICHIGAN
ANN ARBOR, MICHIGAN 48109-1340
(313) 764-6270

ROBBEN W. FLEMING
Interim President

April 1, 1988

Mr. Donald B. Canham
Director
Intercollegiate Athletics
1000 South State Street
Campus Mail - 3717

Dear Don:

    I have your letter of March 22, with copies to the Regents, about Keith Molin's call to Bruce Madej with respect to the Athletic Director situation. While I would have preferred Keith had not called Bruce, and did not know that he was going to at that point, the situation is not as incredible as it may seem to you.

    It is true that the Regents had not met <u>on March 17</u> to discuss a final decision on the Athletic Director. They <u>had</u>, however, discussed the various options as early as March 5, and again on the night of March 16 and the morning of March 17. I knew, and they knew, before March 17 that there was a consensus on Jack Weidenbach. There were some problems that remained to be ironed out and no final choice had been made.

    Knowing that there would have to be a press conference at some time, I talked to Keith in order to start making the necessary arrangements. At that point, I thought that the remaining problems with respect to an announcement might be resolved in time to have a press conference on Friday afternoon. That turned out not to be the case, but I was in meetings and did not have a chance to tell Keith to put a hold on any immediate press conference. That is doubtless why he talked to Bruce....

    ...I am sorry that Keith apparently said to Bruce that you were opposed to Jack Weidenbach. You would be the first to concede, however, that despite your friendship for him, you thought we were making a mistake in not naming someone who had direct coaching or athletic director experience.

    You and I have been good friends for a long time. You have been very good to us, and Sally and I very much appreciate it. For my part, we will remain good friends and I hope you feel the same way.

Sincerely,

Robben W. Fleming

ss

cc: The Board of Regents

two-page letter. It explains the phone call, but the deliberations on the part of the regents will forever be a mystery. Only Baker of the 1988 board of regents is still in office. In trying to get the scenario I talked with Deane and others. None can clearly recall the exact order of events.

It was a mess. At least two of the regents were furious because they had not been in on the conversation or the vote. Of course there was no comment from the athletic department; we didn't know what was going on. Newspapers and radio and TV people called constantly and for the first time I had nothing to say. The whole thing was bizarre. From the start I had tried to stay out of the selection of my successor, so I had little information.

A few days later the regents changed their minds again and went back to Schembechler. He could coach football for two years and be the director of athletics. Bo refused again, not because he wanted to coach forever, but because he didn't want to be dictated to as to when he would give up football. They then reconsidered and named him athletic director and football coach, a combination simply too difficult these days for one man to handle. Bo and I discussed the matter several times. He has told me since then that the reason he took the dual job was that otherwise he didn't know who he would be working for; and when he took it he intended to concentrate on football and let someone else handle the duties of A.D. This is similar to the way they did it at Texas A&M and Auburn University, and ended up on NCAA probation. Joe Paterno was athletic director and football coach at Penn State for a little while. After he resigned the athletic director's job Joe told me it was just impossible, it drove him "up the wall." Paterno delegated everything concerning the department to others and continued to be the highly successful football coach he is.

One of the best examples of someone trying and failing to carry on both jobs was George Perles at Michigan State, a guy I like. George fought the president, John DiBiaggio, to become athletic director. I told him I thought he was making a mistake, but it became a bitter war and he won. The sad part is that during the year or so Perles was both athletic director and football coach, he was an outstanding athletic director. I've talked to several of the coaches and some of the staff people at Michigan State and they all said Perles was terrific because he understood the problems of the coaches. That is the first requirement, in my opinion, for being a good athletic director. Coaches have enough problems and don't need another in the director's office as Michigan State had when they hired Merilee Baker. The difficulty at Michigan State was that Perles, in being a good athletic director, neglected his football program. It ended, as everyone knows, with his losing both jobs.

There are virtually no major schools that appoint one person to both jobs. In the old days, prior to women's athletics and the big business of college sports, many schools, notably the Big Eight schools, successfully combined them. Demands were far different then.

Subsequently, Weidenbach was named associate athletic director. Schembechler continued to coach football but spent little time as director of athletics, even though he had the title. He attended few, if any, Big Ten meetings. Weidenbach and one or two others ran the department.

Schembechler would have been a top athletic director — had he discontinued coaching and concentrated on administration.

Two years later, Bo left the university and went to work for Tom Monaghan as president of the Detroit Tigers baseball team, not one of the best moves he ever made. Weidenbach then became the interim A.D. for three years and finally was appointed director. What changed Jack's mind about qualifications, I don't know. I never discussed athletics with Jack at all; he certainly never asked my opinion and I have had very limited conversations with him since I left the university.

A major disappointment during my final year at Michigan centered on someone I'd hired just out of college. Fritz Crisler often hired young people. I was one — only 27 when he appointed me Michigan's head track coach. Remembering that, I brought in many myself, providing them at least with a start. During my long span we had hundreds of interns at Michigan before they went on to other jobs in the profession. On occasion if an intern had some qualifications we currently needed, we'd keep him on the staff for several years. Generally, the young people were grateful, conscientious, and loyal. Not so Bob DeCarolis.

The issue involved disloyalty. During my last month on the job, reports came to me that DeCarolis, whom I'd hired directly on graduation from the University of Massachusetts, planned to change various things after I was gone. Not a bad idea, although a little silence until I left would have been better. I wasn't particularly concerned until about a year later, when the reports were confirmed with the publication of a book, *Win At Any Cost: The Sell-Out of College Athletics,* by Francis Dealy. The author quoted DeCarolis at some length, and disappointing it was.

DeCarolis had been my bookkeeper, thus Dealy's interest in interviewing him. Although I had given him the title of business manager, he really wasn't. I always did my own budgets, investments and banking; DeCarolis was not privy to some of the information he expounded upon. Dealy quoted him as saying,

> "If it weren't for Canham's half-assed swimming pool, we'd be okay. It's the annual mortgage payments of $875,000 plus the natatorium's annual maintenance expenses of $500,000 that has caused our deficit."

DeCarolis had the figures wrong and he had misinterpreted the situation. He claimed he was misquoted. He was not.

The real surprise was that DeCarolis apparently didn't read or didn't understand our financial statement. At the time we had $12 million in reserve, plus another million in operating money — money not there, incidentally, when I started as the athletic director 20 years before. We could have written a check from the reserves to pay for the pool. But we didn't because as a tax-free borrower we received a very favorable interest rate; interest on the reserves more than covered the debt service. His math was about as accurate as in the Bud Middaugh situation.

John Beckett, a sports writer for the *Ann Arbor News* who was always on the lookout for a semi-scandal, published a story about the DeCarolis quotes. University accountants and others who could read a balance sheet quickly wrote letters to the university and to the newspaper attempting to set the record straight. Subsequently, acting A.D. Weidenbach issued a statement saying that any deficit the department was running had nothing to do with the Canham Natatorium. He pointed out the financial advantage of using borrowed funds for the pool. Not much damage was done, except for some deep disappointment over the disloyalty. DeCarolis, who wanted to run the athletic department, was to some extent given the chance after I left. When Joe Roberson became A.D. in 1994 he stopped that nonsense and gave DeCarolis some assignments he was more capable of handling, and an office on the golf course.

My last year was not one to celebrate, so I did not allow any retirement banquets or parties. I'm not much of a party guy anyway and most retirement parties are dull. I remembered that Crisler had refused any semblance of retirement celebration, saying, "Don, you can tell the alumni association and all of the people who want to hold retirement parties for Fritz Crisler that that's fine but he won't be there." Then he said, "I'm not going to allow some of the people who gave me the most trouble to attend a farewell party and feel that all is well!" He wasn't bitter; he never liked parties in the first place. And he didn't want his leaving celebrated.

Shapiro asked once if I would let the university have a retirement party for me. Allan Smith, former president, also wanted to organize one. And alumni clubs throughout the middle west thought it would be nice to get someone to make a free speech. But I had lost interest and all I wanted to do was leave as soon as possible. The difficulties toward the end with Shapiro and the search for a successor eroded my enthusiasm. I was upset that the regents as well didn't seem to appreciate what an athletic director's job at Michigan was all about. I never felt it was personal, but maybe it was. They may have wanted a dramatic change and more direct control.

When Fritz left, he only allowed the coaches to offer doughnuts and coffee in the basement of the administration building as his retirement get-away. In my case, one afternoon in June of 1988 the coaches and some of my closest friends came out to School-Tech and presented me with a beautiful painting by John Martin, a leading sports artist. We had a drink or two and talked of the past and the future — and that is how retirement parties should be. I think, as Crisler said, "When you're gone, you're gone." And I would add, "Don't take too long to go and don't return." I never have returned to the athletic department office and probably never will. I talk often with the present athletic director and try to help when I can, but no one needs the "past" trying to influence the "future."

Roberson, the current athletic director, is a Michigan graduate who had an outstanding career as a corporate fund-raiser for the university. As I said when I left in 1988, fund-raising is essential for future athletic survival at Michigan and any other institution if they hope to compete on a level playing surface with other Division I schools.

The times changed from Yost to Crisler and from Crisler to me, a period of a half century. The next half century of Michigan will probably be successful, but it absolutely will be different — and, on most days, nowhere near as much fun.

Chapter 20

Where Do We Go from Here?

◆————————————————————————

Athletic Administration in Crisis

T he dramatic changes in athletics since the days of Fielding Yost
and Fritz Crisler are legion. Television, athletic scholarships,
intensified recruiting, million-dollar gates, women's competition, air travel, and professional influence on the college game are a
few things they never had to be concerned about. The future of athletics at Michigan as well as all the other majors universities is not so
easy to see or predict, but some problems loom on the horizon of college sports.

"Who Will Be in Charge?"

For Michigan the most serious area for the future is how the athletic department will be governed. Throughout this book it has been
shown how faculty control of athletics enabled Michigan to rise to
eminence in athletics. In 1990 after Schembechler left, a move was
started to place control and management in the hands of the president
and not a board made up of faculty, alumni and students, where it had
rested since the days of Yost and before. In 1995 the move became
serious and specific. There were complaints made to the regents by
alumni, faculty, and M-club members to stop the reorganization proposed by President James Duderstadt just months before he left the
university. In the spring of 1996 the regents agreed and took the issue

off the agenda at least temporarily.

Yet on July 8, 1996, following Duderstadt's departure, a draft of Proposed Changes to Regents By-laws for Intercollegiate Athletics was sent forward by Walter Harrison, vice president of university relations. The changes were, as stated in a cover letter, agreed upon by "a consensus of the Board in Control of Intercollegiate Athletics."

What is a consensus? Is it a majority? "The changes vary considerably from the ones proposed in November," Harrison said. That was putting it mildly. They were dramatic changes, even more restrictive and non-functional than those the regents rejected in the spring of 1996. The proposal set forth on July 8, 1996, would be, if accepted, a disaster for Michigan athletics. They were obviously put together by those who know nothing about running an athletic department. The proposal virtually puts all management and authority in the hands of a vice president, not a faculty Board in Control or an athletic director. How could any faculty person be part of a "consensus" for the Harrison committee report, giving away their historical role?

1. The term Board in Control of Intercollegiate Athletics is stricken from the bylaws completely. The board controls nothing; it is advisory only and is referred to as "the board."

2. The athletic director is removed as chairman. In his place "a faculty man or woman shall be elected chairman." The faculty chairman calls the meetings, not the director. What dean would tolerate not being chairman of his department? Can anyone imagine the specter of a faculty member campaigning to be "chairman of the board?"

3. The long-term faculty representatives who gave Michigan such continuity, such as Ralph Aigler and Marc Plant, are remnants of the past. The faculty representative is limited to five years, hardly time to become completely familiar with Big Ten and NCAA rules and regulations. Of course he or she may be re-appointed, or not.

4. The alumni association of the university, not the regional alumni clubs, will select the alumni members to the board. In the past, clubs in Cleveland, Chicago, Detroit and Grand Rapids selected their own representatives. The Alumni Association selected one member. Who is more qualified — the clubs themselves or the association, to select the representatives?

5. The board is no longer "responsible for the business management

of the athletic department" — a vital function of the board since Yost's time.

6. The most ridiculous proposed change in the Harrison draft concerns business proceedings. "All money, regardless of source, shall be deposited in a bank approved by the chief financial officer" — there's nothing new there, but no withdrawal shall be made, "except upon voucher approved first by the advisory board and then the executive vice president and chief financial officer." A Chinese fire drill is more efficient. Formerly, the athletic director could approve normal department expenditures and issue payments. Major items went through the board.

This Ivy League method of running a department is hard to comprehend at Michigan, the largest, most respected, and most successful athletic department in the nation. The administration of athletics as conducted under presidents Alexander Ruthven, Harlan Hatcher, Robben Fleming, Allan Smith, and Harold Shapiro, the structure that made Michigan great, was not good enough for Duderstadt. The hope is that the current regents will reject the Harrison committee report and return to the bylaws as they were in 1988.

Television

The tremendous popularity of athletics in societies throughout the world and particularly in the United States can be traced primarily to television. It has provided revenue beyond comprehension just two decades ago. It has brought new sports into the living room and made fans of women and children in the process (i.e. gymnastics, football, basketball). TV has enabled professional teams and leagues to be formed and flourish with their guaranteed-rights fees. For the universities, it has been the best public relations agency ever as the TV cameras roam the campus on game days and provide free time for public announcements about the schools.

One of the most important contributions, however, is that the money generated has been the savior for many athletic departments. Budgets in hundreds of schools could not be balanced without it. The inconvenience and shortcomings of television are far outweighed by the positive advantages of having the camera on the field or in the arena.

The future, however, may not be as bright. Cable and over-the-air television is certain to change. The viewing audience of the future could be significantly lower. Television rights fees may not be reduced much, but the trend toward very slow increases has started. Surveys show that young people (television's future audience) are watching television at a much lower rate each year. They are sitting in front of computer screens rather than television sets. Not only is over-the-air television losing viewers, but sports news, like business news and shopping news, will be major factors on the Internet to lure more viewers from TV. With fewer viewers, rights fees for intercollegiate athletics cannot be the major factors in athletic budgets it is today. The day may come when young people may develop more enthusiasm for the Internet than they do for Michigan playing Ohio State.

Rising Costs

If television's future hints of financial problems for schools, it will only complicate what everyone knows is the most serious future crisis. That is rising costs. Inflation, while under control in the general economy, is not in control at most NCAA schools. Michigan is a prime example. When I retired in 1988 the athletic budget was $18 million. The budget for 1996-97 was projected at $32 million. Schools no longer earn their budgets; most depend on gifts from friends, corporations, and alumni, plus licensing fees from manufacturers ($6 million to Michigan in 1995) on copyrighted logos and designs.

What happens when football or basketball teams have a tough time winning? History shows that gifts decline and licensing royalties certainly dwindle when teams are not in the hunt on a regular basis. Where that has occurred, universities are forced to bail out the athletic departments with general funds.

That has never happened at Michigan. Bill Battle, owner and genius behind Collegiate Licensing (the company that markets licensed products for 150 of the leading NCAA schools, including Michigan), told me on a 1996 fishing trip in Idaho that in 1995 Michigan led the nation in royalty income. He did point out, however, that Michigan Rose Bowl victories and NCAA final four appearances made the $6 million possible. So performance, as always, is the bottom line when it comes to licensing royalties. "What have you done for me lately," is the guideline in licensing income.

Agents

It is also pretty certain that agents and gambling will continue to threaten collegiate athletic programs. In the increasing competition for athletes to fill pro rosters, colleges will face more problems with agents than ever before. It isn't happenstance that high school players recently have gone directly from their high school gyms to the professional draft in basketball. Agents were at work. Million-dollar contracts are common and an agent's commission is hefty. In baseball it's an old story, as high school and college athletes are signed regularly out of school. The agent is the major factor leading athletes to the pros prior to graduation.

In the last decade we have seen the phenomenon of high school parents driving new Cadillacs and having mortgages paid off by their teenage super stars' supposed future. There are about 1,000 agents, it is said — some will sign anyone with even a little promise. Sports agency is a growth industry and many universities, the NCAA, the Football Coaching Association and other groups, have had many conferences trying to come up with answers on how to protect young athletes from unscrupulous agents. Few of the signed athletes who gave up education for a bonus ever reach the heights agents promise.

The problem is that few people know who the agents are, and new ones spring up each year. Twenty-three or 24 states had enough concerns to put legislation on the books to regulate agents. In some cases some agents have been prosecuted in state courts. In the final analysis, the coach and the institution probably have the best influence and control of the athlete. Some colleges have programs to educate the athlete against agents' abuses. Others have provided free legal service for athletes dealing with agents and pro contracts. Unfortunately, the pre-college contract and the paid-off mortgage as a result of agents are usually beyond detection or regulation.

Gambling

One activity that always concerns athletic administrators is gambling. It has been a problem for basketball since the days of the scandals at Kentucky, Bradley University, University of San Francisco, and more recently at Tulane. In those cases the point-shaving was orchestrated by the gamblers against the odds makers' point-spread for certain games. Players were paid to manipulate the scores. Since that time, almost every year one hears about some football or basketball game where less than full effort was expended by an athlete or two to make sure the point spread was covered or not. How can it be proven?

Periodically the NCAA receives rumors of gamblers' influence. It's a hopeless task to police thousands of athletes, to say nothing of the gamblers. Many feel there have been more thrown games than ever detected or reported, both in football and basketball. If one talks to LasVegas gamblers, they are certain there are still thrown games. Coaches and athletic directors say, "ridiculous." The same denials were made before previous scandals.

In addition to the illegal approach by gamblers to athletes, students on various campuses are sometimes paid to report any unusual team problems. I recall one Big Ten football team where there was a racial problem that obviously was reported to the gamblers. The coaches knew of it but few others did. The spots on that team changed drastically overnight. At Michigan we have from time to time been informed of questionable people who wanted to watch football practice or who became friends with athletes to get inside information. As a result, we never took phone calls from strangers in the training rooms, press box or publicity department concerning injuries or team matters. Tough coaches and tough policies are the only way to combat the gamblers. The laws and legislation haven't helped much. As lottery and casino gambling continue to spread across the nation, the gambling problem in intercollegiate athletics will increase.

Dignity and Class

Like location in business and housing, image in athletics is crucial. The image that's being projected across the land by pros and collegians alike is not pretty; almost daily there is some athlete at some institution who has embarrassed himself and his school. A good deal of that misbehavior is the fault of the institution due to admission policy and, in particular, the coach and his discipline or lack of it. There is no greater threat to college athletics than the uncontrolled behavior, absence of dignity, and the police blotter record at some schools. That is a quick way to lose faculty, administrative, alumni, and fan support.

The University of Miami in Florida set a world record recently for deplorable player behavior.

Michigan was fortunate to have had a disciplinarian like Bo Schembechler coaching its football team for more than 20 years. Where others were having major problems, we had just a few minor ones. Schembechler tolerated nothing that was in violation of the rules of his team or the university. Any disciplinary problems were solved quickly and without headlines. His teams were never an embarrassment. That was a major factor in creating team loyalty and nationwide respect for Michigan. I've seen Bo send players home from the Rose Bowl game for missing curfew at night. That awakened others in a hurry. I've seen him leave players at home from Big Ten football games because of poor class attendance. Once, when several players attended a party where marijuana was used, all were suspended from the team for the season. It never was proven that the athletes themselves used the marijuana, but that didn't matter. Needless to say, Bo had few subsequent problems with questionable party attendance.

Unless the image and behavior of the college athlete is changed, there will be big problems ahead. Fans are fickle. Major league baseball learned that. Fortunately, the rules committees and the various sports groups have started to move. In college hockey, fighting has virtually stopped. Most end zone displays in football have been taken care of by the rules. A few more technical fouls called in basketball straighten out the coach and the athletes. And where they are called, the officials remain in charge. Progress toward a return to control and dignity has just started and must continue. Coaches have a key role, but it's also essential to have the right admission policies, pre-enrollment screening, and an athletic department philosophy that winning at all costs is a trip to oblivion. College presidents who complain about college sports problems had better check on whom they are letting attend their schools.

Amateurism

To traditionalists and most coaches, "pay for play" will be the end of amateur sports as we have known them for more than 100 years. Fans take a different view of the college amateur than they do of the paid pro. At this time it would seem that college athletes in some instances will eventually be paid, a sorry prospect. The message was clearly sent when the U.S. Olympic committee in 1996 awarded cash for medals in Atlanta. The committee, in my time never made up of geniuses, put a final end to amateurism. It had a running start when the pro basketball players became the "dream team." A surprise and a disappointment to me and most others in intercollegiate sports, however, occurred when Walter Byers, the former NCAA executive director, advocated paying college athletes. Byers, in a complete reversal from his days in the NCAA office, advocated "pay for play" because the teams they play on are producing so much revenue.

Walter knows better than anyone that revenue sports support the non-revenue sports for men and women on most campuses. He also knows that many NCAA surveys show only a handful of NCAA athletic departments turn a profit. He also knows a quick way to end up in court is to pay football and basketball players and not pay swimmers or women golfers. So a proposal without a solution hardly flies. To pay some athletes in some sports would mean eliminating teams for both men and women in a search for payroll funds, hardly the way to keep everyone playing. The real question is just how much "pay" do athletes need. At many schools all of the revenue-producing athletes hold scholarships that equal $25,000 a year. That is better than the nations' average workers' income. So how much does "play for pay" need to increase?

One of the last bastions for amateur sports is the NCAA and a crisis has arisen because an Olympic medalist who accepts the prize money is ineligible for future NCAA competition. In 1996 several collegians won medals. Avery Brundage, former Olympic head, must be spinning in his grave.

The Playoff

Every fall there is a campaign by the media for a college football playoff. Michigan was the only school that publicly opposed the Big Ten and Pac-10's forcing the Rose Bowl to join the bowl game coalition. The reason for the opposition is simple. If there are more than two unbeaten teams for a year or two when the regular season ends, the one-game championship will be in jeopardy. The same group that engineered the pressure on the Rose Bowl will begin to lament the unfairness "of only two teams decided by vote playing for the national championship." So, needing more than one game to solve that situation, off we go on a pro-style multiple game play-off series.

Since 1946 the Rose Bowl has been the exclusive property of the Big Ten and Pac-10. In addition, the exposure per team is second to none, and it is foolish to let other schools and conferences get a foot in the door. To jeopardize that situation is to ignore tradition and to gamble with the future. That is what the Pac-10 and the Big Ten did. Some school will be furious in the near future when the coalition takes over the Rose Bowl for their championship game and the Big Ten champion is not first or second in the voters poll and thus is out of the championship game. So, instead of the Rose Bowl, they will be shuffled off to another bowl. A Minnesota, Indiana, or Purdue, who haven't been to the Rose Bowl in decades, would not be ecstatic over the missed chance to play in Pasadena, as Notre Dame and Miami move in. Michigan and Ohio wouldn't turn hand springs, either.

The crux of the matter, however, is that in many areas in this country where great football is played there is no clamor whatsoever for a playoff, and for good reason. They don't want to minimize the great tradition and great impact of Southern Cal-Notre Dame, or Oklahoma-Nebraska, or Michigan-Ohio State, or Florida-Florida State. There is no question that if the bowls are used in the future to determine a playoff, the interest and emphasis will shift from those great regional games in some sections of this country to playoff games.

Where are the Big Ten presidents who were to "control athletics" and prevent over-emphasis? If one looks, they were the very ones who voted to put the Rose Bowl in the mix. Some cited the money that would be made — what other reason could they give? The myth that the financial bonanza would occur on a playoff series like the NFL uses will jolt the collegiate football world. Big money will not be there. The NCAA will not vote for any plan where the money is not shared at least by Division I schools, so divide the revenue by more than 100. It is even more possible the money will be spread over the entire NCAA for programs that benefit all, as is done with Final Four basketball revenue. So much for those who foresee huge revenues for a multi-game playoff in football.

Author's note: Due to the limitations of space, this index contains less than one-third of the individuals mentioned in this book, At the outset I mentioned that thousands, not hundreds, had a part in Michigan lore; just a few are indexed below.